BERLITZ

GREEK
for travellers

By the staff of Berlitz Guides

How best to use this phrase book

● We suggest that you start with the **Guide to pronunciation** (pp. 6-9), then go on to **Some basic expressions** (pp. 10-15). This gives you not only a minimum vocabulary, but also helps you get used to pronouncing the language.

● Consult the **Contents** pages (3-5) for the section you need. In each chapter you'll find travel facts, hints and useful information. Simple phrases are followed by a list of words applicable to the situation.

● Separate, detailed contents lists are included at the beginning of the extensive **Eating out** and **Shopping guide** sections (Menus, p. 39, Shops and services, p. 97).

● If you want to find out how to say something in Greek, your fastest look-up is via the **Dictionary** section (pp. 161-189). This not only gives you the word, but is also cross-referenced to its use in a phrase on a specific page.

● If you wish to learn more about constructing sentences, check the **Basic grammar** (pp. 156-160).

● Note the **colour margins** are indexed in Greek and English to help both listener and speaker. And, in addition, there is also an **index in Greek** for the use of your listener.

● Throughout the book, this symbol ☞ suggests phrases your listener can use to answer you. If you still can't understand, hand this phrase book to the Greek-speaker to encourage pointing to an appropriate answer.

Revised edition—3rd printing 1989   Printed in Switzerland

Contents

Acknowledgments
We are particularly grateful to Andreas Kyriacou and Pantelis Kotatis for their help in the preparation of this book, and to Dr. T.J.A. Bennett who devised the phonetic transcription.

Guide to pronunciation

The alphabet

Here are the characters which comprise the Greek alphabet. The left-hand columns show the printed capital and small letters, while written letters are shown in the centre columns. The column on the right gives you the Greek names of these letters.

Α	α	*A*	*a*	**ah**lfah
Β	β	*B*	*b*	**vee**tah
Γ	γ	*Γ*	*γ*	**ghah**mah
Δ	δ	*Δ*	*d*	**dheh**ltah
Ε	ε	*E*	*e*	**ehp**seelonn
Ζ	ζ	*Z*	*z*	**zee**tah
Η	η	*H*	*n*	**ee**tah
Θ	θ	*Θ*	*d*	**thee**tah
Ι	ι	*I*	*c*	**yee**otah
Κ	κ	*K*	*u*	**kah**pah
Λ	λ	*Λ*	*J*	**lahm**dhah
Μ	μ	*M*	*μ*	**mee**
Ν	ν	*N*	*v*	**nee**
Ξ	ξ	*Ξ*	*ξ*	**ksee**
Ο	ο	*O*	*o*	o**mee**kron
Π	π	*Π*	*d*	**pee**
Ρ	ρ	*P*	*p*	**ro**
Σ	σ ς	*Σ*	*s*	**seegh**mah
Τ	τ	*T*	*τ*	**tahf**
Υ	υ	*Y*	*v*	**eep**seelonn
Φ	φ	*φ*	*φ*	**fee**
Χ	χ	*X*	*γ*	**khee**
Ψ	ψ	*Y*	*ψ*	**psee**
Ω	ω	*Ω*	*ω*	o**mehg**hah

Just knowing the alphabet is not, of course, enough to pronounce Greek. We're offering you a helping hand by providing "imitated pronunciation" throughout this book. This chapter is intended to make you familiar with the transcription we have devised, and to help you get used to the sounds of Greek.

As a minimum vocabulary for your trip, we have selected a number of basic words and phrases under the title "Some basic expressions" (pages 10–15).

An outline of Greek sounds

The imitated pronunciation should be read as if it were English except for any special rules set out below. It is based on Standard British pronunciation, though we have tried to take account of General American pronunciation also. Of course, the sounds of any two languages are never exactly the same; but if you follow carefully the examples given here, you will have no difficulty in reading our transcriptions in such a way as to make yourself understood.

Letters shown in **bold** should be read with more stress (louder) than the others.

Vowels

Letter	Approximate pronunciation	Symbol	Example	
α	like the vowel in car, but pronounced farther forward in the mouth	ah	άρωμα	**ah**rommah
ε	like **e** in sell	eh	μέρα	**meh**rah
η, ι, υ	like **ee** in meet	ee	κύριος	**kee**reeoss
o, ω	like **o** in got	o	παρακαλώ	pahrahkah**lo**

Consonants

β	like v in vine	v	βιβλίο	veevleeo
γ	1) before α, o, ω, ου, and consonants, a voiced version of the ch sound in Scottish loch	gh	μεγάλος	mehghahloss
	2) before ε, αι, η, ι, υ, ει, οι, like y in yet	y	γεμάτος	yehmahtoss
δ	like th in this	dh	δεν	dhehn
ζ	like z in zoo	z	ζεστός	zehstoss
θ	like th in thing	th	θα	thah
κ	like k in kit	k	καλός	kahloss
λ	like l in lemon	l	λάθος	lahthoss
μ	like m in man	m	μέσα	mehssah
ν	like n in new	n	νέος	nehoss
ξ	like x in six	ks	έξω	ehkso
π	like p in pot	p	προς	pross
ρ	like r in red	r	πριν	preen
σ, ς	1) before voiced consonants (β, γ, δ, ζ, μ, ν, ρ) like z in zoo	z	κόσμος	kozmoss
	2) elsewhere, like s in see	s/ss	Πόσο στο	posso sto
τ	like t in tea	t	τότε	totteh
φ	like f in five	f	φέρτε	fehrteh
χ	like ch in Scottish loch	kh	άσχημος	ahskheemoss
ψ	like ps in dropsy	ps	διψώ	dheepso

Groups of letters

αι	like e in get	eh	είναι	eeneh
ει, οι	like ee in see	ee	πείτε	peeteh

ου	like **oo** in r**oo**t	oo	μου	moo
αυ	1) before voiceless consonants (θ, κ, ξ, κ, σ, τ, φ, χ, ψ), like **uff** in p**uff**	ahf	αυτό	ahfto
	2) elsewhere, similar to **ave** in h**ave**	ahv	αυγό	ahvgho
ευ	1) before voiceless consonants, like **ef** in l**ef**t	ehf	ευχή	ehfkhee
	2) elsewhere, like **ev** in l**ev**el	ehv	ευμενής	ehvmehneess
γγ	like **ng** in li**ng**er	ngg	Αγγλία	ahnggleeah
γκ	1) at the beginning of a word like **g** in **g**o	g	γκαμήλα	gahmeelah
	2) in the middle of a word, like **ng** in li**ng**er	ngg	άγκυρα	**ahng**geerah
γξ	like **nks** in li**nks**	ngks	φάλαγξ	**fah**lahngks
γχ	like **ng** followed by the **ch** of Scottish lo**ch**	ngkh	μελαγχολία	mehlahng-kholleeah
μπ	1) at the beginning of a word, like **b** in **b**eer	b	μπορείτε	bor**ree**teh
	2) in the middle of a word, like **mb** in lu**mb**er	mb	Όλυμπος	oll**ee**mboss
ντ	1) at the beginning of a word, like **d** in **d**ear	d	ντομάτα	dom**mah**tah
	2) in the middle of a word, like **nd** in u**nd**er	nd	κέντρο	**keh**ndro
τζ	like **ds** in see**ds**	dz	τζάκι	**dzah**kee

Accent marks

An accent (ά) above a vowel indicates the stressed syllable. A diaeresis (two dots) written over a letter means that the letter is pronounced separately from the previous one, e.g., καιρός is pronounced keh**ross**, but in Κάϊρο, the α and ι are pronounced separately, **kah**eero.

Some basic expressions

Yes.	Ναι.	neh
No.	Όχι.	okhee
Please.	Παρακαλώ.	pahrahkahlo
Thank you.	Ευχαριστώ.	ehfkhahreesto
Thank you very much.	Ευχαριστώ πολύ.	ehfkhahreesto pollee
That's all right/ You're welcome.	Εντάξει/ Ευχαρίστως.	ehndahksee/ ehfkhahreestoss

Greetings *Χαιρετισμοί*

Good morning.	Καλημέρα.	kahleemehrah
Good afternoon.	Καλησπέρα.	kahleespehrah
Good evening.	Καλησπέρα.	kahleespehrah
Good night.	Καληνύκτα.	kahleeneektah
Goodbye.	Αντίο.	ahndeeo
This is Mr./Mrs./ Miss...	Ο κύριος/Η κυρία/ Η δεσποινίδα...	o keereeoss/ee keereeah ee dhehspeeneedhah
How do you do? (Pleased to meet you.)	Τι κάνετε;	tee kahnehteh
How are you?	Πως είστε;	poss eesteh
Very well, thanks. And you?	Πολύ καλά, ευχαριστώ. Και εσείς;	pollee kahlah ehfkhahreesto. keh ehsseess
How's life?	Τι κάνετε;	tee kahnehteh
Fine.	Καλά.	kahlah
I beg your pardon.	Με συγχωρείτε.	meh seengkhorreeteh
Excuse me. (May I get past?)	Συγγνώμη.	seenghnommee
Sorry!	Συγγνώμη!	seenghnommee

Questions *Ερωτήσεις*

Where?	Που;	poo
How?	Πως;	poss
When?	Πότε;	potteh
What?	Τι;	tee
Why?	Γιατί;	yeeahtee
Who?	Ποιος;	peeoss
Which?	Ποιος/Ποια/Ποιο;	peeoss/peeah/peeo
Where is/are...?	Που είναι...;	poo eeneh
Where can I find/get...?	Που μπορώ να βρω/έχω...;	poo borro nah vro/**eh**kho
How far?	Πόσο μακρυά;	posso mahkreeah
How long?	Σε πόσο χρόνο;	seh posso khronno
How much/How many?	Πόσο/Πόσα;	posso/possah
How much does this cost?	Πόσο κοστίζει αυτό;	posso kosteezee ahfto
When does ... open/close?	Πότε ανοίγει/ κλείνει...;	potteh ahneeyee/**klee**nee
What do you call this/that in Greek?	Πως το λένε αυτό/ εκείνο στα Ελληνικά;	poss to **le**hneh ahfto/ ehkeeno stah ehleeneekah
What does this/ that mean?	Τι σημαίνει αυτό/ εκείνο;	tee seemehnee ahfto/ ehkeeno

Do you speak...? *Μιλάτε...;*

Do you speak English?	Μιλάτε Αγγλικά;	meelahteh ahnggleekah
Does anyone here speak English?	Μιλά κανείς Αγγλικά εδώ;	meelah kahneess ahnggleekah ehdho
I don't speak (much) Greek.	Δεν μιλώ (καλά) Ελληνικά.	dhehn meelo (kahlah) ehleeneekah
Could you speak more slowly?	Μπορείτε να μιλάτε πιο αργά;	borreeteh nah meelahteh peeo ahr**gh**ah

Could you repeat that?	Μπορείτε να το επαναλάβετε;	borreeteh nah to ehpahnahlahvehteh
Could you spell it?	Μπορείτε να το συλλαβήσετε;	borreeteh nah to seelahveessehteh
Please write it down.	Γράψτε το, παρακαλώ.	ghrahpsteh to pahrahkahlo
Can you translate this for me/us?	Μπορείτε να μου/ μας το μεταφράσετε;	borreeteh nah moo/mahss to mehtahfrahssehteh
Please point to the... in the book.	Παρακαλώ, δείψτε ... στο βιβλίο.	pahrahkahlo dheeksteh ... sto veevleeo
word	την λέξη	teen lehksee
phrase	την φράση	teen frahssee
sentence	την πρόταση	teen protahsse
Just a moment. I'll see if I can find it in this book.	Μια στιγμή. Να κοιτάζω εάν μπορώ να το βρω σε αυτό το βιβλίο.	meeah steeghmee. nah keetahkso ehahn borro nah to vro seh ahfto to veevleeo
I understand.	Καταλαβαίνω.	kahtahlahvehno
I don't understand.	Δεν καταλαβαίνω.	dhehn kahtahlahvehno
Do you understand?	Καταλαβαίνετε;	kahtahlahvehnehteh

Can/May...?   Μπορώ...;

Can I have...?	Μπορώ να έχω...;	borro nah ehkho
Can we have...?	Μπορούμε να έχουμε...;	borroomeh nah ehkhoomeh
Can you show me?	Μπορείτε να μου δείξετε;	borreeteh nah moo dheeksehteh
I can't.	Δεν μπορώ.	dhehn borro
Can you tell me...?	Μπορείτε να μου πείτε...;	borreeteh nah moo peeteh
Can you help me?	Μπορείτε να με βοηθήσετε;	borreeteh nah meh voeetheessehteh
Can I help you?	Μπορώ να σας βοηθήσω;	borro nah sahss voeetheesso
Can you direct me to...?	Μπορείτε να μου δείξετε...;	borreeteh nah moo dheeksehteh

Wanting... *Ζητώντας...*

I'd like...	Θα ήθελα...	thah eethehlah
We'd like...	Θα θέλαμε...	thah thehlahmeh
What do you want?	Τι θέλετε;	tee thehlehteh
Give me...	Δώστε μου...	dhosteh moo
Give it to me.	Δώστε μου το.	dhosteh moo to
Bring me...	Φέρτε μου...	fehrteh moo
Bring it to me.	Φέρτε μου το.	fehrteh moo to
Show me...	Δείξτε μου...	dheeksteh moo
Show it to me.	Δείξτε μου το.	dheeksteh moo to
I'm looking for...	Ψάχνω...	psahkhno
I'm hungry.	Πεινώ.	peeno
I'm thirsty.	Διψώ.	dheepso
I'm tired.	Είμαι κουρασμένος/-η.	eemeh koorahzmehnoss/-ee
I'm lost.	Χάθηκα.	khahtheekah
It's important.	Είναι σοβαρό.	eeneh sovvahro
It's urgent.	Είναι επείγον.	eeneh ehpeeghonn

It is/There is... *Είναι/Υπάρχει...*

It is...	Είναι...	eeneh
Is it...?	Είναι...;	eeneh
It isn't...	Δεν είναι...	dhehn eeneh
Here it is.	Εδώ είναι.	ehdho eeneh
Here they are.	Εδώ είναι.	ehdho eeneh
There it is.	Εκεί είναι.	ehkee eeneh
There they are.	Εκεί είναι.	ehkee eeneh
There is/There are...	Υπάρχει/Υπάρχουν...	eepahrkhee/eepahrkhoon
Is there/Are there...?	Υπάρχει/Υπάρχουν...;	eepahrkhee/eepahrkhoon
There isn't/aren't...	Δεν υπάρχει/υπάρχουν...	dhehn eepahrkhee/eepahrkhoon
There isn't/aren't any.	Δεν υπάρχει/υπάρχουν καθόλου.	dhehn eepahrkhee/eepahrkhoon kahtholloo

It's... Είναι...

big/small	μεγάλος/μικρός*	meh**ghah**loss/mee**kross**
quick/slow	γρήγορος/αργός	ghree**ghor**ross/ahr**ghoss**
hot/cold	ζεστός/κρύος	zeh**stoss**/**kree**oss
full/empty	γεμάτος/άδειος	yeh**mah**toss/**ah**dheeoss
easy/difficult	εύκολος/δύσκολος	**ehf**kolloss/**dhee**skolloss
heavy/light	βαρύς/ελαφρύς	vah**reess**/ehlah**freess**
open/shut	ανοικτός/κλειστός	ahneek**toss**/klee**stoss**
right/wrong	σωστός/λανθασμένος	so**stoss**/lahnthahz**meh**noss
old/new	παλιός/καινούργιος	pahlee**oss**/keh**noor**yeeoss
old/young	γέρος/νέος	**yeh**ross/**neh**oss
beautiful/ugly	ωραίος/άσχημος	or**reh**oss/**ahs**kheemoss
free (vacant)/ occupied	ελεύθερος/κατειλημένος	ehl**ehf**thehross/ kahteelee**meh**noss
good/bad	καλός/κακός	kah**loss**/kah**koss**
better/worse	καλύτερος/χειρότερος	kah**lee**tehross/ khee**rot**tehross
early/late	νωρίς/αργά	nor**reess**/ahr**ghah**
cheap/expensive	φτηνός/ακριβός	ftee**noss**/ahkree**voss**
here/there	εδώ/εκεί	eh**dho**/eh**kee**

Quantities Ποσότητες

a little/a lot	λίγα/πολλά	**lee**ghah/pol**lah**
few/a few	λίγα/μερικά	**lee**gah/mehree**kah**
much/many	πολύ/πολλοί	pol**lee**/pol**lee**
more/less	περισσότερα/ λιγότερα	pehree**ssot**tehrah/ leegh**ot**tehrah
more than/less than	περισσότερα από/ λιγότερα από	pehree**ssot**tehrah ah**po**/ leegh**ot**tehrah ah**po**
enough/too	αρκετά/πάρα πολύ	ahr**keh**tah/**pah**rah pol**lee**
some/any	μερικά/αρκετά	mehree**kah**/ahr**keh**tah

---

* The endings of adjectives change according to gender and number, see the grammar section for a more detailed explanation.

A few more useful words   *Περισσότερες χρήσι λέξεις*

at	στο	sto
on	επάνω	ehpahno
in	μέσα	**meh**ssah
to	προς	pross
after	μετά	mehtah
before (time)	πριν	preen
before (place)	πριν	preen
for	για	yeeah
from	από	ahpo
with	με	meh
without	χωρίς	khor**reess**
through	δια μέσου	dheeah **meh**ssoo
towards	προς	pross
until	μέχρι	**meh**khree
during	κατά την διάρκεια	kah**tah** teen dheeahr**kee**ah
next to	δίπλα από	**dhee**plah ahpo
near	κοντά	kondah
behind	πίσω από	**pee**sso ahpo
between	ανάμεσα	ah**nah**mehssah
since	από	ahpo
above	επάνω	ehpahno
below	κάτω	**kah**to
under	κάτω από	**kah**to ahpo
inside	μέσα	**meh**ssah
outside	έξω	**ehk**so
up	επάνω	**epah**no
down	κάτω	**kah**to
and	και	keh
or	ή	ee
but	αλλά	ah**lah**
not	δεν	dhehn
never	ποτέ	pot**teh**
nothing	τίποτα	**tee**pottah
very	πολύ	pol**lee**
too (also)	επίσης	eh**pees**seess
yet	ακόμη	ah**kom**mee
soon	σύντομα	seen**dom**mah
now	τώρα	**tor**rah
then	τότε	**tot**teh
perhaps	ίσως	**eess**oss
only	μόνο	**mon**no

Arrival

Passport control *Έλεγχος διαβατηρίου*

Here's my passport.	Ορίστε το διαβατήριο μου.	orreesteh to dheeahvah-teereeo moo
I'll be staying...	Θα μείνω...	thah meeno
a few days	λίγες μέρες	leeyehss mehrehss
a week	μια βδομάδα	meeah vdhommahdhah
two weeks	δύο βδομάδες	dheeo vdhommahdhehss
a month	ένα μήνα	ehnah meenah
I don't know yet.	Δεν ξέρω ακόμα.	dhehn ksehro ahkommah
I'm here...	Είμαι εδώ...	eemeh ehdho
on holiday	για διακοπές	yeeah dheeahkoppehss
on business	για δουλειά	yeeah dhooleeah
on a sightseeing tour	για περιοδεία στα αξιοθέατα	yeeah pehreeodheeah stah ahkseeothehahtah
I'm just passing through.	Είμαι περαστικός/-ή.	eemeh pehrahsteekoss/-ee
I'm sorry, I don't understand.	Συγνώμη δεν, καταλαβαίνω.	seenghnommee dhehn kahtahlahvehno
Does anyone here speak English?	Μιλά κανείς Αγγλικά εδώ;	meelah kahneess ahnggleekah ehdho

---

ΤΕΛΩΝΕΙΟΝ
CUSTOMS

After collecting your luggage at the airport (αεροδρόμιο– ahehro**dhro**mmeeo) you have a choice. Use the green exit if you have nothing to declare, or the red exit if you are carrying items in excess of the permitted limit. Check through the chart on the following page for duty-free allowances into Greece.

εμπορεύματα για δήλωση	τίποτα για δήλωση
goods to declare	nothing to declare

	Cigarettes		Cigars		Tobacco	Spirits (liquor)		Wine
1	200	or	50	or	250 g.	1 l.	or	2 l.
2	300	or	75	or	400 g.	1½ l.	or	5 l.

Perfume:	1) 50 g.	Toilet water:	1) ¹/₄ l.
	2) 75 g.		2) ³/₈ l.

1) visitors entering from non-EEC countries*
2) visitors entering from EEC countries*

I've nothing to declare.	Δεν έχω να δηλώσω τίποτε.	dhehn ehkho nah dheelosso teepotteh
I've...	Έχω...	ehkho
a carton of cigarettes	μια κούτα τσιγάρα	meeah kootah tseeghahrah
a bottle of ...	ένα μπουκάλι ...	ehnah bookahlee
It's for my personal use.	Είναι για προσωπική χρήση.	eeneh yeeah prossoppeekee khreessee
This is a gift.	Αυτό είναι ένα δώρο.	ahfto eeneh ehnah dhorro

Το διαβατήριο σας, παρακαλώ.	Your passport, please.
Έχετε τίποτα να δηλώσετε;	Do you have anything to declare?
Παρακαλώ ανοίξτε αυτή την αποσκευή.	Please open this bag.
Θα πρέπει να πληρώσετε φόρο για αυτό.	You'll have to pay duty on this.
Έχετε και άλλες αποσκευές;	Do you have any more luggage?

---

* All allowances are subject to change without notice.

Baggage – Porter   *Αποσκευές – Αχθοφόρος*

Porter!	Αχθοφόρε!	ahkhthofforreh
Please take this...	Παρακαλώ πάρτε...	pahrahkahlo pahrteh
bag	την τσάντα	teen tsahndah
luggage	τις αποσκευές	teess ahposkehvehss
suitcase	την βαλίτσα	teen vahleetsah
travelling bag	το σακβουαγιάζ	to sahkvooahyeeahz
That's mine.	Αυτή είναι δική μου.	ahftee eeneh dheekee moo
That's not mine.	Αυτή δεν είναι δική μου.	ahftee dhehn eeneh dheekee moo
Take this luggage...	Πάρτε αυτές τις αποσκευές ...	pahrteh ahftehss teess ahposskehvehss
to the bus/train	στο λεωφορείο/τραίνο	sto lehofforreeo/trehno
to the luggage lockers	στο τμήμα αποσκευών	sto tmeemah ahposkehvonn
There's one piece missing.	Λείπει μια αποσκευή.	leepee meeah ahposskehvee
How much is that?	Πόσο κάνει αυτό;	posso kahnee ahfto
Where are the luggage trolleys (carts)?	Που είναι τα καροτσάκια αποσκευών;	poo eeneh tah kahrotsahkeeah ahposkehvonn

Changing money   *Συνάλλαγμα*

Where's the currency exchange office?	Που είναι το γραφείο αλλαγής συναλλάγματος;	poo eeneh to ghrahfeeo ahlahyeess seenahlahghmahtoss
Where can I change some traveller's cheques (checks)?	Που μπορώ να αλλάξω μερικά τράβελερς τσεκς;	poo borro nah ahlahkso mehreekah trahvehlehrs tsehks
I want to change some dollars/pounds.	Θα ήθελα να αλλάξω μερικά δολλάρια/μερικές Αγγλικές λίρες.	thah eethehlah nah ahlahkso mehreekah dhollahreeah/mehreekehss ahngleekehss leerehss
Can you change this into drachmas?	Μπορείτε να αλλάξετε αυτό σε δραχμές;	borreeteh nah ahlahksehteh ahfto seh dhrahkhmehss
What's the exchange rate?	Ποια είναι η τιμή συναλλάγματος;	peeah eeneh ee teemee seenahlahghmahtoss

BANK – CURRENCY, see page 129

Where is...? *Που είναι...;*

Where is the...?	Που είναι το...;	poo **ee**neh to
car hire	γραφείο νοίκιασης αυτοκινήτων	ghrah**fee**o nee**kee**eahsseess ahftokkee**nee**tonn
duty free shop	κατάστημα αφορολογήτων	kah**tah**steemah ahforrolloy**ee**tonn
newsstand	περίπτερο	pe**hree**ptehro
restaurant	εστιατόριο	ehsteeah**tor**reeo
ticket office	γραφείο εισιτηρίων	ghrah**fee**o eesseeteer**ee**onn
tourist office	γραφείο τουρισμού	ghrah**fee**o tooreezmoo
How do I get to...?	Πως μπορώ να πάω στο...;	poss bor**ro** nah **pah**o sto
Is there a bus into town?	Υπάρχει λεωφορείο για την πόλη;	ee**pahr**khee lehofforr**ee**o yee**ah** teen **pol**lee
Where can I get a taxi?	Που μπορώ να βρω ένα ταξί;	poo bor**ro** nah vro **eh**nah **tah**ksee
Where can I hire (rent) a car?	Που μπορώ να νοικιάσω ένα αυτοκίνητο;	poo bor**ro** nah neekee**ah**sso **eh**nah ahftokkee**nee**eto

Hotel reservation *Κράτηση ξενοδοχείου*

Do you have a hotel guide?	Έχετε οδηγό ξενοδοχείου;	**eh**khehteh odhee**gho** ksehnodhokh**ee**oo
Could you reserve a room for me?	Μπορείτε να μου κρατήσετε ένα δωμάτιο;	bor**ree**teh nah moo krah**tee**ssehteh **eh**nah dhomm**ah**teeo
in the centre	στο κέντρο της πόλης	sto **keh**ndro teess **pol**leess
near the railway station	κοντά στο σιδηροδρομικό σταθμό	kon**dah** sto seedheero-dhromm**ee**ko stah**th**mo
a single room	ένα μονό δωμάτιο	**eh**nah monno dhomm**ah**teeo
a double room	ένα διπλό δωμάτιο	**eh**nah dheeplo dhomm**ah**teeo
not too expensive	όχι πολύ ακριβό	okhee pollee ahkree**vo**
Where is the hotel/boarding house?	Που είναι το ξενοδοχείο/πανσιόν;	poo **ee**neh to ksehnodho-**khee**o/pahnsee**onn**
Do you have a street map?	Έχετε οδηκό χάρτη;	**eh**khehteh odhee**ko khahr**tee

HOTEL/ACCOMMODATION, see page 22

Car hire (rental) *Ενοικίαση αυτοκινήτου*

Car hire is fairly expensive. In high season book early, and give advance warning of any special requirements (air conditioning, automatic transmission). In principle, most companies require an international driving licence (Britons excepted), but will normally accept any national licence if it is more than 1 year old. Third party insurance is usually included.

I'd like to hire (rent) a car.	Θα ήθελα να νοικιάσω ένα αυτοκίνητο.	thah **ee**thehlah nah neekee**ah**sso **eh**nah ahfto**kkee**neeto
small	μικρό	mee**kro**
medium-sized	μετρίου μεγέθους	meh**tree**oo mehye**h**thooss
large	μεγάλο	meh**ghah**lo
automatic	αυτόματο	ahf**tom**mahto
I'd like it for a day/a week.	Θα το ήθελα για μια μέρα/βδομάδα.	thah to **ee**thehlah yeeah **mee**ah **meh**rah/vdhom**mah**dhah
Are there any weekend arrangements?	Υπάρχουν διευκόλυνσεις για το Σαββατοκύριακο;	ee**pahr**khoon dheeehfko**lleen**seess yeeah to sahvahto**kkee**reeahko
Do you have any special rates?	Έχετε ειδικές τιμές;	**eh**khehteh eedhee**kehss** tee**mehss**
What's the charge per day/week?	Ποια είναι η τιμή για μια μέρα/βδομάδα;	**pee**ah **ee**neh ee tee**mee** yeeah **mee**ah **meh**rah/vdhom**mah**dhah
Is mileage included?	Συμπεριλαμβάνονται τα χιλιόμετρα;	seembehreelahm**vah**nondeh tah kheelee**om**mehtrah
What's the charge per kilometre?	Ποια είναι η τιμή για κάθε χιλιόμετρο;	**pee**ah **ee**neh ee tee**mee** yeeah **kah**theh kheelee**om**mehtro
I want full insurance.	Θέλω μικτή ασφάλεια.	**theh**lo meek**tee** ahs**fah**leeah
I've a credit card.	Έχω μια πιστωτική κάρτα.	**eh**kho **mee**ah peestottee**kee** **kah**rtah
What's the deposit?	Πόση είναι η εγγύηση;	**pos**see **ee**neh ee ehngg**ee**eessee
Here's my driving licence.	Ορίστε η άδεια οδηγήσεως μου.	or**ree**steh ee **ah**dheeah odhee**yee**eessehoss moo

CAR, see page 75

Taxi *Ταξί*

Taxis are metered in cities and are reasonably cheap, but additional charges (for night travel, luggage, waiting or over special holidays) are not shown. In the country, taxis are not always metered, but fixed rates do exist. Negotiate the approximate fare before leaving.

Where can I get a taxi?	Που μπορώ να βρω ένα ταξί;	poo borro nah vro ehnah tahksee
Please get me a taxi.	Βρέστε μου ένα ταξί, παρακαλώ.	vrehsteh moo ehnah tahksee pahrahkahlo
What's the fare to...?	Ποια είναι η τιμή για...;	peeah eeneh ee teemee yeeah
How far is it to...?	Πόσο μακρυά είναι...;	posso mahkreeah eeneh
Take me to...	Να με πάτε...	nah meh pahteh
this address	σε αυτή την διεύθυνση	seh ahftee teen dheeehftheensee
the airport	στο αεροδρόμιο	sto ahehrodhrommeeo
the town centre	στο κέντρο της πόλης	sto kehndro teess polleess
the ... Hotel	στο ξενοδοχείο...	sto ksehnodhokheeo
Turn left/right at the next corner.	Στρίψτε αριστερά/δεξιά στην επόμενη γωνία.	streepsteh ahreestehrah/dhehkseeah steen ehpommehnee ghonneeah
Go straight ahead.	Πηγαίνετε ίσια.	peeyehnehteh eesseeah
Please stop here.	Παρακαλώ σταματήστε εδώ.	pahrahkahlo stahmahteesteh ehdho
I'm in a hurry.	Είμαι βιαστικός/-ή.	eemeh veeahsteekoss/-ee
Could you drive more slowly?	Μπορείτε να οδηγήτε πιο αργά;	borreeteh nah odheeyeeteh peeo ahrghah
Could you help me carry my luggage?	Μπορείτε να με βοηθήσετε να μεταφέρω τις αποσκευές μου;	borreeteh nah meh voeetheessehteh nah mehtahfehro teess ahposskehvehss moo
Could you wait for me?	Μπορείτε να με περιμένετε;	borreeteh nah meh pehreemehnehteh
I'll be back in 10 minutes.	Θα επιστρέψω σε 10 λεπτά.	thah ehpeestrehpso seh 10 lehptah

TIPPING, see inside back-cover

Hotel — Other accommodation

Hotel reservations are essential during the high season. But if you arrive without one, go to the EOT (national tourist board). The local tourist police will also advise on accommodation throughout the area.

Ξενοδοχείο (ksehnodho**khee**o)	Hotel. There's a high proportion of new hotels in Greece. The government classifies them in six categories according to comfort offered. After luxury class, there are categories A to E. Most hotels can insist on half or full board.	
Μοτέλ (mo**ttehl**)	Motel. There are a few motels which have sprung up in the past years along principal highways.	
Πανδοχείο (pahndho**khee**o)	Inn. These are found in small towns and offer simple but good accommodation.	
Πανσιόν (pahnsee**onn**)	Boarding house. Located in cities, room and board is available at a modest price.	
Ξενώνας νεότητος (ksehnonnahss nehotteetoss)	Youth hostel. These are sometimes known as "youth hostels" in English. They are cheap and clean, and accommodation is usually dormitory-style. Your stay may be limited to five days. You will need an international membership card.	
Διαμερίσματα (dheeahmeh-reezmahtah)	Apartment, bungalow. These are plentiful, particularly on the islands and in coastal resorts. However, you should book well in advance for the high season.	
Δωμάτια (dhommahteeah)	Rooms. These are often advertised in English, mainly on the islands. Accommodation will be cheap and clean, usually with use of the family bathroom and kitchen.	

Can you recommend a hotel/boarding house?	Μπορείτε να μου συστήσετε ένα ξενοδοχείο/πανσιόν;	bor**ree**teh nah moo seest**ee**ssehteh **eh**nah ksehnodho**khee**o/ pahnsee**onn**
Are there any flats (apartments) vacant?	Υπάρχουν άδεια διαμερίσματα;	eepahrkhoon ahdheeah dheeahmehreezmahtah

Checking in – Reception *Στην ρεσεπσιόν*

My name is...	Το όνομα μου είναι...	to onnommah moo eeneh
I've a reservation.	Έχω κρατήσει δωμάτιο.	ehkho krahteessee dhommahteeo
We've reserved two rooms.	Έχομε κρατήσει δύο δωμάτια.	ehkhommeh krahteessee dheeo dhommahteeah
Here's the confirmation.	Εδώ είναι η επιβεβαίωση.	ehdho eeneh ee ehpeevehvehossee
Do you have any vacancies?	Έχετε ακόμη άδεια δωμάτια;	ehkhehteh ahkommee ahdheeah dhommahteeah
I'd like a ... room.	Θα ήθελα ένα... δωμάτιο.	thah eethehlah ehnah... dhommahteeo
single/double	μονό/διπλό	monno/dheeplo
I'd like a room with...	Θα ήθελα ένα δωμάτιο με...	thah eethehlah ehnah dhommahteeah meh
twin beds	δύο κρεββάτια	dheeo krehvahteeah
a double bed	ένα διπλό κρεββάτι	ehnah dheeplo krehvahtee
a bath	μπάνιο	bahneeo
a shower	ντους	dooss
a balcony	μπαλκόνι	bahlkonnee
a view	θέα	thehah
We'd like a room...	Θα θέλαμε ένα δωμάτιο...	thah thehlahmeh ehnah dhommahteeo
in the front	στη πρόσοψη	stee prossopsee
at the back	στο πίσω μέρος	sto peesso mehross
facing the lake/ the mountains/ the sea	προς την λίμνη/ τα βουνά/ την θάλασσα	pross teen leemnee/ tah voonah/ teen thahlahssah
on the ground floor	στο ισόγειον	sto eessoyeeonn
It must be quiet.	Πρέπει να είναι ήσυχο.	prehpee nah eeneh eesseekho
Is there (a)...?	Υπάρχει...;	eepahrkhee
air conditioning	κλιματισμός	kleemahteezmoss
heating	θέρμανση	thehrmahnsee
hot water	ζεστό νερό	zehsto nehro
laundry service	πλυντήριο	pleendeereeo
room service	σέρβις δωματίου	sehrveess dhommahteeoo
private toilet	ιδιωτική τουαλέττα	eedheeotteekee tooahlehtah

CHECKING OUT, see page 31

HOTEL

Could you put... in the room?	Μπορείτε να βάλετε ... στο δωμάτιο;	borreeteh nah vahlehteh ... sto dhommahteeo
an extra bed	ένα επιπρόσθετο κρεββάτι	ehnah ehpeeprosthehto krehvahtee
a cot	ένα παιδικό κρεββάτι	ehnah pehdheeko krehvahtee

How much? *Πόσο;*

What's the price...?	Πόσο κοστίζει...;	posso kosteezee
per week	την βδομάδα	teen vdhommahdhah
per night	την νύκτα	teen neektah
for bed and breakfast	το δωμάτιο και το πρόγευμα	to dhommahteeo keh to proyehvmah
excluding meals	χωρίς τα γεύματα	khorreess tah yehvmahtah
for full board (A.P.)	με πλήρης διατροφή	meh pleereess dheeahtroffee
for half board (M.A.P.)	με ημιδιατροφή	meh eemeedheeahtroffee
Does that include...?	Η τιμή συμπεριλαμβάνει...;	ee teemee seembehreelahmvahnee
breakfast	το πρόγευμα	to proyehvmah
meals	τα γεύματα	tah yehvmahtah
service	το ποσοστό υπηρεσίας	to possosto eepeerehsseeahss
Is there any reduction for children?	Υπάρχει έκπτωση για τα παιδιά;	eepahrkhee ehkptossee yeeah tah pehdheeah
Do you charge for the baby?	Το μωρό πληρώνει;	to morro pleeronnee
That's too expensive.	Είναι πολύ ακριβά.	eeneh pollee ahkreevah
Do you have anything cheaper?	Έχετε άλλο πιο φτηνό;	ehkhehteh ahlo peeo fteeno

How long? *Πόσο καιρό;*

We'll be staying...	Θα μείνουμε...	thah meenoomeh
overnight only	μόνο μια νύκτα	monno meeah neektah
a few days	λίγες μέρες	leeyehss mehrehss
a week (at least)	μια βδομάδα (τουλάχιστον)	meeah vdhommahdhah (toolahkheestonn)
I don't know yet.	Δεν ξέρω ακόμα.	dhehn ksehro ahkommah

NUMBERS, see page 146

Ξενοδοχείο

Decision *Απόφαση*

May I see the room?	Μπορώ να δω το δωμάτιο;	borro nah dho to dhommahteeo
That's fine. I'll take it.	Είναι εντάξει. Θα το πάρω.	eeneh ehndahksee. thah to pahro
No, I don't like it.	Όχι, δεν μου αρέσει.	okhee dhehn moo ahrehssee
It's too...	Είναι πολύ...	eeneh pollee
cold/hot	κρύο/ζεστό	kreeo/zehsto
dark/small	σκοτεινό/μικρό	skotteeno/meekro
It's too noisy.	Έχει πολύ θόρυβο.	ehkhee pollee thorreevo
I asked for a room with a bath.	Ζήτησα δωμάτιο με μπάνιο.	zeeteessah dhommahteeo meh bahneeo
Do you have anything...?	Έχετε κάτι...;	ehkhehteh kahtee
better	καλύτερο	kahleetehro
bigger	μεγαλύτερο	mehghahleetehro
cheaper	φτηνότερο	fteenottehro
quieter	πιο ήσυχο	peeo eesseekho
Do you have a room with a better view?	Έχετε δωμάτιο με καλύτερη θέα;	ehkhehteh dhommahteeo meh kahleetehree thehah

Registration *Καταγραφή*

Upon arrival at a hotel or boarding house you'll be asked to fill in a registration form (έντυπο-**ehn**deepo). The desk clerk may keep your passport overnight.

Επώνυμο/Όνομα	Name/First name
Διεύθυνση/Οδός/Αριθμός	Home address/Street/Number
Εθνικότητα/Επάγγελμα	Nationality/Profession
Τόπος/Ημερομηνία γεννήσεως	Place/Date of birth
Έρχεστε απο.../Προορισμός...	Coming from .../Going to...
Αριθμός διαβατηρίου	Passport number
Τόπος/Ημερομηνία	Place/Date
Υπογραφή	Signature

What does this mean?	Τι σημαίνει αυτό;	tee seemehnee ahfto

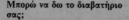

Μπορώ να δω το διαβατήριο σας;	May I see your passport?
Παρακαλώ, συμπληρώστε αυτό το έντυπο.	Would you mind filling in this registration form?
Υπογράψτε εδώ, παρακαλώ.	Sign here, please.
Πόσο καιρό θα μείνετε;	How long will you be staying?

What's my room number?	Ποιος είναι ο αριθμός του δωμάτιου μου;	peeooss eeneh o ahreethmoss too dhommahteeoo moo
Will you have our luggage sent up?	Θα στείλετε τις αποσκευές μας επάνω;	thah steelehteh teess ahposskehvehss mahss ehpahno
Where can I park my car?	Που μπορώ να σταθμεύσω το αυτοκίνητο μου;	poo borro nah stahthmehfso to ahftokkeeneeto moo
Does the hotel have a garage?	Μήπως έχει το ξενοδοχείο γκαράζ;	meeposs ehkhee to ksehnodhokheeo gahrahz
I'd like to leave this in your safe.	Θα ήθελα να αφήσω αυτό στο χρηματοκιβώτιο σας.	thah eethehlah nah ahfeesso ahfto sto khreemahtokkeevotteeo sahss
What time is the front door locked?	Τι ώρα κλείνει η εξώπορτα;	tee orrah kleenee ee ehksopportah

Hotel staff *Υπάλληλοι ξενοδοχείου*

maid	η καμαριέρα	ee kahmahreeehrah
manager	ο διευθυντής	o dheeehftheendeess
porter	ο θυρωρός	o theerorross
receptionist	ο/η* υπάλληλος υποδοχής/ ρεσεπσιονίστ	o/ee eepahleeloss eepodhokheess/ rehsehpsionneest

When calling for service, the best thing to say is παρακαλώ (pahrahkahlo – please).

---

* If referring to a man say ο (o), if to a woman use η (ee).

General requirements   *Γενικές ανάγκες*

The key to room..., please.	Το κλειδί του δωματίου..., παρακαλώ.	to kleedhee too dhommah-teeoo... pahrahkahlo
Is there a bath on this floor?	Υπάρχει μπάνιο σε αυτόν τον όροφο;	eepahrkhee bahneeo seh ahftonn tonn orroffo
What's the voltage here?	Πόσα βολτ είναι το ρεύμα εδώ;	possah volt eeneh to rehvmah ehdho
Where's the socket (outlet) for the shaver?	Που είναι η υποδοχή πρίζας για την ξυριστική μηχανή;	poo eeneh ee eepodhokhee preezahss yeeah teen kseereesteekee meekhahnee
Can you find me a...?	Μπορείτε να μου βρείτε...;	borreeteh nah moo vreeteh
babysitter	μια μπέϊμπυ σίτερ	meeah "babysitter"
secretary	μια γραμματέα	meeah ghrahmahtehah
typewriter	μια γραφομηχανή	meeah ghrahfommee-khahnee
May I have a/an/ some...?	Μπορώ να έχω...;	borro nah ehkho
ashtray	ένα σταχτοδοχείο	ehnah stahktodhokheeo
bath towel	μια πετσέτα του μπάνιου	meeah pehtsehtah too bahneeoo
(extra) blanket	μια κουβέρτα (επιπρόσθετο)	meeah koovehrtah (ehpeeprosthehto)
envelopes	μερικούς φακέλλους	mehreekooss fahkehlooss
(more) hangers	(περισσότερες) κρεμάστρες	(pehreessottehrehss) krehmahstrehss
hot-water bottle	μια θερμοφόρα	meeah thermofforrah
ice cubes	παγοτιέρα	pahghotteeehrah
needle and thread	βελόνι και κλωστή	vehlonnee keh klostee
pillow	μαξιλάρι	mahkseelahree
reading lamp	μια λάμπα για διάβασμα	meeah lahmbah yeeah dheeahvahzmah
soap	σαπούνι	sahpoonee
writing paper	χαρτί αλληλογραφίας	khahrtee ahleeloghrah-feeahss
Where's the...?	Που είναι...;	poo eeneh
bathroom	το μπάνιο	to bahneeo
dining room	η τραπεζαρία	ee trahpehzahreeah
emergency exit	η έξοδος κινδύνου	ee ehksodhoss keendheenoo
hairdresser's	το κομμωτήριο	to kommotteereeo
lift (elevator)	το ασανσέρ	to ahssahnsehr

NUMBERS, see page 146

Telephone – Post (mail) *Τηλέφωνο – Ταχυδρομείο*

Can you get me Athens 1234567?	Μπορείτε να καλέσετε Αθήνα 1234567;	borreeteh nah kahleh-sehteh ahtheenah 1234567
Do you have any stamps?	Έχετε γραμματόσημα;	ehkhehteh ghrahmah-tosseemah
Would you post (mail) this for me, please?	Μπορείτε να μου ταχυδρομήσετε αυτό σας, παρακαλώ;	borreeteh nah moo tahkheedhrommeessehteh ahfto sahss pahrahkahlo
Are there any letters for me?	Υπάρχουν γράμματα για μένα;	eepahrkhoon ghrah-mahtah yeeah mehnah
Are there any messages for me?	Υπάρχει καμμιά παραγγελία για μένα;	eepahrkhee kahmeeah pahrahnggehleeah yeeah mehnah
How much are my telephone charges?	Πόσος είναι ο λογαριασμός του τηλεφώνου μου;	possoss eeneh o loghahreeahzmoss too teelehfonnoo moo

Difficulties *Δυσκολίες*

The... doesn't work.	... δεν λειτουργεί.	... dehn leetooryee
air conditioner	Το σύστημα κλιματισμού	to seesteemah kleemahteezmoo
light	Το φως	to foss
radio	Το ράδιο	to rahdheeo
television	Η τηλεόραση	ee teelehorrahssee
The tap (faucet) is dripping.	Η βρύση στάζει.	ee vreessee stahzee
There's no hot water.	Δεν υπάρχει ζεστό νερό.	dhehn eepahrkhee zehsto nehro
The washbasin is blocked.	Ο νιπτήρας είναι βουλωμένος.	o neepteerahss eeneh voolommehnoss
The window is jammed.	Το παράθυρο δεν ανοίγη.	to pahrahtheero dhehn ahneeyee
The curtains are stuck.	Οι κουρτίνες είναι σκαλωμένες.	ee koorteenehss eeneh skahlommehnehss
The bulb is burned out.	Ο λαμπτήρας κάηκε.	o lahmbteerahss kaheekeh
My room has not been made up.	Το δωμάτιο μου δεν ετοιμάστηκε.	to dhommahteeo moo dhehn ehteemahsteekeh

POST OFFICE AND TELEPHONE, see page 132

The... is broken.	... έσπασε.	... ehspahssee
blind	Το ρολό	to rollo
lamp	Η λάμπα	ee lahmbah
plug	Η πρίζα	ee preezah
shutter	Το εξώφυλλο	to ehksoffeelo
switch	Ο διακόπτης	o dheeahkopteess
Can you get it repaired?	Μπορείτε να το διορθώσετε;	borreeteh nah to dheeorthossehteh

Laundry – Dry cleaner's   Πλυντήριο – Στεγνοκαθριστήριο

I want these clothes...	Θα ήθελα να δώσω αυτά τα ρούχα για...	thah eethehlah nah dhosso ahftah tah rookhah yeeah
cleaned	καθάρισμα	kahthahreezmah
ironed/pressed	σιδέρωμα	seedhehrommah
washed	πλύσιμο	pleesseemo
When will they be ready?	Πότε θα είναι έτοιμα;	potteh thah eeneh ehteemah
I need them...	Τα χρειάζομαι...	tah khreeahzommeh
today	σήμερα	seemehrah
tomorrow	αύριο	ahvreeo
before Friday	πριν την Παρασκευή	preen teen pahrahskehvee
Can you ... this?	Μπορείτε να... αυτό;	borreeteh nah... ahfto
mend	διορθώσετε	dheeorthossehteh
patch	μπαλώσετε	bahlossehteh
stitch	ράψετε	rahpsehteh
Can you sew on this button?	Μπορείτε να ράψετε αυτό το κουμπί;	borreeteh nah rahpsehteh ahfto to koombee
Can you get this stain out?	Μπορείτε να καθαρίσετε αυτόν τον λεκέ;	borreeteh nah kahthah-reessehteh ahftonn tonn lehkeh
Is my laundry ready?	Είναι έτοιμα τα ρούχα μου;	eeneh ehteemah tah rookhah moo
This isn't mine.	Αυτό δεν είναι δικό μου.	ahfto dhehn eeneh dheeko moo
There's something missing.	Κάτι λείπει.	kahtee leepee
There's a hole in this.	Υπάρχει μια τρύπα σε αυτό.	eepahrkhee meeah treepah seh ahfto
It's shrunk.	Μάζεψε.	mahzehpsee

Hairdresser – Barber *Κομμωτήριο – Κουρείο*

Is there a hairdresser/ beauty salon in the hotel?	Υπάρχει κομμωτήριο/ ινστιτούτο καλλονής στο ξενοδοχείο;	eepahrkhee kommo-teereeo/eensteetooto kahlonneess sto ksehnodhokheeo
Can I make an appointment for ...?	Μπορώ να κλείσω ραντεβού για την ...;	borro nah kleesso rahndehvoo yeeah teen
I'd like it cut and shaped.	Θα ήθελα κόψιμο και φορμάρισμα.	thah eethehlah kopseemo keh formahreezmah
I want a haircut, please.	Θέλω να με κουρέψετε, παρακαλώ.	thehlo nah meh kooreh-psehteh pahrahkahlo
bleach	ξέβαμμα	ksehvahmah
blow-dry	στέγνωμα	steghnommah
colour rinse	ένα ρενάζ	ehnah rehnsahz
dye	μια βαφή	meeah vahfee
face pack	μια μάσκα για το πρόσωπο	meeah mahskah yeeah to prossoppo
manicure	μανικιούρ	mahneekeeoor
permanent wave	μια περμανάντ	meeah pehrmahnahnd
setting lotion	αφρό-λακ	ahfro-lahk
shampoo and set	σαμπουάν και μιζ αν πλι	sahmbooahn keh meez ahn plee
with a fringe (bangs)	με φράντζα	meh frahndzah
I'd like a shampoo for ... hair.	Θα ήθελα ένα σαμπουάν για ... μαλλιά.	thah eethehlah ehnah sahmbooahn yeeah ... mahleeah
normal/dry/greasy (oily)	κανονικά/ξηρά/ λιπαρά	kahnonneekah/kseerah/ leepahrah
Do you have a colour chart?	Έχετε ένα δειγματολόγιο;	ehkhehteh ehnah dheeghmahtolloyeeo
Don't cut it too short.	Μη τα κόψετε πολύ κοντά.	mee tah kopsehteh pollee kondah
A little more off the...	Να τα κόψετε λίγο ακόμη...	nah tah kopsehteh leegho ahkommee
back	πίσω	peesso
neck	στο σβέρκο	sto svehrko
sides	στα πλάγια	stah plahyeeah
top	επάνω	ehpahno
I don't want any hairspray.	Δεν θέλω λακ.	dhehn thehlo lahk
I'd like a shave.	Ξύρισμα, παρακαλώ.	kseereezmah pahrahkahlo

DAYS OF THE WEEK, see page 150

Would you trim my..., please?	Παρακαλώ, μου κόβετε λίγο...	pahrahkahlo moo kovvehteh leegho
beard	τα γένεια	tah yehneeah
moustache	το μουστάκι	to moostahkee
sideboards (sideburns)	τις φαβορίτες	teess fahvorreetehss

Checking out *Αναχώρηση*

May I have my bill, please?	Μπορώ να έχω τον λογαριασμό, παρακαλώ;	borro nah ehkho tonn loghahreeahzmo pahrahkahlo
I'm leaving early in the morning.	Φεύγω αύριο νωρίς το πρωί.	fehvgho ahvreeo norreess to proee
Please have my bill ready.	Μπορείτε να μου ετοιμάσετε τον λογαριασμό, παρακαλώ.	borreeteh nah moo ehteemahssehteh tonn loghahreeahzmo pahrahkahlo
We'll be checking out around noon.	Θα φύγουμε κατά το μεσημέρι.	thah feeghoomeh kahtah to mehsseemehree
I must leave at once.	Πρέπει να φύγω αμέσως.	prehpee nah feegho ahmehssoss
Is everything included?	Συμπεριλαμβάνονται τα πάντα;	seembehreelahmvahnondeh tah pahndah
Can I pay by credit card?	Μπορώ να πληρώσω με πιστωτική κάρτα;	borro nah pleerosso meh peestotteekee kahrtah
I think there's a mistake in this bill.	Νομίζω κάνατε λάθος στο λογαριασμό.	nommeezo kahnahteh lahthoss sto loghahreeahzmo
Can you get us a taxi?	Μπορείτε να μας βρείτε ένα ταξί;	borreeteh nah mahss vreeteh ehnah tahksee
Would you send someone to bring down our baggage?	Θα μπορούσατε να στείλετε κάποιον να κατεβάσει τις αποσκευές μας;	thah borroossahteh nah steelehteh kahpeeonn nah kahtehvahssee teess ahposkehvehss mahss
Here's the forwarding address.	Αυτή είναι η επόμενη μου διεύθυνση.	ahftee eeneh ee ehpommehnee moo dheeehftheensee
You have my home address.	Έχετε τη διεύθυνση κατοικίας μου.	ehkhehteh tee dheeehftheensee kahteekeeahss moo
It's been a very enjoyable stay.	Η διαμονή ήταν πολύ ευχάριστη.	ee dheeahmonnee eetahn pollee ehfkhahreestee

TIPPING, see inside back-cover

Camping   *Κατασκήνωση (Κάμπινγκ)*

There are camp sites all over Greece (except on Rhodes), and it is illegal to camp anywhere else. They are usually clean and imaginatively planned, with good facilities.

Is there a camp site near here?	Υπάρχει ένα μέρος για κάμπινγκ εδώ κοντά;	eepahrkhee ehnah mehross yeeah "camping" ehdho kondah
Can we camp here?	Μπορούμε να κατασκηνώσουμε εδώ;	borroomeh nah kahtahskeenossoomeh ehdho
Do you have room for a tent/caravan (trailer)?	Έχετε μέρος για την σκηνή/τροχόσπιτο;	ehkhehteh mehross yeeah teen skeenee/trokhospeeto
What's the charge...?	Πόσο κοστίζει...;	posso kosteezee
per day	την μέρα	teen mehrah
per person	το άτομο	to ahtommo
for a car	ένα αυτοκίνητο	ehnah ahftokkeeneeto
for a tent	μια σκηνή	meeah skeenee
for a caravan (trailer)	ένα τροχόσπιτο	ehnah trokhospeeto
Is the tourist tax included?	Συμπεριλαμβάνετε και ο τουριστικός φόρος;	seembehreelahmvahnehteh keh o tooreesteekoss forross
Is there/Are there (a)...?	Υπάρχει/ Υπάρχουν...;	eepahrkhee/ eepahrkhoon
drinking water	πόσιμο νερό	posseemo nehro
electricity	ρεύμα	rehvmah
playground	γήπεδο	gheepehdho
restaurant	εστιατόριο	ehsteeahtorreeo
shopping facilities	ευκολίες για ψώνια	ehfkolleeehss yeeah psonneeah
swimming pool	πισίνα	peesseenah
Where are the showers/toilets?	Που είναι τα ντους/οι τουαλέττες;	poo eeneh tah dooss/ee tooahlehtehss
Where can I get butane gas?	Που μπορώ να βρω υγραέριο;	poo borro nah vro eeghrahehreeo

ΑΠΑΓΟΡΕΥΕΤΑΙ ΤΟ ΚΑΜΠΙΝΓΚ CAMPING PROHIBITED	ΑΠΑΓΟΡΕΥΟΝΤΑΙ ΤΑ ΤΡΟΧΟΣΠΙΤΑ NO CARAVANS (TRAILERS)

CAMPING EQUIPMENT, see page 106

Eating out

There are many types of places where you can eat and drink in Greece.

Γαλακτοπωλείο (ghahlahktopolleeo)	This is a shop selling milk, butter, and yoghurt; you can also buy pastries and ice-cream.
Εστιατόριο (ehsteeahtorreeo)	This is the general, collective word for restaurants.
Ζαχαροπλαστείο (zahkhahroplahsteeo)	A tea-room, where you can also buy sweets.
Καφενείο (kahfehneeo)	A coffee house.
Ουζερί (oozehree)	A bar. The name is inspired by the typically Greek aperitif, *ouzo*.
Σνακ-μπαρ ("snack bar")	A snack-bar. The Greeks have taken over the word.
Ταβέρνα (tahvehrnah)	This is the sign to look for if you want to try some real Greek dishes.
Χασαποταβέρνα (khahssahpottah-vehrnah)	A grill-room attached to a butcher's shop.
Ψαροταβέρνα (psahrottahvehrnah)	This is a *taverna* specializing in seafood.
Ψησταριά (pseestahreeah)	Again, a kind of *taverna*, but specializing in charcoal-grilled food.

Greek cuisine *Ελληνική κουζίνα*

Although Greek cuisine cannot be compared to that of France, nevertheless it has a long and honorable tradition, going back to Plato and even further. In terms of simply-prepared dishes made from the freshest ingredients, it cannot be beaten.

Many Greek dishes have Turkish names and indeed are also found in Turkey. Both countries claim the existing cuisine as their own, but it seems more likely that it was evolved by the Greeks and taken on by the Turks during the many years that they occupied Greece. The Greeks were great travellers and exchanged culinary knowledge with many of the countries they passed through.

The principal elements of Greek cuisine are vegetables such as artichokes and aubergines, tomatoes and olives, olive oil, and seasonings like lemon juice, garlic, basil, oregano and rosemary.

Although meat dishes are limited (mutton and poultry are the most common), vegetables are fresh and inventively combined. Fish and seafood are excellent, the former possibly best when grilled and served with lemon wedges, but prices can go very high.

Care must be taken when having an aperitif before a meal not to eat too many hors d'oeuvres. These are very tempting ranging from whitebait to tiny parcels of stuffed vine leaves, numerous dips and canapés.

And when the heat of the afternoon sun has abated, what better way of waking from a siesta than with a strong black coffee and a very, very sweet pastry like *baclava*.

Meal times Ώρες φαγητού

The Greeks like to eat quite late, it's not unusual to start dinner at 10 p.m. However, in most restaurants you can usually get a meal as early as you would at home.

Breakfast (το πρόγευμα – to **pro**yehvmah) is generally served between 7 and 10 a.m.

Lunch (το γεύμα – to **yehv**mah) is from about 12.30 to 3 p.m.

Dinner (ο δείπνος – ο **dhee**pnoss) is from around 7 until midnight or 1 a.m. In nightclubs you can usually get served even later.

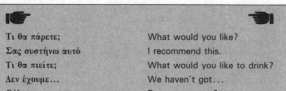

Τι θα πάρετε;	What would you like?
Σας συστήνω αυτό	I recommend this.
Τι θα πιείτε;	What would you like to drink?
Δεν έχουμε...	We haven't got...
Θέλετε...;	Do you want...?

Hungry? *Πεινασμένος;*

I'm hungry.	Πεινώ.	peeno
I'm thirsty.	Διψώ.	dheepso
Can you recommend a good restaurant?	Μπορείτε να μου συστήσετε ένα καλό εστιατόριο;	borreeteh nah moo seesteessehteh ehnah kahlo ehsteeahtorreeo
Where can I get a typical Greek meal?	Που μπορώ να βρω Ελληνικό φαγητό;	poo borro nah vro ehleeneeko fahyeeto
Are there any inexpensive restaurants around here?	Υπάρχουν φθηνά εστιατόρια εδώ κοντά;	eepahrkhoon ftheenah ehsteeahtorreeah ehdho kondah
Where can I get a snack?	Που μπορώ να έχω ένα σνακ;	poo borro nah ehkho ehnah "snack"

If you want to be sure of getting a table in well-known restaurants, it may be better to telephone in advance.

I'd like to reserve a table for 4.	Θα ήθελα να κρατήσω ένα τραπέζι για 4.	thah eetehlah nah krahteesso ehnah trahpehzee yeeah 4
I'd like to reserve a table for...	Θα ήθελα να κρατήσω ένα τραπέζι για...	thah eetehlah nah krahteesso ehnah trahpehzee yeeah
this evening	απόψε	ahpopseh
for tomorrow	αύριο	ahvreeo
for lunch	γεύμα	yehvmah
We'll come at 8.	Θα έλθουμε στις 8.	thah ehlthoomeh steess 8
My name is...	Το όνομα μου είναι...	to onommah moo eeneh

Could we have a table...?	Μπορούμε να έχουμε ένα τραπέζι...;	borroomeh nah ehkhoomeh ehnah trahpehzee
in the corner	στη γωνία	stee ghonneeah
by the window	στο παράθυρο	sto pahrahtheero
outside	έξω	ehkso
on the terrace	στη ταράτσα	stee tahrahtsah
in a non-smoking area	στη περιοχή των μη καπνιστών	stee pehreeokhee tonn mee kahpneestonn

Asking and ordering   Ερωτώ και παραγγέλω

Waiter/Waitress!	Σερβιτόρε/Σερβιτόρα!	sehrveetorreh/ serveetorrah
I'd like something to eat/drink.	Θα ήθελα κάτι να φάω/πίνω.	thah eethehlah kahtee nah faho/peeno
May I have the menu, please?	Μπορώ να έχω την κάρτα με τα μενού, παρακαλώ;	borro nah ehkho teen kahrtah meh tah mehnoo pahrahkahlo
Do you have a set menu/local dishes?	Έχετε έτοιμο μενού/ ντόπια φαγητά;	ehkhehteh ehteemo mehnoo/doppeeah fahyeetah
What do you recommend?	Τι μας συστήνετε;	tee mahss seesteenehteh
Do you have anything ready quickly?	Έχετε κάτι που να γίνεται γρήγορα;	ehkhehteh kahtee poo nah yeenehteh ghreeghorrah
I'm in a hurry.	Είμαι βιαστικός/-ή.	eemeh veeahsteekoss/-ee
Could we have a/an... please?	Θα μπορούσαμε να έχουμε... παρακαλώ;	thah borroossahmeh nah ehkhoomeh... pahrahkahlo
ashtray	ένα σταχτοδοχείο	ehnah stahkhtodhokheeo
cup	ένα φλιτζάνι	ehnah fleedzahnee
fork	ένα πηρούνι	ehnah peeroonee
glass	ένα ποτήρι	ehnah potteeree
knife	ένα μαχαίρι	ehnah mahkhehree
napkin (serviette)	μια πετσέτα	meeah pehtsehtah
plate	ένα πιάτο	ehnah peeahto
spoon	ένα κουτάλι	ehnah kootahlee
May I have some...?	Μπορώ να έχω...;	borro nah ehkho
bread	ψωμί	psommee
butter	βούτυρο	vooteero

NUMBERS, see page 146

Εστιατόριο – Φαγητά

37

lemon	λεμόνι	lehmonnee
oil	λάδι	lahdhee
pepper	πιπέρι	peepehree
seasonings	καρύκευματα	kahreekehvmahtah
vinegar	ξύδι	kseedhee

Some useful expressions for dieters and special requirements:

I'm on a diet.	Κάνω δίαιτα.	kahno dheeehtah
I don't drink alcohol.	Δεν πίνω αλκοόλ.	dhehn peeno ahlko-ol
I mustn't eat food containing...	Δεν πρέπει να τρώγω φαγητά που περιέχουν...	dhehn prehpee nah trogho fahyeetah poo pehreeehkhoon
flour/fat	αλεύρι/λίπος	ahlehvree/leeposs
salt/sugar	αλάτι/ζάχαρη	ahlahtee/zahkhahree
Do you have... for diabetics?	Έχετε... για διαβητικούς;	ehkhehteh... yeeah dheeahveeteekooss
cakes	κέικς	"cakes"
fruit juice	χυμούς φρούτων	kheemooss frootonn
a special menu	ειδικά μενού	eedheekah mehnoo
Do you have vegetarian dishes?	Έχετε πιάτα για χορτοφάγους;	ehkhehteh peeahtah yeeah khortofahghooss
Could I have... instead of dessert?	Μπορώ να έχω... αντί του επιδορπίου;	borro nah ehkho... ahndee too ehpeedhorpeeoo
Can I have an artificial sweetener?	Μπορώ να έχω ζαχαρίνη;	borro nah ehkho zahkhahreenee

And...

I'd like some more.	Θα ήθελα λίγο ακόμη.	thah eethehlah leegho ahkommee
Can I have more..., please?	Μπορώ να έχω περισσότερα..., παρακαλώ;	borro nah ehkho pehreessottehrah... pahrahkahlo
Just a small portion.	Μόνο μια μικρή μερίδα.	monno meeah meekree mehreedhah
Nothing more, thanks.	Τίποτε άλλο, ευχαριστώ.	teepotteh ahlo ehfkhahreesto
Where are the toilets?	Που είναι οι τουαλέττες;	poo eeneh ee tooahlehtehss

Breakfast *Πρόγευμα*

For Greeks the first meal of the day is the least important. It usually comprises a few cups of strong, black coffee and maybe some sweet rolls or cakes. However, visitors are normally given a continental breakfast, and some hotels will even provide an English breakfast with bacon and eggs.

I'd like breakfast, please.	Θέλω να προγευματίσω, παρακαλώ.	thehlo nah proyehvmah-teesso pahrahkahlo
I'll have a/an/ some...	Θέλω...	thehlo
bacon and eggs	αυγά με μπέικον	ahvghah meh "bacon"
boiled egg	ένα βραστό αυγό	ehnah vrahsto ahvgho
soft/hard	μελάτα/σφικτά	mehlahtah/sfeektah
eggs	αυγά	ahvghah
fried eggs	τηγανιτά αυγά	teeghahneetah ahvghah
scrambled eggs	χτυπητά αυγά	khteepeetah ahvghah
fruit juice	ένα χυμό φρούτων	ehnah kheemo frootonn
grapefruit	κρέιπφρουτ	"grapefruit"
orange	πορτοκάλι	portokahlee
ham and eggs	αυγά με ζαμπόν	ahvghah meh zahmbonn
jam	μαρμελάδα	mahrmehlahdhah
marmalade	μια μαρμελάδα πορτοκάλι	meeah mahrmehlahdhah portokkahlee
toast	ένα τοστ	ehnah tost
yoghurt	γιαούρτι	yeeahoortee
May I have some...?	Μπορώ να έχω...;	borro nah ehkho
bread	ψωμί	psommee
butter	βούτυρο	vooteero
(hot) chocolate	(ζεστή) σοκολάτα	(zehstee) sokkollahtah
coffee	καφέ	kahfeh
decaffeinated	χωρίς καφεΐνη	khorreess kahfeheenee
black/ with milk	μαύρο/με γάλα	mahvro/meh ghahlah
honey	μέλι	mehlee
milk	γάλα	ghahlah
cold/hot	κρύο/ζεστό	kreeo/zehsto
pepper	πιπέρι	peepehree
rolls	ψωμάκια	psommahkeeah
salt	αλάτι	ahlahtee
tea	τσάι	tsahee
with milk	με γάλα	meh ghahlah
with lemon	με λεμόνι	meh lehmonnee
(hot) water	(ζεστό) νερό	(zehsto) nehro

What's on the menu?   *Τι περιέχει η κάρτα με τα μενού;*

When ordering, one of the possibilities is to stroll into the kitchen and have a look at what's cooking in the various pots and pans. This is acceptable and even encouraged in some restaurants.

However, if you don't want to do that, under the headings below you'll find alphabetical lists of food and dishes that might be offered on a Greek menu with their English equivalent. You can simply show the book to the waiter. If you want some fruit, for instance, let him point to what's available on the appropriate list. Use pages 36 and 37 for ordering in general.

Reading the menu   *Διαβάζοντας το μενού*

Επιπλέον...	... extra
Κατά παραγγελία	Made to order
Κατά προτίμηση	Of your choice
Κρύα πιάτα	Cold dishes
Μενού της μέρας	Set menu of the day
Ο μάγειρας σας συστήνει...	The chef recommends...
Πιάτο της μέρας	Dish of the day
Σπεσιαλιτέ	Specialities
Σπιτίσιο	Home made
Συστήνομε...	We recommend...
Η σπεσιαλιτέ του καταστήματος	Speciality of the house
Σπεσιαλιτέ της περιοχής	Local specialities

αναψυκτικό	ahnahpseekteeko	soft drink
αστρακοειδή	ahstrahkoeedhee	shellfish
επιδόρπια	ehpeedhorpeeah	desserts
θαλασσινά	thahlahseenah	seafood
κυνήγι	keeneeyee	game
κρασί	krahssee	wine
κρέας	krehahss	meat
κρέας στη σχάρα	krehahss stee skhahrah	grilled meat
λαχανικά	lahkhahneekah	vegetables
ομελέττες	ommehlehtehss	omelets
παγωτό	pahghotto	ice cream
πάστες	pahstehss	pastries
παστίτσιο	pahsteetseeo	pasta
πατάτες	pahtahtehss	potatoes
πατάτες τηγανιτές	pahtahtehss teeghahneetehss	chips (french fries)
πουλερικά	poolehreekah	poultry
ποτά	pottah	drinks
πρώτο πιάτο	protto peeahto	first course
ψάρι	psahree	fish
ρίζι	reezee	rice
σαλάτες	sahlahtehss	salads
σούπες	soopehss	soups
τυρί	teeree	cheese
φρούτα	frootah	fruit

Starters (Appetizers)   *Ορεκτικά*

I'd like an appetizer.	Θα ήθελα ένα ορεκτικό.	thah **ee**thehlah **eh**nah orrehk**tee**ko
What do you recommend?	Τι μας συστήνετε;	tee mahss seesteenehteh
αβοκάδο	ahvo**kkah**dho	avocado
αγγινάρες	ahnggee**nah**rehss	artichokes
αντζούγιες	ahn**dzoo**yee-ehss	anchovies
αυγά (με μαγιονέζα)	ahv**ghah** (meh mahyeeo**nneh**zah)	eggs (with mayonnaise)
γαρίδες	ghah**reed**hehss	prawns (shrimp)
γαρίδες κοκταίηλ	ghah**reed**hehss kok**teh**eel	prawn cocktail
ελιές (γεμιστές)	ehlee**ehss** (yehmees**tehss**)	(stuffed) olives
ζαμπόν (βραστό/ καπνιστό)	zahm**bonn** (vrah**sto**/ kahpnee**sto**)	ham (boiled/ smoked)
καβούρι	kahv**oo**ree	crab
καραβίδα	kahrah**veed**hah	crawfish
κρύο κρέας	**kree**o **kreh**ahss	cold meat
μανιτάρια	mahnee**tah**reeah	mushrooms
σκουμπρί	skoom**bree**	mackerel
πατέ	pah**teh**	pâté
πεπόνι	peh**po**nnee	melon
ποικιλία ορεκτικών	peekee**lee**ah orrehktee**konn**	assorted appetizers
ραπανάκια	rahpah**nah**keeah	radishes
ρέγγα (καπνιστή)	**rehn**ggah (kahpnees**tee**)	(smoked) herring
σαλάμι	sah**lah**mee	salami
σαλάτα	sah**lah**tah	salad
σαρδέλλες	sahrd**heh**lehss	sardines
σολωμός (καπνιστός)	sollom**moss** (kahpnees**toss**)	(smoked) salmon
σπαράγγια	spah**rahn**ggeeah	asparagus
στρείδια	**stree**dheeah	oysters
τόννος	**ton**noss	tuna (tunny)
χαβιάρι	khahvee**ah**ree	caviar
χέλι (καπνιστό)	**kheh**lee (kahpnee**sto**)	(smoked) eel
χυμός φρούτου	khee**moss froo**too	fruit juice

ντολμαδάκια (dolmah**dhah**keeah)	vine leaves stuffed with rice and onions and flavoured with herbs.
ταραμοσαλάτα (tahrahmossah**lah**tah)	paté made from fish roe blended with bread, olive oil and onions.
κολοκύθια τηγανιτά (kolo**kee**theeah teeghahnee**tah**)	courgettes sliced into rounds, dipped into batter and fried.

Salads   Σαλάτες

Salads are plentiful and very varied. Many are a meal in themselves, while others are more like dips than salads, served with flat bread or raw vegetables.

What salads do you have?	Τι σαλάτες έχετε;	tee sahlahtehss ehkhehteh

σαλάτα	sahlahtah	salad
αγγινάρες	ahnggeenahrehss	artichoke
κοκκινογούλια	kokkeenoghooleeah	beetroot
ντομάτες και	dommahtehss keh	tomato and
αγγούρια	ahnggooreeah	cucumber
μαρούλι	mahroolee	lettuce
μελιτζάνες	mehleedzahnehss	aubergine

γαριδοσαλάτα (ghahreedhossahlahtah)	shrimp in oil and lemon sauce
τζατζίκι (dzahdzeekee)	a salad made of yoghurt, cucumber, garlic, olive oil and mint
σκορδαλιά (skordhahleeah)	chopped garlic and potatoes in olive oil
χόρτα σαλάτα (khortah sahlahtah)	''herb salad''; boiled herbs with olive oil and lemon sauce, especially as a dressing for fish
χωριάτικη σαλάτα (khorreeahteekee sahlahtah)	a typically Greek salad made of olives, tomatoes, cucumber, onions, parsley, green peppers and *feta* (white goat cheese)
χούμους (khoomooss)	chick peas blended with tahini (sesame seed paste), oil, lemon and garlic

Egg dishes – Omelets   Πιάτα αυγών – Ομελέττες

I'd like an omelet.	Θα ήθελα μια ομελέττα.	thah eethehlah meeah ommehlehtah

αυγά	ahvghah	eggs
μελάτα	mehlahtah	soft-boiled
σφικτά	sfeektah	hard-boiled
τηγανιτά (μάτια)	teeghahneetah (mahteeah)	fried
ποσσέ	posseh	poached
ομελέττα με αγκινάρες	ommehlehtah meh ahnggeenahrehss	artichoke omelet
ομελέττα με ζαμπόν	ommehlehtah meh zahmbonn	ham omelet

ομελέττα με λουκάνικα	ommehlehtah meh lookahneekah	sausage omelet
ομελέττα με ντομάτα	ommehlehtah meh dommahtah	tomato omelet
ομελέττα με πατάτες	ommehlehtah meh pahtahtehss	potato omelet
ομελέττα με συκωτάκια πουλιών	ommehlehtah meh seekottahkeeah pooleeonn	chicken liver omelet
ομελέττα με τυρί	ommehlehtah meh teeree	cheese omelet

Soups *Σούπες*

You can find very tasty fish soups made either with tomato sauce or with eggs and lemon sauce.

| I'd like some soup. | Θα ήθελα μια σούπα. | thah eethehlah meeah soopah |
| What do you recommend? | Τι μου συστήνετε; | tee moo seesteenehteh |

κοτόσουπα	kottossoopah	clear chicken soup
κρεατόσουπα	krehahtossoopah	clear meat soup
μαγειρίτσα	mahyeereetsah	typical Easter soup made of minced lamb entrails
ρεβύθια	rehveetheeah	chick-pea soup
σούπα αυγολέμονο	soopah ahvghollehmonno	soup with rice, eggs and lemon juice
σούπα πατσάς	soopah pahtsahss	tripe soup
σούπα τραχανάς	soopah trahkhahnahss	semolina soup
σούπα φακές	soopah fahkehss	lentil soup
σούπα χυλοπίττες	soopah kheelohpeetehss	noodle soup
τοματόσουπα	tommahtossoopah	tomato soup
ταχινόσουπα	tahkheenossoopah	"tahini" (sesame seed) soup
φασολάδα	fahssollahdhah	kidney bean soup with tomatoes
χορτόσουπα	khortossoopah	vegetable soup

Particularly on the coast and the islands, fish soup and stew are favourite dishes. Try one of these:

| κακαβιά | kahkahveeah | spicy fish stew |
| ψαρόσουπα | psahrossoopah | fish soup |

Fish and seafood Ψάρι και θαλασσινά

Aegean and Ionian waters supply coastal towns with a wealth
of fish and seafood, while freshwater fish is available inland in
lakeside areas. Fish is usually grilled or fried, basted with oil and
served with lemon juice.

Certain fish dishes can turn out very expensive so make sure
you know what you're ordering.

I'd like some fish.	Θα ήθελα λίγο ψάρι.	thah **ee**thehlah **lee**gho **psah**ree
What kinds of seafood do you have?	Τι είδη θαλασσινών έχετε;	tee **ee**dhee thahlahssee**nonn eh**khehteh
αντζούγιες	ahnd**zoo**yee-ehss	anchovies
αστακός	ahstah**koss**	lobster
αχινός	ahkhee**noss**	sea urchin
γαλέος	ghah**leh**hoss	lamprey
γαρίδες	ghah**ree**dhehss	prawns (shrimp)
γλώσσα	**ghlos**sah	sole
γόπα	**ghop**pah	large sardine
καβούρι	kah**voo**ree	crab
καλαμάρι	kahlah**mah**ree	squid
καραβίδα	kahrah**vee**dhah	crawfish
κέφαλος	**keh**fahloss	mullet
λακέρδα	lah**kehr**dhah	salted tuna (tunny)
λυθρίνι	leeth**ree**nee	grey mullet
μπακαλιάρος	bahkahlee**ah**ross	fresh cod
μπακαλιάρος παστός	bahkahlee**ah**ross pah**stoss**	cured cod
μπαρμπούνι	bahr**boo**nee	red mullet
μύδια	**meed**heeah	mussels
πέρκα	**pehr**kah	perch
πέστροφα	**pehs**troffah	trout
ρέγγα	**rehn**ggah	herring
σαρδέλλα	sahr**dheh**lah	sardine
σκουμπρί	skoom**bree**	mackerel
σουπιά	soo**peeah**	cuttlefish
στρείδια	**stree**dheeah	oysters
συναγρίδα	seenah**ghree**dhah	sea bream
σφυρίδα	sfee**ree**dhah	whiting
τόννος	**ton**noss	tuna (tunny)
τσιπούρα	tsee**poo**rah	gilthead fish
χελιδονόψαρο	khehleedhon**nop**sahro	flying fish
χέλι	**kheh**lee	eel
χταπόδι	khtah**pod**hee	octopus

baked	του φούρνου	too foornoo
cured	παστός	pahstoss
deep fried	τηγανισμένος σε πολύ λάδι	teeghahneezmehnoss seh pollee lahdhee
fried	τηγανιτός	teeghahneetoss
grilled	της σχάρας	teess skahrahss
marinated	μαρινάτος	mahreenahtoss
poached	ποσέ	posseh
smoked	καπνιστός	kahpneestoss
steamed	του ατμό	too ahtmo
stewed	βραστός	vrahstoss

αστακός
(ahstahkoss)
: crawfish often served with oil and lemon sauce or garlic mayonnaise, expensive

γαρίδες με φέτα
(ghahreedhehss meh fehtah)
: sautéed onions, tomatoes and seasonings baked with shrimp and topped with *feta* cheese.

μαρίδες
(mahreedhehss)
: fried smelt

ξιφίας
(kseefeeahss)
: swordfish, sometimes flavoured with oregano and grilled on a skewer

σουπιές με σπανάκι
(soopeeehss meh spahnahkee)
: cuttlefish with spinach

σουφλέ από θαλασσινά
(soofleh ahpo thahlahsseenah)
: shellfish soufflé

χταπόδι κρασάτο
(khtahpodhee krahssahto)
: octopus stewed in wine sauce

ψάρι μαγιονέζα Αθηναϊκή
(psahree mahyeeonnehzah atheenaheekee)
: flaked fish mixed with mayonnaise

ψάρι μαρινάτο
(psahree mahreenahto)
: mullet, sole or mackerel, fried and served with a piquant sauce of wine, tomato juice, vinegar and herbs

ψάρι στα κάρβουνα
(psahree stah kahrvoonah)
: fish baked in coals

Meat *Κρέας*

Even the simplest restaurant can do an honourable job with veal, lamb or pork chops. Pieces of meat are delicious when skewered and grilled over charcoal.

What kind of meat do you have?	Τι είδη κρέατα έχετε;	tee **ee**dhee **kreh**ahtah **eh**khehteh
I'd like some...	Θα ήθελα...	thah **ee**thehlah
beef	βοδινό	vodh**ee**no
pork	χοιρινό	kheer**ee**no
veal	μοσχάρι	mosk**hah**ree
lamb	αρνί	ahr**nee**
αρνάκι του γάλακτος	ahrn**ah**kee too **ghah**lahktoss	baby lamb
αρνίσιες μπριζόλες	ahrn**ee**ssee-ehss breez**oll**ehss	lamb chops
γλώσσα	**ghl**ossah	tongue
εντρεκότ	ehndreh**kott**	rib or rib-eye steak
εσκαλόπ	ehskah**lopp**	cutlet (scallop)
ζαμπόν	zahm**bonn**	ham
καρδιά	kahrdh**ee**ah	heart
καρρέ	**kah**reh	rack
κεφάλι	kehf**ah**lee	head
κιμάς	kee**mahss**	minced meat
κοτολέττες	kott**olleh**tehss	cutlets
λαρδί	lahr**dhee**	bacon
λουκάνικα	look**ah**neekah	sausages
μοσχαρίσιες μπριζόλες	moskhahr**ee**ssee-ehss breez**oll**ehss	veal chops
μπιφτέκι	beef**teh**kee	beef steak
μπριζόλα	breez**oll**ah	chop
μυαλό	meeah**hlo**	brains
νεφρά	neh**frah**	kidneys
νεφραμιά	nehfrahm**ee**ah	sirloin
ουρά βοδινή	oorah vodh**ee**nee	oxtail
παϊδάκια	paheedh**ah**keeah	cutlets
πλάτη	**plah**tee	shoulder
ροσμπίφ	roz**beef**	roast beef
σατωμπριάν	sahtobree**ahn**	thick fillet
σέλλα	**seh**lah	saddle
στήθος	**stee**thoss	breast
συκώτι	seek**ott**ee	liver
φιλέτο	feel**eh**to	fillet
χοιρινές μπριζόλες	kheeree**nehss** breez**oll**ehss	pork chops

baked	του φούρνου	too **foor**noo
barbecued	της σχάρας	teess **skhah**rahss
boiled	βραστός	vrah**stoss**
braised	μαγειρευμένος στη σάλτσα του	mahyeerahv**meh**noss stee **sahl**tsah too
broiled	της σχάρας	teess **skhah**rahss
en casserole	της κατσαρόλας	teess kahtsah**rol**lahss
fried	τηγανιτός	teeghahnee**toss**
grilled	της σχάρας	teess **skhah**rahss
roasted	ψητός	psee**toss**
stewed	βραστός	vrah**stoss**
stuffed	γεμιστός	yehmee**stoss**
rare	λιγοψημένος	leeghopsee**meh**noss
medium	μισοψημένος	meessopsee**meh**noss
well-done	καλοψημένος	kahlopsee**meh**noss

Meat dishes *Κρέατα*

αρνάκι εξοχικό
(ahr**nah**kee ehkso-
kheeko)
spiced lamb baked in a parchment envelope

γιουβέτσι
(yeeoo**veht**see)
meat with Greek noodles or macaroni baked in
the oven

κοκορέτσι
(kokko**reht**see)
kidneys, tripe and liver roasted on a spit

μουσακάς (moossah-
kahss)
layers of sliced aubergine and minced meat,
oven-browned with a creamy cheese mixture

ντολμάδες
(dolmah**dhehss**)
minced meat and rice wrapped in vine or
cabbage leaves with white sauce

ντομάτες γεμιστές
(dommah**tehss**
yehmee**stehss**)
tomatoes stuffed with rice and parsley or with
minced meat

παπουτσάκια
(pahpoot**sah**keeah)
vegetable marrow (zucchini) stuffed with rice
and/or meat, onions and white sauce and then
baked

σουβλάκι
(soov**lah**kee)
chunks of meat marinated in olive oil and lemon
juice, and grilled on a skewer

σουτζουκάκια
(soodzoo**kah**keeah)
minced-meat balls with cumin in tomato sauce

Game and poultry Κυνήγι και πουλερικά

While chicken is found throughout the year and prepared in a variety of different ways, birds such as quail and woodcock only start to appear regularly on the menu in September.

I'd like some game.	Θα ήθελα κυνήγι.	thah **ee**thehlah **keenee**yee
γαλοπούλα	ghahlo**ppoo**lah	turkey
καπόνι	kah**ponn**ee	capon
κοτόπουλο	kott**oppoo**lo	chicken
κοτόπουλο ψητό	kott**oppoo**lo pseeto	roast chicken
κουνέλι	koon**eh**lee	rabbit
λαγός	lah**ghoss**	hare
λαγός σιβέ	lah**ghoss** seeveh	jugged hare
μπεκάτσα	beh**kah**tsah	woodcock
μπούτι	**boo**tee	leg
ορτύκι	or**tee**kee	quail
παπάκι	pah**pah**kee	duckling
πάπια	**pah**peeah	duck
πέρδικα	**pehr**dheekah	partridge
περιστέρι	pehree**steh**ree	pigeon
στήθος	**stee**thoss	breast
φασιανός	fahss**eeah**noss	pheasant
φτερούγα	ftehr**oo**ghah	wing
χήνα	**khee**nah	goose

κοτόπουλο της κατσαρόλας (kott**oppoo**lo teess kahtsah**rol**lahss)	casserole of chicken with lemon sauce
κοτόπουλο της σούβλας (kott**oppoo**lo teess **soov**lahss)	spit-roasted chicken
λαγός στιφάδο (lah**ghoss** stee**fah**dho)	hare cooked with spring onions, wine or tomatoes
πάπια γεμιστή (**pah**peeah yehmee**stee**)	stuffed duck
μπεκάτσα (beh**kah**tsah)	woodcock casseroled in a sauce made of onions, butter, olive oil and wine
ορτύκι (or**tee**kee)	quail baked in a wine sauce and served on a bed of rice

Vegetables Λαχανικά

Vegetables occupy an important place in Greek cuisine, and are served in a multitude of different ways. A wide variety of vegetables is grown, but the season is relatively short. Keep your eyes open for artichokes, broad beans and peas in summer. Vegetables are usually eaten cold (raw or boiled, and then cooled), or tepid. Greeks like to eat them with an oil and vinegar or oil and lemon dressing. The latter is an acquired taste, but worth persevering with.

What vegetables do you recommend?	Τι λαχανικά μας συστήνετε;	tee lahkhahnee**kah** mahss see**stee**nehteh
αγγούρι	ahng**goo**ree	cucumber
αγκινάρες	ahnggee**nah**rehss	artichokes
καλαμπόκι	kahlahm**bok**kee	sweetcorn
κάρδαμο	**kahr**dhahmo	watercress
καρόττα	kah**rot**tah	carrots
κολοκύθα	kollo**kkee**thah	pumpkin
κολοκύθι	kollo**kkee**thee	marrow (zucchini)
κουνουπίδι	koonoo**pee**dhee	cauliflower
κουκιά	koo**kee**ah	broad beans
κρεμμύδια	krehmee**dhee**ah	onions
λαχανάκια Βρυξελλών	lahkhah**nah**keeah vreekseh**lonn**	Brussels sprouts
λάχανο	**lahk**hahno	cabbage
κόκκινο λάχανο	**kok**keeno **lahk**hahno	red cabbage
μαϊντανός	maheendah**noss**	parsley
μανιτάρια	mahnee**tah**reeah	mushrooms
μαρούλι	mah**roo**lee	Cos lettuce
μελιτζάνα	mehleed**zah**nah	aubergine (eggplant)
μπάμιες	**bah**mee-ehss	okra
μπιζέλια	beez**eh**leeah	peas
ντομάτες	dom**mah**tehss	tomatoes
παντζάρι	pahnd**zah**ree	beetroot
πατάτες	pah**tah**tehss	potatoes
πιπεριές	peepehree**ehss**	sweet peppers
πιπεριές πράσινες	peepehree**ehss prahs**seenehss	green peppers
πράσσα	**prahs**sah	leeks
ραδίκι	rah**dhee**kee	chicory (endive)
ραπανάκι	rahpah**nah**kee	radish
ρεβύθια	rehv**ee**theeah	chick peas
ρύζι	**ree**zee	rice

σέλινο	sehleeno	celery
σπαράγγια	spahrahnggeeah	asparagus
σπανάκι	spahnahkee	spinach
φακές	fahkehss	lentils
φασολάκια φρέσκα	fahssollahkeeah frehskah	green beans
φασόλια γίγοντες	fahsolleeah yeeghondehss	butter beans
χόρτα	khortah	wild, green leaf
(αντίδια)	(ahndeedheeah)	vegetable

αγγινάρες με κουκιά (ahnggeenahrehss meh kookeeah)	trimmed artichokes up-ended in a pan, cooked with broad beans, sauteed onions and herbs
κολοκύθια κεφτέδες (kollokkeetheeah kehftehdhehss)	rissoles made of minced courgettes (zucchini), potatoes, onions, cheese and herbs
κολοκύθια τηγανιτά (kollokkeetheeah teeghahneetah)	cauliflower florets deep fried in batter
μουσακάς χωρίς κρέας (moossahkahss khoreess krehahss)	vegetarian moussaka made of aubergines, tomatoes, onions and cheese, with a béchamel sauce
μπάμιες (bahmee-ehss)	ladies' fingers (okra) cooked in a tomato and onion sauce
μπριάμ (breeahm)	a selection of summer vegetables sliced and arranged in a pan, seasoned and baked
ντομάτες γεμιστές με ρίζι (dommahtehss yehmeestehss meh reezee)	tomatoes stuffed with rice, currants, pine nuts and herbs, then baked
πατάτες γεμιστές (pahtahtehss yehmeestehss)	hollowed-out boiled potatoes stuffed with cheese and bacon and covered with a béchamel sauce, and baked
σπανακόπιττα (spahnahkoppeetah)	spinach and leeks with onions and feta cheese baked in a phyllo pastry case
σπανακόριζο (spahnahkorreezo)	spinach cooked with rice and dill
φασόλια γιαχνί (fahsolleeah yeeahkhnee)	dried beans in a tomato sauce

Herbs and spices *Βότανα και μπαχαρικά*

άνηθος	**ahneethoss**	dill
βασσιλικός	**vahsseeleekoss**	basil
δάφνη	**dhahfnee**	bay leaves
δεντρολίβανο	dhehndhroleevahno	rose
διόσμος	**dheeozmoss**	mint
κάππαρη	**kahpahree**	capers
μαϊντανός	maheendahnoss	parsley
μουστάρδα	moostahrdhah	mustard
ρίγανη	reeghahnee	oregano
σαφράνη	sahfrahnee	saffron
σκόρδο	skordho	garlic

Sauces and dressings *Σάλτσες*

λαδόξυδο (lahdhokseedho)	vinegar and oil
μαγιονέζα (mahyeeonnehzah)	mayonnaise
σάλτσα άσπρη (sahltsah ahspree)	meat stock with milk, butter, flour
σάλτσα αυγολέμονο (sahltsah ahvghollehmonno)	meat stock with eggs, flour and lemon juice
σάλτσα κίτρινη (sahltsah keetreenee)	mayonnaise, hard-boiled egg yolks and white wine
σάλτσα λαδολέμονο (sahltsah lahdhollehmonno)	olive oil with lemon and salt to which parsley or oregano is sometimes added
σάλτσα ντομάτα (sahltsah dommahta)	tomato with olive oil, parsley, onion
σάλτσα πράσινη (sahltsah prahsseenee)	mayonnaise with minced parsley
σάλτσα ψητού (sahltsah pseetoo)	meat broth with flour and butter
τζατζίκι (dzahdzeekee)	yoghurt with cucumber, garlic, oil, mint
σκορδαλιά (skordhahleeah)	garlic with bread or potatoes, oil, parsley

Cheese *Τυρί*

Greece produces many varieties of cheese, though most of them are unknown outside the country.

The Greeks are very fond of cheese and frequently eat it with the meal, depending on the type of cheese. The most popular cheese is φέτα (**feh**tah), a white cheese made from goat's milk. You can find many varieties of *feta*: soft, hard, very creamy or very salty.

What kinds of cheese do you have?	Τι είδη τυριών έχετε;	tee **ee**dhee teeree**onn eh**khehteh
γραβιέρα (ghrahvee**ee**hrah)		Swiss-style cheese; best varieties made in Corfu and Crete
κασέρι (kah**ss**ehree)		light, yellow cheese, rich in cream with a soft texture
κασκαβάλι (kahskahvahlee)		yellow cheese, very creamy and rich
κεφαλοτύρι (kehfahlotteeree)		yellow cheese, very strong and salty with tiny holes
μανούρι (mahnooree)		sort of cottage cheese, makes a tasty dessert when mixed with honey
μυζήθρα (mee**zee**thrah)		salted white soft cheese made from ewe's milk
τελεμές (tehleh**mehss**)		tinned (canned) white cheese

And you will probably come across these cheese dishes:

πουρέκια από τυρί (poo**reh**keeah ahpo teeree)	rolls of *phyllo* (very thin) pastry containing a mixture of Gruyère and *feta*, with eggs, parsley and nutmeg
τυράκια τηγανιτά (tee**rah**keeah teeghahneetah)	small squares of bread topped with a cheesy mixture and deep fried
τυροπιττάκια (teeroppee**tah**keeah)	baked triangular pastries containing *feta* and another hard cheese

Fruit *Φρούτα*

Rather than finishing the meal with a sweet dessert, Greeks like to have some fruit, of which there is a great variety.

Do you have fresh fruit?	Έχετε φρέσκα φρούτα;	ehkhehteh **frehs**kah **froo**tah
What kind of fruit do you have?	Τι είδη φρούτων έχετε;	tee **ee**dhee **froo**tonn **eh**khehteh
I'd like a (fresh) fruit cocktail.	Θα ήθελα μια φρουτο-σαλάτα από (φρέσκα) φρούτα.	thah **ee**thehlah meeah frootossah**lah**tah ah**po** (**frehs**kah) **froo**tah

αμύγδαλο	ah**meegh**dhahlo	almond
ανανάς	ahnah**nahss**	pineapple
αχλάδι	ahkh**lah**dhee	pear
βατόμουρο	vah**tom**mooro	raspberry
βερύκοκο	veh**ree**kokko	apricot
δαμάσκηνο	dhah**mahs**keeno	plum
γκρέιπφρουτ	**greh**eepfroot	grapefruit
καρύδα	kah**ree**dhah	coconut
καρύδι	kah**ree**dhee	walnut
καρπούζι	kahr**poo**zee	watermelon
κεράσι	keh**rahs**see	cherry
κίτρο	**kee**tro	citron
κομπόστα φρούτων	kom**bos**tah **froo**tonn	fruit compote
κυδώνι	kee**dhon**nee	quince
λεμόνι	leh**mon**nee	lemon
μανταρίνι	mahndah**ree**nee	tangerine
μήλο	**mee**lo	apple
μούρο	**moo**ro	blackberry
μπανάνα	bah**nah**nah	banana
πεπόνι	peh**pon**nee	melon
πορτοκάλι	portok**kah**lee	orange
ροδάκινο	rodhah**kee**no	peach
ρόδι	**ro**dhee	pomegranate
σταφίδα	stah**fee**dhah	raisin
σταφίδα σουλτανίνα	stah**fee**dhah sooltah**nee**nah	sultana raisin
σταφύλι	stah**fee**lee	grape
άσπρο σταφύλι	**ahs**pro stah**fee**lee	white grape
κόκκινο σταφύλι	**kok**keeno stah**fee**lee	red grape
μαύρο σταφύλι	**mah**vro stah**fee**lee	black grape
σύκο	**see**ko	fig
φουντούκι	foon**doo**kee	hazelnut
φράουλα	**frah**oolah	strawberry
χουρμάς	khoor**mahss**	date

Dessert *Επιδόρπιο*

Traditionally Greeks do not have cakes or sweets at the end of a meal, instead they eat fresh fruit or ice cream. However, they do enjoy something sweet, usually with coffee, after their siesta – and, indeed, at almost any other time of day.

I'd like a dessert, please.	Θα ήθελα ένα επιδόρπιο, παρακαλώ.	thah **ee**thehlah **eh**nah ehpee**dhor**peeo pahrahkah**lo**
Something light, please.	Κάτι ελαφρό, παρα-καλώ.	**kah**tee ehlah**fro** pahrahkah**lo**
Just a small portion.	Μόνο μια μικρή μερίδα.	**mo**nno **mee**ah mee**kree** meh**ree**dhah
Nothing more, thanks.	Τίποτε άλλο, ευχα-ριστώ.	**tee**potteh **ah**lo ehf khah**ree**sto
What do you have for dessert?	Τι έχετε για επιδόρπιο;	tee **eh**khehteh yeeah ehpee**dhor**peeo
γρανίτα	ghrah**nee**tah	water-ice (sherbet)
καραμέλες	kahrah**meh**lehss	sweets (candy)
καρυδόπιττα	kah**reed**hoppeetah	walnut bar
κέικ	"cake"	cake
κρέμα καραμελέ	**kreh**mah kahrah**meh**leh	caramel custard
μηλόπιττα	mee**lop**peetah	apple pie
μους	mooss	mousse (custard)
μπισκότα	bees**kott**ah	biscuits (cookies)
παγωτό	pah**ghott**o	ice-cream
παγωτό βανίλια	pah**ghott**o vah**nee**leeah	vanilla ice-cream
παγωτό κασάτα	pah**ghott**o kah**ssah**tah	spumoni, cassata
παγωτό σοκολάτα	pah**ghott**o sok**koll**ahtah	chocolate ice-cream
παγωτό φράουλα	pah**ghott**o **frah**oolah	strawberry ice-cream
πάστα	**pah**stah	tart
πάστα αμυγδάλου	**pah**stah ahmeegh-**dhah**loo	almond tart
πάστα με καρύδα	**pah**stah meh kah-**reed**hah	coconut tart
πάστα σοκολάτα	**pah**stah sok**koll**ahtah	chocolate tart
πες μελμπά	pehss mehl**bah**	peach melba
πουτίγκα	poo**teeng**gah	pudding
ρυζόγαλο	reezo**ghah**lo	rice pudding
φρουί γκλασέ	fro**oee** glah**sseh**	crystallized fruit
φρουτοσαλάτα	frootossah**lah**tah	fruit cocktail

αμυγδαλωτό (ahmeeghdhahlotto)	almond paste with sugar (marzipan)
γαλακτομπούρεκο (ghahlahktomboorehko)	flaky pastry filled with custard, steeped in syrup
καταΐφι (kahtaheefee)	shredded pastry roll filled with walnuts and steeped in syrup
κουραμπιές (koorahmbeeehss)	biscuit (cookie)
λουκουμάδες (lookoomahdhehss)	light and fluffy honey puffs powdered with cinnamon and dripping with honey
λουκούμι (lookoomee)	Turkish delight
μελομακάρονο (mehlomahkahronno)	honey and nut biscuit (cookie)
μπακλαβάς (bahklahvahss)	baklava; a flaky pastry with a nut filling
παστέλι (pahstehlee)	sesame and honey bars
ρεβανί (rehvahnee)	sponge cake
χαλβάς (khahlvahss)	pudding made of farina, chopped almonds, honey and sugar

To accompany your pastry you will be offered several different kinds of coffee, ranging from instant (known as warm Nescafe – ζεστό Nescafe, zeh**sto** Nescafe) to American and French brews. But the one drunk by Greeks is known as Greek coffee.

The beans are reduced to a fine powder which is boiled with water, and then poured, grounds and all, into a cup. You should let the grounds settle and then only drink about half the cup.

Ελληνικό καφέ	ehleeneeko kah**feh**	Greek coffee

and depending on the quantity of sugar you want, ask for:

σκέτο	**skeh**to	without sugar
μέτριο	**meh**treeo	slightly sweet
γλυκό	ghlee**ko**	sweet

Aperitifs *Απεριτίφ*

The usual Greek aperitif is ούζο (**oo**zo). It's a spirit with an aniseed flavour, containing 50° alcohol. In the provinces it's generally served neat (straight) in thimblefuls, but in town you get larger quantities and most people prefer to add water, which clouds it.

Almost always and everywhere, when you order *ouzo*, the waiter will bring you some olives, cheese, sardines, dried octopus, etc., to eat with it. These titbits are generally called μεζέδες (meh**zeh**dhess).

You'll also have the chance to taste:

ούζο μαστίχα (oozo mah**stee**khah)	sweet and scented with mastic; you can find the best *mastiha* on the isle of Chios
I'd like some *ouzo*.	Θα ήθελα λίγο ούζο. thah **ee**thehlah **lee**gho **oo**zo

> **ΣΤΗΝ ΥΓΕΙΑ ΣΑΣ**
> (steen ee**yee**ah sahss)
> YOUR HEALTH / CHEERS!

Beer *Μπύρα*

Most of the beer available in Greece is very good, and there's a large variety of foreign, as well as Greek, brands. If you want to try some Greek beer, ask for one of the following: Φιξ (feeks), Άλφα (**ahl**fah).

I'd like a beer, please.	Θα ήθελα μια μπύρα, παρακαλώ.	thah **ee**thehlah **mee**ah **bee**rah pahrahkah**lo**
Do you have ... beer?	Έχετε ... μπύρα;	**eh**khehteh ... **bee**rah
bottled	εμφιαλωμένη	ehmfeeahlo**mmeh**nee
draught	βαρελιού	vahrehlee**oo**
foreign	εισαγώμενη	eesagho**mmeh**nee
light / dark	ξανθή / μαύρη	ksahn**thee** / **mahv**ree

Wine   Κρασί

Many visitors are amazed by the wide range of wines available in Greece, few of which are well known abroad.

The ancient Greeks carried the love of wine to an extreme, considering it a sign of civilization. No sooner had Greek colonists set foot on foreign soil than they planted grape vines. Down through the ages, however, the custom of drinking fermented beverages became largely lost among the Greeks.

Nevertheless, ancient Greece must be considered a pioneer of viniculture, for it was the Greeks who first learned the best size for vineyards and the best terrain for the cultivation of grapes.

Today vineyards are found throughout the country, producing over 500 000 tonnes of wine annually. Following often archaic methods of wine production, the regions of Attica, Corfu, Crete, Epirus, Peloponnesus, Thrace and the islands of the Aegean Sea have extensive vineyards.

Greece produces red, white and dessert wine, and, beyond that, a typically Greek one—its resinated wine. The latter is, usually, a white wine to which a resin—from pine needles—is added during the fermentation process to preserve it in the hot Greek climate. Because of its exotic taste you may find it difficult to get used to resinated wine. Since this wine takes on a bitter taste after its first year, try a young *retsina* to start off with.

However, if you can't get used to it, ask for unresinated wine everywhere. An unfavourable latitude and hot climate often produce full-bodied wine which is too alcoholic and somewhat harsh in taste. On the other hand, Greece generally offers quite good dessert wine, best known of which is doubtless the *Muscat* of Samos which is a sweet white wine. The red *Mavrodaphni* and white *Muscat Rion* from Patras and *Vino Santo* from Santorin are among other examples.

In Athens, on the islands and in small towns you'll easily find *tavernas* that store their wine in large barrels.

I'd like a bottle of white wine/red wine.	Θα ήθελα ένα μπουκάλι άσπρο κρασί/κόκκινο κρασί.	thah eethehlah ehnah bookahlee ahspro krahssee/kokkeeno krahssee
a carafe	μια καράφα	meeah kahrahfah
a half bottle	μισό μπουκάλι	meesso bookahlee
a glass	ένα ποτήρι	ehnah potteeree
a litre	ένα λίτρο	ehnah leetro
I'd like some un-resinated wine.	Θα ήθελα λίγο αρετσίνωτο κρασί.	thah eethehlah leegho ahrehtseenotto krahssee
A glass of retsina, please.	Ένα ποτήρι ρετσίνα, παρακαλώ.	ehnah potteeree rehtseenah pahrahkahlo
Please bring me another...	Παρακαλώ φέρτε μου ακόμη...	pahrahkahlo fehrteh moo ahkommee
What's the name of this wine?	Πως λέγεται αυτό το κρασί;	poss lehyehteh ahfto to krahssee
Where does this wine come from?	Από ποια περιοχή είναι αυτό το κρασί;	ahpo peeah pehreeokhee eeneh ahfto to krahsee
How old is this wine?	Πόσο παλιό είναι αυτό το κρασί;	posso pahleeo eeneh ahfto to krahssee
How much is a bottle of...?	Πόσο κάνει ένα μπουκάλι...;	posso kahnee ehnah bookahlee
I don't want anything too sweet.	Δεν θέλω κάτι πολύ γλυκό.	dhehn thehlo kahtee pollee ghleeko

red	κόκκινο	kokkeeno
white	άσπρο	ahspro
rosé	ροζέ	rozzeh
dry	ξηρό	kseero
light	ελαφρύ	ehlahfree
full-bodied	δυνατό	dheenahto
very dry	πολύ ξηρό	pollee kseero
sweet	γλυκό	ghleeko
resinated	ρετσινομένο	rehtseenommehno
unresinated	αρετσίνωτο	ahrehtseenotto
chilled	παγωμένο	pahghomehno
at room temperature	σέ θερμοκρασία δωματίου	seh thehrmokrahsseeah dhomahteeoo

Other alcoholic drinks Άλλα οινοπνευματώδη ποτά

Most of the well-known after-dinner drinks can be found in Greece, or as an alternative try a Greek brandy. Some taste a little rough, but others, like Metaxa, are quite good, even though they don't taste like French brandy.

You will probably see a range of rather lurid liqueurs – these are based on synthetic fruit syrups and don't live up to expectations.

I'd like a...	Θα ήθελα...	thah **ee**thehlah
I'd like to try a glass of...	θα ήθελα να δοκιμάσω ένα ποτήρι...	thah **ee**thehlah nah dhokkeemahsso **eh**nah pot**tee**ree
Are there any local specialities?	Υπάρχουν σπεσιαλιτέ της περιοχής;	ee**pahr**khoon spehsseeahl**ee**teh teess pehreeo**khees**s
Bring me a glass of Metaxa, please.	Φέρτε μου ένα ποτήρι Μεταξά, παρακαλώ.	**fehr**teh moo **eh**nah pot**tee**ree mehtah**ksah** pahrahkah**lo**

κίτρο (**keet**ro)		rather sweet, with a citrus flavour; found on the island of Naxos
Μεταξά (mehtah**ksah**)		a Greek brandy, quite enjoyable
κουμ-κουάτ (koomkoo**aht**)		yellow-coloured brandy, found on the isle of Corfu and made from tiny oranges

brandy	ένα κονιάκ	**eh**nah konn**ee**ahk
gin	ένα τζιν	**eh**nah tzeen
and tonic	και τόνικ	keh **tonn**eek
liqueur	ένα λικέρ	**eh**nah lee**kehr**
rum	ένα ρούμι	**eh**nah **roo**mee
sherry	ένα τσέρι	**eh**nah **tseh**ree
vermouth	ένα βερμούτ	**eh**nah vehr**moot**
vodka	μια βότκα	**mee**ah **vot**kah
whisky	ένα ουίσκι	**eh**nah "whisky"
neat (straight)	σκέτο	**skeh**to
on the rocks	με παγάκια	meh pah**ghah**keeah
and soda	και σόδα	keh **so**dhah

glass	ένα ποτήρι	**eh**nah pot**tee**ree
bottle	ένα μπουκάλι	**eh**nah boo**kah**lee
double (shot of)	ένα διπλό	**eh**nah dhee**plo**

EATING OUT

Εστιατόριο – Φαγητά

Nonalcoholic drinks   *Μη οινοπνευματώδη ποτά*

Tap water in Greece is good and not calcareous but bottled water is also available.

I'd like a/an...	Θα ήθελα...	thah **ee**thehlah
We'd like a/an...	Θα θέλαμε...	thah **the**hlahmeh
apple juice	ένα χυμό μήλου	**eh**nah kheemo **mee**loo
(hot) chocolate	μια (ζεστή) σοκολάτα	**mee**ah (zeh**stee**) sokkol**lah**tah
coffee *	ένα καφέ	**eh**nah kah**feh**
instant	στιγμιαίο	steegh**mee**eeho
Greek	ελληνικό	ehlee**nee**ko
black	μαύρο	**mah**vro
with cream	με κρέμα	meh **kreh**mah
with milk	με γάλα	meh **ghah**lah
decaffeinated	χωρίς καφεΐνη	khor**eess** kahfeh**ee**nee
fruit juice	ένα χυμό φρούτων	**eh**nah kheemo **froo**tonn
grapefruit juice	ένα χυμό κρέιπφρουτ	**eh**nah kheemo "grapefruit"
herb tea	ένα τσάι από βότανα	**eh**nah **tsah**ee ahpo **vo**ttahnah
lemon juice	ένα χυμό λεμονιού	**eh**nah kheemo lehmonn**eeo**o
lemonade	μια λεμονάδα	**mee**ah lehmonn**nah**dhah
milk	ένα ποτήρι γάλα	**eh**nah pott**ee**ree **ghah**lah
milkshake	ένα μιλκσέικ	**eh**nah "milkshake"
mineral water	ένα μεταλλικό νερό	**eh**nah mehtahl**lee**ko neh**ro**
fizzy (carbonated)	αεριούχο	aheh**ree**ooko
still	κανονικό	kahnonn**nee**ko
orange juice	ένα χυμό πορτοκαλιού	**eh**nah kheemo portokkah**lee**oo
orangeade	μια πορτοκαλάδα	**mee**ah portokkah**lah**dhah
tea	ένα τσάι	**eh**nah **tsah**ee
cup of tea	ένα φλιτζάνι τσάι	**eh**nah fleed**zah**nee **tsah**ee
with milk	με γάλα	meh **ghah**lah
with lemon	με λεμόνι	meh leh**monn**nee
iced tea	ένα παγωμένο τσάι	**eh**nah pahgho**mmeh**no **tsah**ee
tomato juice	ένα χυμό ντομάτας	**eh**nah kheemo domm**mah**tahss
tonic water	ένα τόνικ	**eh**nah **tonn**neek

---

* read about coffee on page 55

Complaints *Παράπονα*

There is a plate/ glass missing.	Λείπει ένα πιάτο/ ποτήρι.	leepee ehnah peeahto/ potteeree
I don't have a knife/ fork/spoon.	Δεν έχω μαχαίρι/ πηρούνι/κουτάλι.	dhehn ehkho mahkhehree/ peeroonee/kootahlee
That's not what I ordered.	Δεν είναι αυτό που παράγγειλα.	dhehn eeneh ahfto poo pahrahnggeelah
I asked for...	Ζήτησα...	zeeteessah
There must be some mistake.	Πρέπει να έγινε κάποιο λάθος.	prehpee nah ehyeeneh kahpeeo lahthoss
May I change this?	Μπορώ να αλλάξω αυτό;	borro nah ahlahkso ahfto
I asked for a small portion (for the child).	Ζήτησα μια μικρή μερίδα (για το παιδί).	zeeteessah meeah meekree mehreedhah (yeeah to pehdhee)
The meat is...	Το κρέας είναι...	to krehahss eeneh
overdone	πολύ ψημένο	pollee pseemehno
underdone	άψητο	ahpseeto
too tough	πολύ σκληρό	pollee skleero
This is too...	Αυτό είναι πολύ...	ahfto eeneh pollee
bitter/salty/sweet	πικρό/αλμυρό/γλυκό	peekro/ahlmeero/ ghleeko
I don't like this.	Δεν μου αρέσει αυτό.	dhehn moo ahrehssee ahfto
The food is cold.	Το φαγητό είναι κρύο.	to fahyeeto eeneh kreeo
This isn't fresh.	Δεν είναι φρέσκο.	dhehn eeneh frehsko
What's taking so long?	Γιατί αργεί τόσο;	yeeahtee ahrghee tosso
Have you forgotten our drinks?	Έχετε ξεχάσει τα ποτά μας;	ehkhehteh ksehkhahssee tah pottah mahss
The wine tastes of cork.	Το κρασί μυρίζει φελλό.	to krahssee meereezee fehlo
This isn't clean.	Αυτό δεν είναι καθαρό.	ahfto dhehn eeneh kahthahro
Would you ask the head waiter to come over?	Μπορείτε να ζητήσετε στον αρχισερβιτόρο να έλθη εδώ;	borreeteh nah zeeteessehteh stonn ahrkheessehrveetorro nah ehlthee ehdho

The bill (check)   *Ο λογαριασμός*

By law all service charges must be included in the bill, but there is nothing to stop you offering a tip if the service has been particularly attentive.

I'd like to pay.	Θα ήθελα να πληρώσω.	thah **ee**thehlah nah pleerosso
We'd like to pay separately.	Θα θέλαμε να πληρώσουμε χωριστά.	thah **the**lahmeh nah pleerossoomeh khorreestah
I think there is a mistake in this bill.	Νομίζω υπάρχει λάθος σε αυτό τον λογαριασμό.	nomm**ee**zo eep**ah**rkhee **lah**thoss seh ahfto tonn loghahreeah**z**mo
What's this amount for?	Γιατί είναι αυτή η τιμή;	yeeaht**ee** **ee**neh ahft**ee** ee teem**ee**
Is service included?	Συμπεριλαμβάνεται το ποσοστό υπηρεσίας;	seembehreelahm**vah**nehteh to poss**o**sto eepeerehss**ee**-ahss
Is the cover charge included?	Συμπεριλαμβάνεται το κουβέρ;	seembehreelahm**vah**-nehteh to koov**ehr**
Is everything included?	Συμπεριλαμβάνονται τα πάντα;	seembehreelahm**vah**-nondheh tah **pah**ndah
Do you accept traveller's cheques?	Δέχεστε τράβελερς τσεκ;	dheh**kh**ehsteh trahvehlehrss tsehk
Can I pay with this credit card?	Μπορώ να πληρώσω με αυτή την πιστωτική κάρτα;	borro nah pleerosso meh ahft**ee** teen peestoteek**ee** **kah**rtah
Thank you, this is for you.	Ευχαριστώ, αυτό είναι για σας.	ehfkahree**sto** ahfto **ee**neh yeeah sahss
Keep the change.	Κρατήστε τα ρέστα.	kraht**ee**steh tah **reh**stah
That was a delicious meal.	Το γεύμα ήταν πολύ νόστιμο.	to **yeh**vmah **ee**tahn poll**ee** **no**steemo
We enjoyed it, thank you.	Το απολαύσαμε, ευχαριστούμε.	to ahpoll**ah**fsahmeh ehfkahree**sto**omeh

> **ΤΟ ΦΙΛΟΔΩΡΗΜΑ ΣΥΜΠΕΡΙΛΑΜΒΑΝΕΤΑΙ**
> SERVICE INCLUDED

TIPPING, see inside back-cover

Snacks – Picnic   Σνακς – πικ-νικ

There is a wide variety of snacks available in Greece, and many of them are made with layers of wafer-thin *phyllo* pastry. They are usually baked or deep-fried, and fillings range from spinach and cheese to chicken and other kinds of meat.

Another typically Greek snack is σουβλάκι (soo**vlah**kee) which consists of slices of meat grilled on a spit and served with tomatoes, onions and parsley, all wrapped in a type of bread called πίττα (**pee**tah). It's very cheap and tasty and can be found almost anywhere in the country.

I'll have one of these, please.	Θα πάρω ένα από αυτά, παρακαλώ.	thah **pah**ro **eh**nah ahpo ahftah pahrahkahlo
Give me two of these and one of those, please.	Δώστε μου δύο από αυτά και ένα από αυτό, παρακαλώ.	**dhos**teh moo **dhee**o ahpo ahftah keh **eh**nah ahpo ahfto pahrahkahlo
to the left/right/ above/below	στα αριστερά/δεξιά/ από πάνω/από κάτω	stah ahreesteh**rah**/ dhehk**see**ah/ ahpo **pah**no/ahpo **kah**to
It's to take-away.	Είναι για να το πάρω μαζί μου.	**ee**neh **yeeah** nah to **pah**ro mah**zee** moo
Do you have any cold drinks?	Έχετε παγομένα ποτά;	**ehkh**ehteh pahgho**mmeh**nah pottah
May I have a straw?	Μπορώ να έχω ένα καλαμάκι;	borro nah **ehkh**o **eh**nah kahlah**mah**kee
How much is that?	Πόσο κάνει αυτό;	**posso kah**nee ahfto
I'd like a...	Θα ήθελα...	thah **ee**thehlah
cheese pie	μια τυρόπιττα	**meeah** teeroppeetah
chicken pie	μια κοτόπιττα	**meeah** kottoppeetah
meat pie	μια κρεατόπιττα	**meeah** krehahtoppeetah
spinach pie	μια σπανακόπιττα	**meeah** spahnahkoppeetah
hamburger	ένα χάμπουργκερ	**eh**nah **khahm**boohrgehr
hot dog	ένα χοτ-ντογκ	**eh**nah "hot-dog"
pastry	μια πάστα	**meeah** **pah**stah
pie	μια πίττα	**meeah** **pee**tah
roll	ένα ψωμάκι	**eh**nah psomahkee
salad	μια σαλάτα	**meeah** sahlahtah
sandwich	ένα σάντουϊτς	**eh**nah sahndooeetss
cheese	από τυρί	ahpo teeree
ham	από ζαμπόν	ahpo zahmbonn

Here's a basic list of food and drink that might come in useful when shopping for a picnic.

May I help myself?	Μπορώ να εξυπηρετηθώ μόνος/-η μου;	borro nah ehksee peereh-teetho monnass/-ee moo
Please give me a/ an/some...	Παρακαλώ, μου δίνετε...	pahrahkahlo moo dheenehteh
apples	μήλα	meelah
bananas	μπανάνες	bahnahnehss
biscuits	μπισκότα	beeskottah
beer	μια μπύρα	meeah beerah
bread	ψωμί	psommee
butter	βούτυρο	vooteero
cake	ένα κέικ	ehnah "cake"
cheese	τυρί	teeree
chips (Am.)	τσιπς (πατατάκια)	"chips" (pahtahtahkeeah)
chocolate bar	μια σοκολάτα	meeah sokkollahtah
coffee	καφέ	kahfeh
cold cuts	αλαντικά κομμένα σε φέτες	ahlahndeekah kommehnah seh fehtehss
cookies	μπισκότα	beeskottah
crackers	κράκερς	krahkehrss
crisps	τσιπς (πατατάκια)	"chips" (pahtahtahkeeah)
eggs	αυγά	ahvghah
gherkins (pickles)	αγγούρια ξυδάτα	ahnggooreeah kseedhahtah
grapes	σταφύλια	stahfeeleeah
ham	ζαμπόν	zahmbonn
ice-cream	παγωτό	pahghotto
lemon	ένα λεμόνι	ehnah lehmonnee
lemonade	μια λεμονάδα	meeah lehmonnahdhah
milk	γάλα	ghahlah
mineral water	μεταλλικό νερό	mehtahleeko nehro
mustard	μουστάρδα	moostahrdhah
oranges	πορτοκάλια	portokkahleeah
pastries	πάστες	pahstehss
pepper	πιπέρι	peepehree
roll	ένα ψωμάκι	ehnah psommahkee
salt	αλάτι	ahlahtee
sausages	λουκάνικα	lookahneekah
soft drink	ένα αναψυκτικό	ehnah ahnahpseekteeko
sugar	ζάχαρη	zahkhahree
tea	τσάι	tsahee
wine	κρασί	krahssee
yoghurt	γιαούρτι	yeeahoortee

Travelling around

Plane *Αεροπλάνο*

Is there a flight to Athens?	Υπάρχει πτήση για την Αθήνα;	eepahrkhee pteessee yeeah teen ahtheenah
Is it a direct flight?	Είναι κατευθείας η πτήση;	eeneh kahtehftheeahss ee pteessee
When's the next plane to Rhodes?	Πότε είναι το επόμενο αεροπλάνο για τη Ρόδο;	potteh eeneh to ehpomehno ahehroplahno yeeah tee rodho
Do I have to change planes?	Πρέπει να αλλάξω αεροπλάνα;	prehpee nah ahlahkso ahehroplahnah
Can I make a connection to Cos?	Μπορώ να έχω ανταπόκριση για τη Κω;	borro nah ehkho ahndahpokreessee yeeah tee ko
What time do we take off?	Τι ώρα απογειώνεται το αεροπλάνο;	tee orrah ahpoyeeonnehteh to ahehroplahno
What time do I have to check in?	Τι ώρα πρέπει να είμαι στο αεροδρόμιο;	tee orrah prehpee nah eemeh sto ahehrodhrommeeo
Is there a bus to the airport?	Υπάρχει λεωφορείο για το αεροδρόμιο;	eepahrkhee lehofforreeo yeeah to ahehrodhrommeeo
What's the flight number?	Ποιος είναι ο αριθμός της πτήσης;	peeoss eeneh o ahreethmoss teess pteesseess
What time do we arrive?	Τι ώρα φθάνουμε;	tee orrah fthahnoomeh
I'd like to ... my reservation on flight no 123.	Θα ήθελα να... την κράτηση μου για την πτήση υπ'αριθμό 123.	thah eethehlah nah... teen krahteessee moo yeeah teen pteessee eepahreethmo 123
cancel	ακυρώσω	ahkeerosso
change	αλλάξω	ahlahkso
confirm	επιβεβαιώσω	ehpeevehvehosso

ΑΦΙΞΗ ARRIVAL	**ΑΝΑΧΩΡΗΣΗ** DEPARTURE

TICKETS, see page 68

Train   *Τραίνο*

The Greek rail network is not particularly extensive. However, there are lines between Athens and northern Greece, and Athens and the Peloponnese. Always book in advance as trains get very crowded.

To the railway station   *Για τον σιδηροδρομικό σταθμό*

Where's the railway station?	Που είναι ο σιδη-ροδρομικός σταθμός;	poo **ee**neh o seedheero-dhrommee**koss** stahth**moss**
Taxi!	Ταξί!	tah**ksee**
Take me to the railway station.	Να με πάτε στο σιδηροδρομικό σταθμό.	nah meh **pah**teh sto seedheerodhrommee**ko** stahth**mo**
What's the fare?	Πόσο κάνει;	posso **kah**nee

ΕΙΣΟΔΟΣ	ENTRANCE
ΕΞΟΔΟΣ	EXIT
ΠΡΟΣ ΤΙΣ ΑΠΟΒΑΘΡΕΣ	TO THE PLATFORMS
ΠΛΗΡΟΦΟΡΙΕΣ	INFORMATION

Where's the...?   *Που είναι...;*

Where is/are the...?	Που είναι...;	poo **ee**neh
bar	το μπαρ	to ''bar''
booking office	το γραφείο κρατήσεως	to ghrah**fee**o krah**tees**sehoss
left luggage office (baggage check)	το γραφείο αποσκευών	to ghrah**fee**o ahposkeh**vonn**
lost property (lost and found) office	το γραφείο απωλεσθέν-των αντικειμένων	to ghrah**fee**o ahpollehs-**thehn**donn ahndeekee-**meh**nonn
luggage lockers	το τμήμα αποσκευών	to **tmee**mah ahposkeh**vonn**
newsstand	το περίπτερο	to peh**reep**tehro
platform 7	η αποβάθρα 7	ee ahpo**vvah**thrah 7
reservations office	το γραφείο κρατήσεως	to ghrah**fee**o krah**tees**sehoss
restaurant	το εστιατόριο	to ehsteeah**tor**reeo
snack bar	το σνακ-μπαρ	to ''snack bar''

TAXI, see page 21

ticket office	το γραφείο εισιτηρίων	to ghrahfeeo eesseeteereeonn
waiting room	η αίθουσα αναμονής	ee ehthoossah ahnahmonneess
Where are the toilets?	Που είναι οι τουα-λέττες;	poo eeneh ee tooahlehtehss

Inquiries Πληροφορίες

When is the ... train to Patras?	Πότε είναι το... τραίνο για τη Πάτρα;	potteh eeneh to... trehno yeeah tee pahtrah
first/last/next	πρώτο/τελευταίο/επόμενο	protto/tehlehfteho/ehpommehno
What time does the train to Athens leave?	Τι ώρα φεύγει το τραίνο για Αθήνα;	tee orrah fehvyee to trehno yeeah ahtheenah
What's the fare to Volos?	Πόσο κάνει το εισιτήριο για Βόλο;	posso kahnee to eesseeteereeo yeeah vollo
Is it an express train?	Είναι εξπρές το τραίνο;	eeneh ehksprehss to trehno
Is there a connection to...?	Υπάρχει ανταπόκριση για...;	eepahrkhee ahndahpokreessee yeeah
Do I have to change trains?	Πρέπει να αλλάξω τραίνο;	prehpee nah ahlahkso trehno
Is there enough time to change?	Είναι αρκετός ο χρόνος για την αλλαγή τραίνου;	eeneh ahrkehtoss o khronnoss yeeah teen ahlahyee trehnoo
Is the train running on time?	Φεύγουν τα τραίνα στην ώρα τους;	fehvghoon tah trehnah steen orrah tooss
What time does the train arrive in Patras?	Τι ώρα φθάνει το τραίνο στην Πάτρα;	tee orrah fthahnee to trehno steen pahtrah
Does the train stop in Argos?	Αυτό το τραίνο σταματά στο Άργος;	ahfto to trehno stahmahtah sto ahrghoss
What platform does the train to Patras leave from?	Από ποια αποβάθρα φεύγει το τραίνο για την Πάτρα;	ahpo peeah ahpovvahthrah fehvyee to trehno yeeah teen pahtrah
What platform does the train from Paris arrive at?	Σε ποια αποβάθρα φθάνει το τραίνο από το Παρίσι;	seh peeah ahpovvahthrah fthahnee to trehno ahpo to pahreessee
I'd like to buy a timetable.	Θα ήθελα να αγοράσω ένα ωράριο.	thah eethehlah nah ahghorrahsso ehnah orrahreeo

Το τραίνο είναι κατευθείαν.	It's a direct train.
Πρέπει να αλλάξετε στο...	You have to change at...
Να αλλάξετε στο... και να πάρετε ένα τοπικό τραίνο.	Change at ... and get a local train.
Η αποβάθρα 7 είναι...	Platform 7 is...
προς τα εκεί/πάνω αριστερά/δεξιά	over there/upstairs on the left/on the right
Υπάρχει τραίνο για... στις...	There's a train to... at...
Το τραίνο σας φεύγει από την αποβάθρα 8.	Your train will leave from platform 8.
Υπάρχει καθυστέρηση ... λεπτών.	There will be a delay of ... minutes.
Η πρώτη θέση μπροστά/στο κέντρο/στο πίσω μέρος.	First class at the front/in the middle/at the end.

Tickets Εισιτήρια

I'd like a ticket to ...	Θα ήθελα ένα εισιτήριο για ...	thah **ee**thehlah **eh**nah eesseet**ee**reeo yeeah
single (one-way)	απλό	ahplo
return (roundtrip)	μετ' επιστροφής	meht ehpeestro**ffeess**
first/second class	πρώτη/δεύτερη θέση	prottee/dhehftehree thehssee
half price	μισή τιμή	meessee teemee

Reservation Κράτηση

I'd like to reserve a...	Θα ήθελα να κρατήσω...	thah **ee**thehlah nah krah**tee**sso
seat (by the window)	μια θέση (στο παράθυρο)	meeah thehssee (sto pahrahtheero)
berth	ένα κρεββάτι	ehnah krehvahtee
upper	στο πάνω μέρος	sto pahno mehross
middle	στη μέση	stee mehssee
lower	στο κάτω μέρος	sto kahto mehross
berth in the sleeping car	ένα κρεββάτι στο βαγκόν-λι	ehnah krehvahtee sto vahgonn lee

All aboard *Επιβίβαση*

Is this the right platform for the train to Paris?	Είναι αυτή η σωστή αποβάθρα για το τραίνο για το Παρίσι;	eeneh ahftee ee sostee ahpovvahthrah yeeah to trehno yeeah to pahreessee
Is this the train to Tripolis?	Είναι αυτό το τραίνο για την Τρίπολη;	eeneh ahfto to trehno yeeah teen treepollee
Excuse me. May I get by?	Με συγχωρείτε. Μπορώ να περάσω;	meh seengkhorreeteh. borro nah pehrrahsso.
Is this seat taken?	Είναι κατειλημμένη αυτή η θέση;	eeneh kahteeleemehnee ahftee ee thehssee

ΚΑΠΝΙΣΤΕΣ SMOKER	ΜΗ ΚΑΠΝΙΣΤΕΣ NONSMOKER

I think that's my seat.	Νομίζω ότι αυτή είναι η θέση μου.	nommeezo ottee ahftee eeneh ee thehssee moo
Would you let me know before we get to Mycenae?	Μπορείτε να με ειδοποιήσετε πριν φθάσουμε στις Μυκήνες;	borreeteh nah meh eedhoppeeeessehteh preen fthahssoomeh steess meekeenehss
What station is this?	Ποιος σταθμός είναι αυτός;	peeoss stahthmoss eeneh ahftoss
How long does the train stop here?	Για πόση ώρα σταματά το τραίνο εδώ;	yeeah possee orrah stahmahtah to trehno ehdho
When do we arrive in Athens?	Πότε φθάνουμε στην Αθήνα;	potteh fthahnoomeh steen ahtheenah

Sleeping *Στο βαγκόν-λι*

Are there free compartments in the sleeping car?	Υπάρχουν ελεύθερα διαμερίσματα στο βαγκόν-λι;	eepahrkhoon ehlehf-thehrah dheeahmehreez-mahtah sto vahgonn lee
Where's the sleeping car?	Που είναι το βαγκόν-λι;	poo eeneh to vahgonn lee
Where's my berth?	Που είναι το κρεββάτι μου;	poo eeneh to krehvahtee moo

I'd like a lower berth.	Θα ήθελα ένα κρεββάτι στο κάτω μέρος.	thah **ee**thehlah **eh**nah krehv**ah**tee sto **kah**to **mehr**oss
Would you make up our berths?	Θα μπορούσατε να μας φτιάξετε τα κρεββάτια;	thah borr**oo**ssahteh nah mahss ftee**ah**ksehteh tah krehv**ah**teeah
Would you wake me at 7 o'clock?	Μπορείτε να με ξυπνήσετε στις 7;	borr**ee**teh nah meh kseep**nee**ssehteh steess 7

Eating *Γεύμα*

| Is there a dining-car/buffet on the train? | Υπάρχει βαγόνι-εστιατόριο/μπουφέ στο τραίνο; | eepahr**khee** vahgonnee-ehsteeah**tor**reeo/''buffet'' sto **treh**hno |

Baggage and porters *Αποσκευές και αχθοφόροι*

Porter!	Αχθοφόρε!	ahkhthof**forr**eh
Can you help me with my luggage?	Μπορείτε να με βοηθήσετε με τις αποσκευές μου;	borr**ee**teh nah meh voee**thee**ssehteh meh teess ahposkeh**vehss** moo
Where are the luggage trolleys (carts)?	Που είναι τα καρο-τσάκια αποσκευών;	poo **ee**neh tah kahro-**tsah**keeah ahposkeh**vonn**
Where are the luggage lockers?	Που είναι το τμήμα αποσκευών;	poo **ee**neh to **tmee**mah ahposkeh**vonn**
Where's the left-luggage office (baggage check)?	Που είναι το γραφείο διαφυλάξεως αποσκευών;	poo **ee**neh to grah**fee**o dheeahfee**lah**ksehoss ahposkeh**vonn**
I'd like to leave my luggage, please.	Θα ήθελα να αφήσω τις αποσκευές μου, παρακαλώ.	thah **ee**thehlah nah ah**fee**sso teess ahposkeh**vehss** moo pahrahkah**lo**
I'd like to register (check) my luggage.	Θα ήθελα να παραδώσω συστημένες τις αποσκευές μου.	thah **ee**thehlah nah pahrah**dho**sso seesteeme**mehnehss** teess ahposkeh**vehss** moo

---

ΚΑΤΑΓΡΑΦΗ ΑΠΟΣΚΕΥΩΝ
REGISTERING (CHECKING) BAGGAGE

PORTERS, see also page 18

Coach (long-distance bus) *Υπεραστικό λεωφορείο*

Coach is the ideal way of getting around Greece, as there is only a very limited rail network. Even the smallest towns can be reached, although the service is not so frequent. Coaches are cheap, fast, comfortable, and often crowded.

To find out about schedules, go to one of the larger bus stations.

For more phrases look under the train section, they should also apply to coach travel.

Inquiries *Πληροφορίες*

When is the... coach to Patras?	Πότε φεύγει το... λεωφορείο για Πάτρα;	potteh **fehvyee** to... lehofforreeo yeeah pahtrah
first/last/next	πρώτο/τελευταίο/ επόμενο	protto/tehlefteho/ ehpommehno
What time does the coach to Volos leave?	Τι ώρα φεύγει το λεωφορείο για Βόλο;	tee orrah **fehvyee** to lehofforreeo yeeah vollo
What's the fare to Argos?	Πόσο κάνει το εισιτήριο για Άργος;	posso **kahnee** to eesseeteereeo yeeah ahrghoss
Do I have to change coaches?	Πρέπει να αλλάξω λεωφορείο;	prehpee nah ahlahkso lehofforreeo
What time does the coach arrive in ...?	Τι ώρα φθάνει το λεωφορείο στην ...;	tee orrah fthahnee to lehofforreeo steen
Does the coach stop in Volos?	Σταματά το λεωφορείο στον Βόλο;	stahmahtah to lehofforreeo stonn vollo
How long does the journey (trip) take?	Πόση ώρα διαρκεί το ταξίδι;	possee orrah dheeahrkee to tahkseedhee
I'd like to buy a time table.	Θα ήθελα να αγοράσω ένα ωράριο.	thah eethehlah nah aghorrahsso ehnah orrahreeo

Kilometres into miles													
1 kilometre (km.) = 0.62 miles													
km.	10	20	30	40	50	60	70	80	90	100	110	120	130
miles	6	12	19	25	31	37	44	50	56	62	68	75	81

Bus *Λεωφορείο*

Local buses are cheap and cheerful. If you want a seat then you should get to the bus stop early. In big cities enter the bus at the front and deposit the correct fare in the box provided. When you want to get off, press a button that makes a "stop" sign light up. Travel in Athens is free before 8 a.m.

Which bus goes to the centre of town?	Ποιο λεωφορείο πηγαίνει στο κέντρο της πόλης;	peeo lehofforreeo peeyehnee sto kehndro teess polleess
Where can I get a bus to the opera?	Που μπορώ να πάρω το λεωφορείο για την Όπερα;	poo borro nah pahro to lehofforreeo yeeah teen oppehrah
Which bus do I take to Syntagma?	Ποιο λεωφορείο πρέπει να πάρω για το Σύνταγμα;	peeo lehofforreeo prehpee nah pahro yeeah to seendahghmah
How often do the buses to ... run?	Πόσο συχνά υπαρχει λεωφορείο για ...;	posso seekhnah eepahrkhee lehofforreeo yeeah
Where's the bus stop?	Που σταματά το λεωφορείο;	poo stahmahtah to lehofforreeo
When is the ... bus to Halandri?	Πότε είναι το ... λεωφορείο για το Χαλάνδρι;	potteh eeneh to... lehofforreeo yeeah to khahlahndhree
first/last/next	πρώτο/τελευταίο/ επόμενο	protto/tehlehfteho/ ehpommehno
How much is the fare to...?	Πόσο κάνει το εισιτήριο για...;	posso kahnee to eesseeteereeo yeeah
Do I have to change buses?	Πρέπει να αλλάξω λεωφορείο;	prehpee nah ahlahkso lehofforreeo
How many bus stops are there to...?	Πόσες στάσεις είναι μέχρι...;	possehss stahsseess eeneh mehkhree
Will you tell me when to get off?	Θα μου πείτε που να κατέβω;	thah moo peeteh poo nah kahtehvo
I want to get off at the National Garden.	Θέλω να κατέβω στον Εθνικό κήπο.	thehlo nah kahtehvo stonn ethneeko keepo

```
ΣΤΑΣΗ ΛΕΩΦΟΡΕΙΟΥ
BUS STOP
```

Underground (subway) Ηλεκτρικός

There is a long underground line in Athens called Ηλεκτρικός (eelehktreekoss). It is fast and economical, but should be avoided during lunch hours. Cancel your ticket just before going on the platform, and keep it until the end of your journey as you will be asked for it at the exit.

Where's the nearest underground station?	Που είναι ο κοντινό-τερος σταθμός του Ηλεκτρικού;	poo **ee**neh o kondee-**not**tehross staht**hmoss** too eelehktree**koo**
Does this train go to...?	Πηγαίνει αυτό το τραίνο στο...;	pee**yeh**nee ah**fto** to **treh**no sto
Is the next station ...?	Ο επόμενος σταθμός είναι...;	o ehpom**mehnoss** staht**hmoss eeneh**

Boat service Υπηρεσία πλοίου

Most people like to do a bit of island-hopping while on holiday, and it's certainly not expensive to do so. There are up to four fare classes – the cheapest is usually fine for a daytrip. If you are travelling overnight then it makes sense to book a first or second class cabin. If you want to get around more quickly then catch a hydrofoil from Zéa harbour in Athens – but it's more expensive.

For those on a budget, buy soft drinks and sandwiches before boarding.

When does the next boat to ... leave?	Πότε φεύγει το επόμενο πλοίο για...;	**pot**teh **fehv**yee to ehpomm**ehno pleeo** yeeah
Where's the embarkation point?	Που είναι το σημείο επιβιβάσεως;	poo **ee**neh to seem**eeo** ehpeeveev**ahss**sehoss
How long does the crossing take?	Πόση ώρα διαρκεί η διαδρομή;	**poss**ee **orrah** dheeahr-**kee** ee dheeahdhrommee
At which ports do we stop?	Σε ποια λιμάνια σταματάμε;	seh peeah leemahneeah stahmaht**ahmeh**
Does the boat stop at...?	Σταματά το πλοίο στο...;	stahmaht**ah** to **pleeo** sto

I'd like a... ticket.	Θα ήθελα ένα εισητήριο...	thah **ee**thehlah **eh**nah eesseet**ee**reeo
first/second/third/ fourth class	πρώτης/δεύτερης/ τρίτης/τέταρτης θέσης	**prot**teess/**dehf**teh-reess/**tree**teess/ **teh**tahrteess **theh**sseess
I'd like to take a tour of the harbour/ cruise.	Θα ήθελα να κάνω ένα γύρο του λιμανιού/ μια κρουαζιέρα.	thah **ee**thehlah nah **kah**no **eh**nah **yee**ro too leemahn**eeoo**/m**eeah** krooahz**eeeh**rah
boat	η βάρκα	ee **vahr**kah
cabin	η καμπίνα	ee kahm**bee**nah
single/double	μονή/διπλή	mon**nee**/dhee**plee**
deck	το κατάστρωμα	to kah**tah**strommah
ferry	το φέρρυ-μποτ	to "ferry boat"
hydrofoil	το ιπτάμενο δελφίνι	to eep**tah**mehno dhehl-**fee**nee
life belt/boat	το σωσίβιο/η ναυαγο-σωστική λέμβος	to sos**see**veeo/ee nahvah-ghos**sos**teek**ee lehm**voss
ship	το πλοίο	to **plee**o

Bicycle hire *Ενοικίαση ποδηλάτου*

Bicycles have become popular over the last few years, particularly on the islands, but it's not always possible to hire one in high season. In low season you may be able to get a reduction.

| I'd like to hire a bicycle. | Θα ήθελα να νοικιάσω ένα ποδήλατο. | thah **ee**thehlah nah neekee**ah**sso **eh**nah podh**ee**lahto |

Other means of transport *Άλλα μέσα μεταφοράς*

cable car	εναέριο βαγκόνι	ehnah**eh**reeo vah**gon**nee
helicopter	ελικόπτερο	ehlee**kop**tehro
moped	μοτοποδήλατο	mottoppodh**ee**lahto
motorbike	μοτοσυκλέτα	mottosseek**leh**tah
scooter	βέσπα	**vehs**pah

Or perhaps you prefer:

| to hitchhike | κάνω ωτοστόπ | **kah**no otto**stop** |
| to walk | περπατώ | pehrpah**to** |

Car *Αυτοκίνητο*

The condition of roads varies in Greece. Motorways (express-ways) tend to be good, and tolls are charged according to distance. Secondary roads on the main tourist routes are also reasonably well-maintained, but many country roads may be little more than dirt tracks. Carry a red warning-triangle, first-aid kit and fire extinguisher, and wear your seat belt.

Where's the nearest filling station?	Που είναι το κοντινό-τερο πρατήριο βενζί-νης;	poo **ee**neh to kondee-**nott**ehro prahteereeo vehnz**ee**neess
Full tank, please.	Γέμισμα, παρακαλώ.	**yeh**meezmah pahrah-kah**lo**
I'd like ... litres of petrol (gasoline).	Θα ήθελα ... λίτρα βενζίνη.	thah **ee**tehlah ... **lee**trah vehnz**ee**nee
super (premium/ regular/unleaded/ diesel	σούπερ/απλή/χωρίς μόλυβδο/πετρέλαιο	**soo**pehr/ah**plee**/ khor**reess** molleevdho/ pehtr**eh**leho
Please check the...	Παρακαλώ ελέγξτε...	pahrahkah**lo** ehl**ehng**ksteh
battery	την μπαταρία	teen bahtahr**ee**ah
brake fluid	το λάδι των φρένων	to **lah**dhee tonn **freh**nonn
oil	το λάδι	to **lah**dhee
water	το νερό	to **neh**ro
Would you check the tyre pressure?	Μπορείτε να ελέγξετε την πίεση των τροχών;	bor**ree**teh nah ehl**ehng**-ksehteh teen **pee**-ehssee tonn trok**honn**
1.6 front, 1.8 rear.	1.6 μπροστά, 1.8 πίσω.	1 **kommah** 6 bro**sstah** 1 **kommah** 8 **pee**sso
Please check the spare tyre, too.	Παρακαλώ ελέγξτε και την ρεζέρβα.	parahkah**lo** ehl**ehng**ksteh keh teen rehz**ehr**vah
Can you mend this puncture (fix this flat)?	Το λάστιχο έχει τρυ-πήσει. Μπορείτε να το διορθώσετε;	to **lah**steekho **eh**khee tree**pee**sseh. bor**ree**teh nah to dheeortho-**sseh**teh
Would you change the ..., please?	Μπορείτε να αλλάξετε ..., παρακαλώ;	bor**ree**teh nah ahl**lah**-ksehteh ... pahrahkah**lo**
bulb	τα φώτα	tah **fott**ah
fan belt	τον ιμάντα του ανεμιστήρα	tonn eem**ahn**dah too ahnehmee**stee**rah

CAR HIRE, see page 20

spark(ing) plugs	τα μπουζί	tah boozee
tyre	το λάστιχο	to lahsteekho
wipers	τους καθαριστήρες	tooss kahthahreesteerehss

| Would you clean the windscreen (windshield)? | Μπορείτε να καθαρίσετε το παρ-μπριζ; | borreeteh nah kahthahreessehteh to pahrbreez |

Asking the way – Directions *Ερωτώντας για την κατεύθυνση*

Can you tell me the way to...?	Μπορείτε να μου δείξετε το δρόμο για...;	borreeteh nah moo dheeksehteh to dhrommo yeeah
How do I get to...?	Πως μπορώ να πάω στο...;	poss borro nah paho sto
Are we on the right road for...?	Είμαστε στο σωστό δρόμο για...;	eemahsteh sto sosto dhrommo yeeah
How far is the next village?	Πόσο μακρυά είναι το επόμενο χωριό;	posso mahkreeah eeneh to ehpommehno khorreeo
Is there a road with little traffic?	Υπάρχει δρόμος με λιγότερη κίνηση;	eepahrkhee dhrommoss meh leegottehree keeneessee
How far is it to... from here?	Πόσο μακρυά είναι... από εδώ;	posso mahkreeah eeneh ... ahpo ehdho
Is there a motorway (expressway)?	Υπάρχει αυτοκινητόδρομος;	eepahrkhee ahftokkeeneetodhrommoss
How long does it take by car/on foot?	Πόσο μακρυά είναι με το αυτοκίνητο/ με τα πόδια;	posso mahkreeah eeneh meh to ahftokkeeneeto/ meh tah podheeah
Can I drive to the centre of town?	Μπορώ να οδηγήσω μέχρι το κέντρο της πόλης;	borro nah odheeyeesso mehkhree to kehndro teess polleess
Can you tell me where ... is?	Μπορείτε να μου πείτε που είναι...;	borreeteh nah moo peeteh poo eeneh
How can I find this place/address?	Πως μπορώ να βρω αυτό το μέρος/αυτήν την διεύθυνση;	poss borro nah vro ahfto to mehross/ahfteen teen dheeehftheensee
Where's this?	Που είναι αυτό;	poo eeneh ahfto
Can you show me on this map where I am?	Μπορείτε να μου δείξετε που είμαι σ'αυτό το χάρτη;	borreeteh nah moo dheeksehteh poo eemeh sahfto to khahrtee

Έχετε πάρει λάθος δρόμο.	You're on the wrong road.
Να πάτε ίσια.	Go straight ahead.
βορράς/νότος/ανατολή/δύσις	north/south/east/west
Είναι εκεί κάτω αριστερά/δεξιά.	It's down there on the left/right.
αντίθετα/πίσω... δίπλα από/μετά...	opposite/behind... next to/after...
Να πάτε στο πρώτο/δεύτερο σταυροδρόμι.	Go to the first/second crossroads (intersection).
Στρίψτε αριστερά στα φανάρια.	Turn left at the traffic lights.
Στρίψτε δεξιά στην επόμενη γωνία.	Turn right at the next corner.
Πάρτε την οδό...	Take the ... road.
Πρέπει να γυρίσετε πίσω στο...	You have to go back to...
Ακολουθήστε τα σήματα για Αθήνα.	Follow signs for Athens.

Parking Στάθμευση

Parking in the capital can be a bit of a problem, although some hotels have car parks. Traffic police can give on-the-spot fines for parking offences.

Where can I park?	Που μπορούμε να σταθμεύσουμε;	poo borroomeh nah stahthmehfsoomeh
Is there a car park nearby?	Υπάρχει εδώ κοντά πάρκινγκ;	eepahrkhee ehdho kondah "parking"
May I park here?	Μπορώ να σταθμεύσω εδώ;	borro nah stahthmehfso ehdho
How long can I park here?	Πόση ώρα μπορώ να σταθμεύσω εδώ;	possee orrah borro nah stahthmehfso ehdho
What's the charge per hour?	Πόσο κάνει την ώρα;	posso kahnee teen orrah
Do you have some change for the parking meter?	Μήπως έχετε ψιλά για το παρκόμετρο;	meeposs ehkhehteh pseelah yeeah to pahrkommehtro

Breakdown – Road assistance   Βλάβη – Οδική βοήθεια

Where's the nearest garage?	Που είναι το κοντινότερο γκαράζ;	poo eeneh to kondeenottehro gahrahz
Excuse me. My car has broken down.	Με συγχωρείτε. Το αυτοκίνητο μου έχει μια βλάβη.	meh seengkhorreeteh. to ahftokkeeneeto moo ehkhee meeah vlahvee.
I've had a break-down at...	Έπαθα μια βλάβη στο...	ehpahthah meeah vlahvee sto
Can you send a mechanic?	Μπορείτε να στείλετε ένα μηχανικό;	borreeteh nah steelehteh ehnah meekhahneeko
My car won't start.	Το αυτοκίνητο μου δεν ξεκινά.	to ahftokkeeneeto moo dhehn ksehkeenah
The battery is dead.	Μου τελείωσε η μπαταρία.	moo tehleeosseh ee bahtahreeah
I've run out of petrol (gasoline).	Μου τελείωσε η βενζίνη.	moo tehleeosseh ee vehnzeenee
I have a flat tyre.	Έμεινα από λάστιχο.	ehmeenah ahpo lahsteekho
The engine is over-heating.	Η μηχανή είναι πολύ ζεστή.	ee meekhahnee eeneh pollee zehstee
There is something wrong with the...	Κάτι συμβαίνει με...	kahtee seemvehnee meh
brakes	τα φρένα	tah frehnah
carburettor	το καρμπυρατέρ	to kahrbeerahtehr
exhaust pipe	την εξάτμηση	teen ehksahtmeessee
radiator	το ψυγείο	to pseeyeeo
wheel	τον τροχό	tonn trokho
Can you send a break-down van (tow truck)?	Μπορείτε να στείλετε ένα ρυμουλκό;	borreeteh nah steelehteh ehnah reemoolko
How long will you be?	Πόση ώρα θα κάνετε;	possee orrah thah kahnehteh

Accident – Police   Δυστύχημα – Αστυνομία

| Please call the police. | Παρακαλώ, καλέστε την αστυνομία. | pahrahkahlo kahlehsteh teen ahsteenommeeah |
| There's been an accident. | Έγινε ένα δυστύχημα. | ehyeeneh ehnah dheesteekheemah |

It's about 2 kilometres from...	Περίπου 2 χιλιόμετρα από...	pehreepoo 2 kheeleeommeehtrah ahpo
Where is there a telephone?	Υπάρχει εδώ κοντά τηλέφωνο;	eepahrkhee ehdho kondah teelehfonno
Call a doctor/an ambulance, quickly.	Καλέστε ένα γιατρό/ ένα ασθενοφόρο, γρήγορα.	kahlehsteh ehnah yeeahtro/ehnah ahsthehnofforro ghreeghorrah
There are people injured.	Υπάρχουν τραυματίες.	eepahrkhoon trahvmahteeehss
What's your name and address?	Ποιο είναι το όνομα και η διεύθυνση σας;	peeo eeneh to onnommah keh ee dheeehftheensee sahss
What's your insurance company?	Ποια είναι η ασφαλιστική εταιρία σας;	peeah eeneh ee ahsfahleesteekee ehtehreeah sahss

Road signs Σήματα τροχαίας

ΑΛΑΓΗ ΠΟΡΕΙΑΣ	Diversion (detour)
ΑΝΑΨΤΕ ΤΑ ΦΩΤΑ	Switch on headlights
ΑΠΑΓΟΡΕΥΕΤΑΙ Η ΣΤΑΘΜΕΥΣΗ	No parking
ΑΠΑΓΟΡΕΥΕΤΑΙ ΤΟ ΠΡΟΣΠΕΡΑΣΜΑ	No overtaking (no passing)
ΑΠΟΤΟΜΗ ΑΝΩΦΕΡΕΙΑ/ ΚΑΤΩΦΕΡΕΙΑ	Steep hill
ΑΡΓΑ/ΚΟΨΤΕ ΤΑΧΥΤΗΤΑ	Slow down
ΒΑΡΕΙΑ ΟΧΗΜΑΤΑ	Heavy vehicles
ΔΙΑΣΤΑΥΡΩΣΗ ΜΕ ΣΙΔΗΡΟΔΡΟΜΙΚΗ ΓΡΑΜΜΗ	Level (railroad) crossing
ΔΙΟΔΙΑ	Toll
ΔΥΣΚΟΛΗ ΔΙΑΒΑΣΗ/ΑΡΓΑ	Slow traffic
ΔΩΣΤΕ ΠΡΩΤΟΠΟΡΕΙΑ	Give way (yield)
ΕΠΙΤΡΕΠΕΤΑΙ Η ΣΤΑΘΜΕΥΣΗ	Parking allowed
ΕΡΓΑ ΕΠΙ ΤΗΣ ΟΔΟΥ	Road works ahead
ΕΞΟΔΟΣ ΒΑΡΕΩΝ ΟΧΗΜΑΤΩΝ	Lorry (truck) exit
ΚΑΤΟΛΙΣΘΗΣΗ ΛΙΘΩΝ	Falling rocks
ΚΙΝΔΥΝΟΣ	Danger
ΚΡΑΤΑΤΕ ΔΕΞΙΑ	Keep right
ΛΑΚΟΥΒΕΣ	Potholes
ΜΟΝΟ ΓΙΑ ΠΕΖΟΥΣ	Pedestrians only
ΟΔΙΚΗ ΓΡΑΜΜΗ ΓΙΑ ΔΗΜΟΣΙΕΣ ΜΕΤΑΦΟΡΕΣ	Lane reserved for public transport
ΠΡΟΣΟΧΗ ΣΧΟΛΕΙΟ	Caution, school
ΣΤΡΟΦΕΣ	Bends (curves)
ΤΕΛΟΣ ΑΠΑΓΟΡΕΥΜΕΝΗΣ ΖΩΝΗΣ	End of restricted area
ΧΑΛΑΣΜΕΝΟΣ ΔΡΟΜΟΣ	Poor road surface

Sightseeing

Where's the tourist office?	Που είναι το γραφείο τουρισμού;	poo **ee**neh to ghrah**fee**o tooreez**moo**
What are the main points of interest?	Ποια είναι τα πιο ενδιαφέροντα μέρη;	**pee**ah **ee**neh tah **pee**o ehndheeah**feh**ronndah **meh**ree
We're only here for...	Είμαστε εδώ μόνο για...	**ee**mahsteh ehdho monno yeeah
a few hours	λίγες ώρες	**lee**yehss orrehss
a day	μια μέρα	**mee**ah **meh**rah
a week	μια βδομάδα	**mee**ah vdhom**mah**dhah
Can you recommend a sightseeing tour / an excursion?	Μπορείτε να προτείνετε μια περιοδεία στα αξιοθέατα/μια εκδρομή;	bor**ree**teh nah prot**tee**nehteh **mee**ah pehreeo**dhee**ah stah ahkseeo**the**hahtah/**mee**ah ehk**dhromm**ee
Where do we leave from?	Από που θα φύγουμε;	ah**po** poo thah **fee**ghoomeh
Will the bus pick us up at the hotel?	Μπορεί να μας πάρει το λεωφορείο από το ξενοδοχείο;	bor**ree** nah mahss **pah**ree to lehoffor**ree**o ah**po** to ksehnodho**khee**o
How much does the tour cost?	Πόσο κοστίζει η εκδρομή;	**posso** kost**ee**zee ee ehk**dhromm**ee
What time does the tour start?	Τι ώρα αρχίζει η εκδρομή;	tee **orr**ah ahr**khee**zee ee ehk**dhromm**ee
Is lunch included?	Συμπεριλαμβάνεται το γεύμα;	seembehreelahm**vah**nehteh to **yehv**mah
What time do we get back?	Τι ώρα θα επιστρέψουμε;	tee **orr**ah thah ehpee**streh**psoomeh
Do we have free time in...?	Έχουμε ελεύθερη ώρα στο...;	**ehk**hoomeh eh**lehf**thehree **orr**ah sto
Is there an English-speaking guide?	Υπάρχει ξεναγός που να μιλάει Αγγλικά;	eep**ahr**khee ksehnah**ghoss** poo nah mee**lah**ee ahnggle**ek**ah
I'd like to hire a private guide for...	Θα ήθελα να νοικιάσω έναν ιδιωτικό ξεναγό για...	thah **ee**thehlah nah nee**kee**ahsso **eh**nahn eedheeot**teek**o ksehnah**gho** yeeah
half a day	μισή μέρα	mee**ssee** **meh**rah
a full day	μια μέρα	**mee**ah **meh**rah

Where's/Where are the...?	Πού είναι...;	poo eeneh
abbey	το μοναστήρι	to monnahsteeree
art gallery	η γκαλερί τέχνης	ee gahlehree tehkhneess
artists' quarter	η συνοικία των καλλιτεχνών	ee seeneekeeah tonn kahleetehkhnonn
botanical gardens	ο βοτανικός κήπος	o vottahneekoss keeposs
building	το κτίριο	to kteereeo
business quarter	το εμπορικό κέντρο	to ehmborreeko kehndro
castle	ο πύργος	o peerghoss
cathedral	η μητρόπολη	ee meetroppollee
cave	το σπήλαιο	to speeleho
cemetery	το νεκροταφείο	to nehkrottahfeeo
chapel	το παρεκκλήσι	to pahrehkleessee
church	η εκκλησία	ee ehkleesseeah
city centre	το κέντρο της πόλης	to kehndro teess polleess
concert hall	η αίθουσα συναυλιών	ee ehthoossah seenahvleeonn
convent	το μοναστήρι	to monnahsteeree
court house	το δικαστήριο	to dheekahsteereeo
downtown area	το κέντρο της πόλης	to kehndro teess polleess
embankment	το φράγμα	to frahghmah
exhibition	η έκθεση	ee ehkthehssee
factory	το εργοστάσιο	to ehrghostahsseeo
fair	το πανηγύρι	to pahneeyeeree
flea market	η λαϊκή αγορά	ee laheekee aghorrah
fortress	το φρούριο	to frooreeo
fountain	η πηγή	ee peeyee
gardens	το πάρκο	to pahrko
harbour	το λιμάνι	to leemahnee
library	η βιβλιοθήκη	ee veevleeotheekee
market	η αγορά	ee aghorrah
monastery	το μοναστήρι	to monnahsteeree
monument	το μνημείο	to mneemeeo
museum	το μουσείο	to moosseeo
old town	η παλιά πόλη	ee pahleeah pollee
opera house	η όπερα	ee oppehrah
palace	το παλάτι	to pahlahtee
park	το πάρκο	to pahrko
parliament building	η βουλή	ee voolee
planetarium	το αστεροσκοπείο	to ahstehrosskoppeeo
royal palace	το βασιλικό παλάτι	to vahsseeleeko pahlahtee
ruins	τα ερείπια	tah ehreepeeah
shopping area	η περιοχή για ψώνια	ee pehreeookhee yeeah psonneeah

square	η πλατεία	ee plah**tee**ah
stadium	το στάδιο	to **stah**dheeo
statue	το άγαλμα	to **ahg**hahlmah
stock exchange	το χρηματιστήριο	to khreemahtees**tee**reeo
theatre	το θέατρο	to **the**hahtro
tomb	ο τάφος	o **tah**foss
tower	ο πύργος	o **peerg**hoss
town hall	το δημαρχείο	to dheemahr**kee**o
university	το πανεπιστήμιο	to pahnehpees**tee**meeo
zoo	ο ζωολογικός κήπος	o zo-olloyee**koss kee**poss

Admission Η είσοδος

Is ... open on Sundays?	Είναι ανοικτό... τις Κυριακές;	**ee**neh ahnee**kto**... teess keeree-ah**kehss**
What are the opening hours?	Ποιες ώρες είναι ανοικτά τα καταστήματα;	pee**ehss** orrehss **ee**neh ahnee**ktah** tah kahtah**stee**mahtah
When does it close?	Πότε κλείνει;	**pot**teh **klee**nee
How much is the entrance fee?	Πόσο κοστίζει η είσοδος;	**poss**o kost**ee**zee ee **e**ssodhoss
Is there any reduction for...?	Υπάρχει έκπτωση για...;	ee**pahr**khee **ehk**ptossee **yeah**...
children	τα παιδιά	tah pehd**hee**ah
the disabled	τους ανάπηρους	tooss ah**nah**peerooss
groups	τις ομάδες	teess om**mah**dhehss
pensioners	τους συνταξιούχους	tooss seendahk**seeoo**khooss
students	τους φοιτητές	tooss feetee**tehss**
Do you have a guidebook in English?	Έχετε οδηγό στα Αγγλικά;	**ehk**hehteh odhee**gho** stah ahnggleek**ah**
Can I buy a catalogue?	Μπορώ να αγοράσω ένα κατάλογο;	borr**o** nah ahghorr**ahs**so **eh**nah kah**tah**logho
Is it all right to take pictures?	Επιτρέπεται να πάρω φωτογραφίες;	ehpeet**reh**pehteh nah **pah**ro fottoghrah**fee**ehss

| ΕΙΣΟΔΟΣ ΕΛΕΥΘΕΡΑ | ADMISSION FREE |
| ΑΠΑΓΟΡΕΥΕΤΑΙ Η ΦΩΤΟΓΡΑΦΗΣΗ | TAKING PHOTOGRAPHS IS PROHIBITED |

Who – What – When? *Ποιος – Τι – Πότε;*

What's that building?	Ποιο είναι αυτό το κτίριο;	peeo **ee**neh ahfto to **ktee**reeo
Who was the...?	Ποιος ήταν ο...;	pee**oss ee**tahn o
architect	αρχιτέκτονας	ahrkhee**tehk**tonnahss
artist	καλλιτέχνης	kahlee**tehk**hneess
painter	ζωγράφος	zogh**rah**foss
sculptor	γλύπτης	**ghleep**teess
Who built it?	Ποιος το έκτισε;	pee**oss** to eh**ktee**sseh
Who painted that picture?	Ποιος ζωγράφισε αυτό τον πίνακα;	pee**oss** zogh**rah**feesseh ahfto tonn **pee**nahkah
When did he live?	Πότε έζησε;	**potteh** eh**zee**sseh
When was it built?	Πότε κτίστηκε;	**potteh ktee**steekeh
Where's the house where ... lived?	Που είναι το σπίτι που έζησε ο/η...;	poo **ee**neh to **spee**tee poo eh**zee**sseh o/ee*
We're interested in...	Ενδιαφερόμαστε για...	ehndeeahfeh**rom**mahsteh yeeah
antiques	αντίκες	ahn**dee**kehss
archaeology	αρχαιολογία	ahrkheholloy**ee**ah
art	τέχνη	**tehk**hnee
botany	βοτανική	vottahnee**kee**
ceramics	κεραμική	kehrahmee**kee**
coins	νομίσματα	nom**meez**mahtah
fine arts	καλές τέχνες	kah**lehss tehk**hnehss
furniture	έπιπλα	**eh**peeplah
geology	γεωλογία	yeholloy**ee**ah
handicrafts	χειροτεχνία	kheerottehkh**knee**ah
history	ιστορία	eestor**ree**ah
medicine	ιατρική	eeahtree**kee**
music	μουσική	moossee**kee**
natural history	φυσική ιστορία	feessee**kee** eestor**ree**ah
ornithology	ορνιθολογία	orneetholloy**ee**ah
painting	ζωγραφική	zoghrahfee**kee**
pottery	αγγειοπλαστική	ahnggeeoplahstee**kee**
religion	θρησκεία	threes**kee**ah
sculpture	γλυπτική	ghleeptee**kee**
zoology	ζωολογία	zo-olloy**ee**ah
Where's the ... department?	Που είναι το τμήμα...;	poo **ee**neh to **tmee**mah

---

* When referring to a man use **o** (o), to a woman say **η** (ee)

It's...	Είναι...	eeneh
amazing	καταπληκτικό	kahtahpleekteeko
awful	τρομερό	trommehro
beautiful	ωραίο	orreho
gloomy	σκοτεινό	skotteeno
impressive	επιβλητικό	ehpeevleeteeko
interesting	ενδιαφέρον	ehndheeahfehronn
magnificent	μεγαλοπρεπές	mehghahloprehpehss
pretty	όμορφο	ommorfo
strange	παράξενο	pahrahksehno
superb	θαυμάσιο	thahvmahsseeo
terrifying	τρομακτικό	trommahkteeko
tremendous	εξαιρετικό	ehksehrehteeko
ugly	άσχημο	ahskheemo

Religious services   *Θρησκευτική λειτουργία*

The national religion is Greek Orthodox. In Athens and other large towns you will also find Catholic and Protestant churches and some synagogues. During the high season, part of the service may be in English, but normally they are held in Greek

Is there a... near here?	Υπάρχει μια... εδώ κοντά;	eepahrkhee meeah... ehdho kondah
Catholic church	καθολική εκκλησία	kahtholleekee ehklee-sseeah
Orthodox church	ορθόδοξη εκκλησία	orthodhoksee ehklee-sseeah
synagogue	συναγωγή	seenahghoyee
mosque	τζαμί	dzahmee
Protestant church	εκκλησία διαμαρ-τυρομένων	ehkleesseeah dheeah-mahrteerommehnonn
At what time is...?	Τι ώρα είναι...;	tee orrah eeneh
mass/the service	η λειτουργία	ee leetooryeeah
Where can I find a... who speaks English?	Που μπορώ να βρω ένα... που να μιλάει Αγγλικά;	poo borro nah vro ehnah... poo nah meelahee ahnggleekah
priest/minister/rabbi	παπά/προτεστάντη κληρικό/ραββίνο	pahpah/prottehstahndee kleereeko/rahveeno
I'd like to visit the church.	Θα ήθελα να επισκεπτώ την εκκλησία.	thah eethehlah nah ehpeeskehpto teen ehkleesseeah

In the countryside Στήν ύπεθρο

Is there a scenic route to...?	Υπάρχει γραφική διαδρομή για...;	eepahrkhee ghrahfeekee dheeahdhrommee yeeah
How far is it to...?	Πόσο μακρυά είναι μέχρι το/τη...;	posso mahkreeah eeneh mehkhree to/tee
Can we walk?	Μπορούμε να περπατήσουμε;	borroomeh nah pehrpah-teessoomeh
How high is that mountain?	Πόσο ύψος έχει αυτό το βουνό;	posso eepsoss ehkhee ahfto to voono
What's the name of that...?	Πως λέγεται αυτό ...;	poss lehyehteh ahfto
animal/bird	το ζώο/το πουλί	to zo-o/to poolee
flower/tree	το λουλούδι/το δέντρο	to looloodhee/to dhehndro

Landmarks Ορόσημα

bridge	γέφυρα	yehfeerah
canal	κανάλι	kahnahlee
cliff	γκρεμός	grehmoss
farm	αγρόκτημα	ahghrokteemah
field	χωράφι	khorrahfee
footpath	μονοπάτι	monnoppahtee
forest	δάσος	dhahssoss
garden	κήπος	keeposs
hill	λόφος	loffoss
house	σπίτι	speetee
lake	λίμνη	leemnee
meadow	λιβάδι	leevahdhee
mountain	βουνό	voono
(mountain) pass	(ορεινή) διάβαση	(orreenee) dheeahvahssee
path	μονοπάτι	monnoppahtee
peak	κορυφή	korreefee
pond	μικρή λίμνη	meekree leemnee
river	ποταμός	pottahmoss
road	δρόμος	dhrommoss
sea	θάλασσα	thahlahssah
spring	πηγή	peeyee
valley	κοιλάδα	keelahdhah
village	χωριό	khorreeo
vineyard	αμπέλι	ahmbehlee
wall	τοίχος	teekhoss
waterfall	καταρράκτης	kahtahrahkteess
wood	δάσος	dhahssoss

ASKING THE WAY, see page 76

Relaxing

Cinema (movies) – Theatre *Κινηματογράφος – Θέατρο*

You may still find some beautiful open-air cinemas in the countryside and suburbs. Foreign films are usually shown in the original version with Greek subtitles. It's not normally possible to reserve seats. Like cinemas, theatres are also often open-air in summer, but here you should book in advance.

What's on at the cinema tonight?	Τι παίζουν στον κινηματογράφο απόψε;	tee **peh**zoon stonn keeneemahto**ghrah**fo ah**pop**seh
What's playing at the ... Theatre?	Τι παίζουν στο... Θέατρο;	tee **peh**zoon sto... **the**hahtro
What sort of play is it?	Τι είδους έργο είναι;	tee **eed**hooss **ehr**gho **ee**neh
Who's it by?	Ποιος είναι ο συγγραφέας;	**pee**oss **ee**neh o seeng-grah**feh**hahss
Can you recommend a ...?	Μπορείτε να μου προτείνετε ...;	bor**ree**teh nah moo prot**tee**nehteh
good film	ένα καλό φιλμ	**eh**nah kah**lo** feelm
comedy	μια κωμωδία	**mee**ah kommod**hee**ah
musical	ένα μουσικοχορευτικό	**eh**nah maosseekokho-**rreh**fteeko
Where's that new film directed by... being shown?	Πού παίζετε αυτό το νέο έργο του...;	poo **peh**zehteh ahf**to** to **neh**o **ehr**gho too
Who's in it?	Ποιος παίζει;	**pee**oss **peh**zee
Who's playing the lead?	Ποιος είναι ο πρωταγωνιστής;	**pee**oss **ee**neh o prottah-ghonnees**teess**
Who's the director?	Ποιος είναι ο σκηνοθέτης;	**pee**oss **ee**neh o skeeno-**theh**teess
At which theatre is that new play by... being performed?	Σε ποιο θέατρο παίζετε αυτό το νέο έργο του...;	seh **pee**o **the**hahtro **peh**zehteh ahf**to** to **neh**o **ehr**gho too

What time does it begin?	Τι ώρα αρχίζει;	tee orrah ahrkheezee
Are there any seats for tonight?	Υπάρχουν θέσεις για απόψε;	eepahrkhoon thehsseess yeeah ahpopseh
How much are the seats?	Πόσο κοστίζει η είσοδος;	posso kosteezee ee eessodhoss
I want to reserve 2 seats for the show on Friday evening.	Θέλω να κρατήσω 2 θέσεις για τη βραδυνή παράσταση της Παρασκευής.	thehlo nah krahteesso 2 thehsseess yeeah tee vrahdheenee pahrahstahssee teess pahrahskehveess
Can I have a ticket for the matinee on Tuesday?	Μπορώ να έχω ένα εισιτήριο για την απογευματινή της Τρίτης;	borro nah ehkho ehnah eesseeteereeo yeeah teen ahpoyehvmahteenee teess treeteess
I want a seat in the stalls (the orchestra).	Θέλω μια θέση στη πλατεία.	thehlo meeah thehssee stee plahteeah
Not too far back.	Όχι πολύ πίσω.	okhee pollee peesso
Somewhere in the middle.	Κάπου στο κέντρο.	kahpoo sto kehndro
How much are the seats in the circle (mezzanine)?	Πόσο κάνουν οι θέσεις στον εξώστη;	posso kahnoon ee thehsseess stonn ehksostee
May I have a programme, please?	Μπορώ να έχω ένα πρόγραμμα, παρακαλώ;	borro nah ehkho ehnah proghrahmah pahrahkahlo
Where's the cloakroom?	Που είναι η γκαρντερόμπα;	poo eeneh ee gahrndehrobah

---

Με συγχωρείτε, δεν υπάρχουν άλλα εισιτήρια.	I'm sorry, we're sold out.
Έχουν μείνει μόνο λίγες θέσεις στον εξώστη.	There are only a few seats left in the circle (mezzanine).
Μπορώ να δω το εισιτήριο σας;	May I see your ticket?
Αυτή είναι η θέση σας.	This is your seat.

DAYS OF THE WEEK, see page 150

Ξεκούραση

Opera – Ballet – Concert   Όπερα – Μπαλέτο – Συναυλία

Can you recommend a/an...?	Μπορείτε να μου προτείνετε...;	borreeteh nah moo protteenehteh
ballet	ένα μπαλέτο	ehnah bahlehto
concert	μια συναυλία	meeah seenahvleeah
opera	μια όπερα	meeah oppehrah
operetta	μια οπερέττα	meeah oppehrehtah
Where's the opera house/the concert hall?	Που είναι η όπερα/ η αίθουσα συναυλίας;	poo eeneh ee oppehrah/ ee ehthoossah seenahvleeahss
What's on at the opera tonight?	Τι παίζεται στην Όπερα απόψε;	tee pehzehteh steen oppehrah ahpopseh
Who's singing/ dancing?	Ποιος τραγουδά/ χορεύει;	peeoss trahghoodhah/ khorrehvee
Which orchestra is playing?	Ποια ορχήστρα παίζει;	peeah orkheestrah pehzee
Who's the conductor/ soloist?	Ποιος είναι ο διευθηντής της ορχήστρας/ ο σολίστας;	peeoss eeneh o dheeehftheendeess teess orkheestrahss/ o solleestahss

Nightclubs – Discos   Νυκτερινά κέντρα – Δισκοθήκη

Can you recommend a good nightclub?	Μπορείτε να μου συστήσετε ένα καλό νυκτερινό κέντρο (νάιτ-κλαμπ);	borreeteh nah moo seesteessehteh ehnah kahlo neektehreeno kehndro ("night club")
Is there a floor show?	Έχει επιθεώρηση πίστας;	ehkhee ehpeethehorreessee peestahss
What time does the show start?	Τι ώρα αρχίζει το πρόγραμμα;	tee orrah ahrkheezee to proghrahmah
Is evening dress required?	Είναι απαραίτητο το βραδυνό ρούχο;	eeneh ahpahrehteeto to vrahdheeno rookho
Where can we go dancing?	Που μπορούμε να πάμε να χορέψουμε;	poo borroomeh nah pahmeh nah khorrehpsoomeh
Is there a discotheque in town?	Υπάρχει δισκοθήκη στην πόλη;	eepahrkhee dheeskotheekee steen pollee
Would you like to dance?	Θα θέλατε να χορέψετε;	thah thehlahteh nah khorrehpsehteh

Sports *Αθλητισμός*

Very popular in Greece are watersports. From swimming to water-skiing, almost every watersport imaginable is available, including water polo. If you want to use underwater equipment, check with the local tourist office as strict rules govern its use.

Yachting: there are plenty of pleasure ports with many facilities where you can dock your own yacht, ship or sailing boat or hire one.

Is there a soccer match anywhere this Sunday?	Υπάρχει πουθενά ποδοσφαιρικός αγώνας αυτή τη Κυριακή;	eepahrkhee poothehnah podhosfehreekoss ahghonnahss ahftee tee keereeahkee
Which teams are playing?	Ποιες ομάδες παίζουν;	peeehss ommahdhehss pehzoon
Can you get me a ticket?	Μπορείτε να μου πάρετε ένα εισητήριο;	borreeteh nah moo pahrehteh ehnah eesseeteereeo

basketball	καλαθόσφαιρα/μπάσκετ	kahlahthossfehrah/"basket"
boxing	πυγμαχία/μποξ	peeghmahkheeah/"box"
cycling	ποδηλασία	podheelahsseeah
football (soccer)	ποδόσφαιρο	podhosfehro
horse racing	ιπποδρομία	eepodhrommeeah
(horseback) riding	ιππασία	eepahsseeah
mountaineering	ορειβασία	orreevahsseeah
sailing	ιστιοπλοΐα	eesteeoploeeah
skiing	χιονοδρομία	kheeonnodhrommeeah
swimming	κολύμβηση	kolleemveessee
tennis	τέννις	"tennis"
volleyball	βόλεϋ	volleh-ee
water polo	υδατόσφαιρα/πόλο	eedhahtosfehrah/"polo"

I'd like to see a boxing match.	Θα ήθελα να δω ένα αγώνα πυγμαχίας.	thah eethehlah nah dho ehnah ahghonnah peeghmahkheeahss
What's the admission charge?	Πόσο κοστίζει η είσοδος;	posso kosteezee ee eessodhoss

Where's the nearest golf course?	Που είναι το κοντινό-τερο γήπεδο γκολφ;	poo **ee**neh to kondeeno-ttehro **yee**pehdho ''golf''
Where are the tennis courts?	Που είναι τα γήπεδα του τέννις;	poo **ee**nah tah yee-pehdhah too ''tennis''
What's the charge per...?	Πόσο κοστίζει...;	**poss**o kost**ee**zee
day/round/hour	την μέρα/τον γύρος/την ώρα	teen **meh**rah/tonn **yee**ross/teen **orr**ah
Can I hire (rent) rackets?	Μπορώ να νοικιάσω ρακέτες;	borro nah neekeee**ah**sso rah**keh**tehss
Where's the race course (track)?	Που είναι ο ιππό-δρομος;	poo **ee**neh o eepo-dhrommoss
Is there any good fishing/hunting around here?	Υπάρχει καλό ψάρεμα/κυνήγι εδώ κοντά;	ee**pah**rkhee kahlo psahrehmah/keeneeyee ehdho kondah
Do I need a permit?	Χρειάζομαι άδεια;	khree**ah**zommeh **ah**dheeah
Where can I get one?	Που μπορώ να βγάλω μια;	poo borro nah **vghah**lo meeah
Is there a swimming pool here?	Υπάρχει πισίνα εδώ;	ee**pah**rkhee peesseenah ehdho
Is it open-air or indoor?	Είναι ανοικτή ή σκεπαστή;	**ee**neh ahneek**tee** ee skehpah**stee**
Is it heated?	Είναι θερμενόμενη;	**ee**neh thehrmehno-mmehnee
What's the tempera-ture of the water?	Ποια είναι η θερμο-κρασία του νερού;	peeah **ee**neh ee thehrmo-kkrahsseeah too nehroo
What's the beach like – sandy, shingle, rocky?	Πως είναι η πλαζ – έχει άμμο, χαλίκια, βράχια;	poss **ee**neh ee plahz – **eh**khee ahmo, khah**lee**keeah, **vrah**kheeah

On the beach Στη παραλία

Is it safe for swim-ming?	Μπορούμε να κολυμπή-σουμε χωρίς κίνδυνο;	bor**roo**meh nah kolleem-beessoomeh khor**reess** **keen**dheeno
Is there a lifeguard?	Υπάρχει ακτοφύ-λακας;	ee**pah**rkhee ahktoffee-lahkahss
Is it safe for children?	Είναι ακίνδυνα για τα παιδιά;	**ee**neh ah**keen**dheenah yeeah tah pehdhee**ah**

The sea is very calm.	Η θάλασσα είναι πολύ ήσυχη.	ee thahlahssah eeneh pollee eesseekhee
There are some big waves.	Υπάρχουν μεγάλα κύματα.	eepahrkhoon mehghah-lah keemahtah
Are there any dangerous currents?	Υπάρχουν επικίνδυνα ρεύματα;	eepahrkhoon ehpeekeen-dheenah rehvmahtah
What time is high tide/low tide?	Τι ώρα έχει παλίρροια/άμπωτη;	tee orrah ehkee pahleereeah/ahmbottee
I want to hire a/an/some...	Θα ήθελα να νοικιάσω...	thah eethehlah nah neekeeahsso
bathing hut (cabana)	μια καμπίνα	meeah kahmbeenah
deck chair	μια πολυθρόνα	meeah polleethronnah
motorboat	μια βάρκα με μηχανή	meeah vahrkah meh meekhahnee
rowing boat	μια βάρκα με κουπιά	meeah vahrkah meh koopeeah
sailing boat	μια βάρκα με πανί	meeah vahrkah meh pahnee
skin-diving equipment	μια εξάρτηση για υποβρύχιο ψάρεμα	meeah ehksahrteessee yeeah eepovreekheeo psahrehmah
sunshade (umbrella)	μια τέντα για τον ήλιο	meeah tehndah yeeah tonn eeleeo
surfboard	ένα κάνω για σερφ	ehnah kahno yeeah sehrf
water-skis	θαλάσσια σκι	thahlahsseah "ski"
windsurfer	ένα γουϊντσέρφερ	ehnah "windsurfer"

ΙΔΙΩΤΙΚΗ ΠΛΑΖ	PRIVATE BEACH
ΑΠΑΓΟΡΕΥΕΤΑΙ Η ΚΟΛΥΜΠΗΣΗ	NO SWIMMING

Winter sports *Χειμερινά σπορ*

Is there a skating rink near here?	Υπάρχει εδώ κοντά πίστα πάγου;	eepahrkhee ehdho kondah peestah pahghoo
Are there ski lifts?	Υπάρχουν σκι αναβατήρες;	eepahrkhoon "ski" ahnahvahteerehss
Can I take skiing lessons?	Μπορώ να παρακο-λουθήσω μαθήματα σκι;	borro nah pahrahko-llootheesso mathee-mahtah "ski"

Making friends

Introductions *Συστάσεις*

May I introduce...?	Μπορώ να σας γνωρίσω...;	borro nah sahss ghnorreesso
John, this is...	Τζων, από εδώ...	"John" ahpo ehdho
My name's...	Ονομάζομαι...	onnommahzommeh
Pleased to meet you.	Χαίρομαι που σας γνωρίζω.	khehrommeh poo sahss ghnorreezo
What's your name?	Πως σας λένε;	poss sahss lehneh
How are you?	Πως είστε;	poss eesteh
Fine, thanks. And you?	Καλά, ευχαριστώ. Και σεις;	kahlah, ehfkhahreesto keh seess

Follow up *Καλύτερη γνωριμία*

Where do you come from?	Από που είστε;	ahpo poo eesteh
I'm from...	Είμαι από το/την...	eemeh ahpo to/teen
What nationality are you?	Ποια είναι η εθνικότητα σας;	peeah eeneh ee ehthneekotteetah sahss
I'm...	Είμαι...	eemeh
American	Αμερικάνος/-ίδα*	ahmehreekahnoss/-eedhah
British	Βρεττανός/-ίδα	vrehtahnoss/-eedhah
Canadian	Καναδός/-έζα	kahnahdhoss/-ehzah
English	Άγγλος/-ίδα	ahnggloss/-eedhah
Irish	Ιρλανδός/-έζα	eerlahndhoss/-ehzah
Scottish	Σκωτζέζος/-α	skotzehzoss/-ah
How long have you been here?	Πόσο καιρό είστε εδώ;	posso kehro eesteh ehdho
Is this your first visit?	Έρχεστε για πρώτη φορά;	ehrkhehsteh yeeah prottee forrah

---

* Where there is a different ending for the feminine gender, we have indicated this by printing first the masculine, and then the feminine ending. For example ahmehreekahnoss/ahmehreekahneedah. See the grammar section for a more detailed explanation.

COUNTRIES, see page 145

Are you enjoying your stay?	Είστε ευχαριστημένος/-η από την διαμονή σας;	eesteh ehfkhahreestee-mehnoss/-ee ahpo teen dheeahmonnee sahss
I like the landscape a lot.	Μου αρέσει πολύ η φύση.	moo ahrehssee pollee ee feessee
What do you think of the country/people?	Τι γνώμη έχετε για την χώρα/τους ανθρώπους;	tee ghnommee ehkheh-teh yeeah teen khorrah/tooss ahnthroppooss
Where are you staying?	Που μένετε;	poo mehnehteh
Are you on your own?	Είστε μόνος/-η σας;	eesteh monnoss/-ee sahss
I'm with my...	Είμαι με... μου.	eemeh meh... moo
wife	την γυναίκα	teen yeenehkah
husband	τον άνδρα	tonn ahndhrah
family	την οικογένεια	teen eekoyehneeah
parents	τους γονείς	tooss ghonneess
boyfriend/girlfriend	τον φίλο/την φίλη	tonn feelo/teen feelee

father/mother	ο πατέρας/η μητέρα	o pahtehrahss/ee meetehrah
son/daughter	ο γιός/η κόρη	o yeeoss/ee korree
brother/sister	ο αδελφός/η αδελφή	o ahdhehlfoss/ee ahdhehlfee
uncle/aunt	ο θείος/η θεία	o theeoss/ee theeah
nephew/niece	ο ανεψιός/η ανεψιά	o ahnehpseeoss/ee ahnehpseeah
cousin	ο ξάδελφος/η ξαδέλφη	o ksahdhehlfoss/ee ksahdhehlfee

Are you married?	Είστε παντρεμένος/-η;	eesteh pahndrehmehnoss/-ee
Are you single?	Είστε ελεύθερος/-η;	eesteh ehlehftheh-ross/-ee
Do you have children?	Έχετε παιδιά;	ehkhehteh pehdheeah
I'm a student.	Είμαι φοιτητής/φοι-τήτρια.	eemeh feeteeteess/feeteetreeah
What are you studying?	Τι σπουδάζετε;	tee spoodhahzehteh
Do you travel a lot?	Ταξιδεύετε πολύ;	tahkseedhehvehteh pollee
Do you play cards/chess?	Παίζετε χαρτιά/σκάκι;	pehzehteh khahrteeah/skahkee

The weather   Ο καιρός

What a lovely day!	Τι υπέροχη μέρα!	tee **ee**pehrokhee **meh**rah
What awful weather!	Τι απαίσιος καιρός!	tee ahpehsseeoss kehross
Isn't it cold/hot today?	Κάνει κρύο/ζέστη σήμερα.	kahnee **kree**o/**zeh**stee **see**mehrah
Is it usually as warm as this?	Συνήθως ο καιρός είναι τόσο ζεστός όπως τώρα;	seeneethoss o kehross eeneh tosso zehstoss oposs torrah
Do you think it's going to ...?	Τι λέτε θα...;	tee **leh**teh thah
be a nice day	είναι ωραία μέρα	eeneh **orr**ehah **meh**rah
rain	βρέξη	**vrehk**see
What is the weather forecast?	Ποια είναι η πρόβλεψη κερού;	peeah eeneh ee **prov**lehpsee kehroo

cloud	το σύνεφο	to **see**nehfo
fog	η ομίχλη	ee **omm**eekhlee
frost	ο παγετός	o pahyeh**toss**
ice	ο πάγος	o **pah**ghoss
lightning	η αστραπή	ee ahstrah**pee**
moon	το φεγγάρι/η σελήνη	to fehnggah**ree**/ee seh**lee**nee
sky	ο ουρανός	o oorah**noss**
snow	το χιόνι	to **khee**onnee
star	το αστέρι/το άστρο	to ah**steh**ree/to **ah**stro
sun	ο ήλιος	o **ee**leeoss
thunder	η βροντή	ee vron**dee**
thunderstorm	η θύελα	ee **thee**ehlah
wind	ο άνεμος	o **ah**nehmoss

Invitations   Προσκλήσεις

Would you like to have dinner with us on...?	Θα θέλατε να δειπνήσετε μαζί μας την...;	thah **theh**lahteh nah dheepnee**sseh**teh mah**zee** mahss teen
May I invite you for lunch?	Μπορώ να σας προσκαλέσω για γεύμα;	borro nah sahss proskah**leh**sso yeeah **yehv**mah
Can you come over for a drink this evening?	Μπορείτε να έλθετε για ένα ποτό απόψε;	borreeteh nah **ehl**thehteh yeeah **eh**nah potto ah**pop**seh

DAYS OF THE WEEK, see page 150

There's a party. Are you coming?	Γίνεται ένα πάρτυ. Έρχεστε;	yeenehteh ehnah pahrtee. ehrkhehsteh
That's very kind of you.	Πολύ ευγενικό από μέρους σας.	pollee ehvyehneeko ahpo mehrooss sahss
Great. I'd love to come.	Περίφημα. Θα ήθελα πολύ να έλθω.	pehreefeemah. thah eethehlah pollee nah ehltho
What time shall we come?	Τι ώρα να έλθουμε;	tee orrah nah ehlthoomeh
May I bring a friend/ a girlfriend?	Μπορώ να φέρω ένα φίλο/μια φίλη;	borro nah fehro ehnah feelo/meeah feelee
I'm afraid we have to leave now.	Νομίζω ότι πρέπει να φύγουμε τώρα.	nommeezo ottee prehpee nah feeghoomeh torrah
Next time you must come to visit us.	Την επόμενη φορά πρέπει εσείς να μας επισκεφτείτε.	teen ehpommehnee fo-rrah prehpee ehseess nah mahss ehpeeskehfteeteh
Thanks for the evening. It was great.	Ευχαριστώ για την βραδυά. Ήταν υπέροχη.	ehfkhahreesto yeeah teen vrahdheeah. eetahn eepehrokhee

Dating Ραντε-βού

Do you mind if I smoke?	Σας ενοχλεί εάν καπνίζω;	sahss ehnokhlee ehahn kahpneezo
Would you like a cigarette?	Θα θέλατε ένα τσιγάρο;	thah thehlahteh ehnah tseeghahro
Do you have a light, please?	Έχετε φωτιά, παρακαλώ;	ehkhehteh fotteeah pahrahkahlo
Why are you laughing?	Γιατί γελάτε;	yeeahtee yehlahteh
Is my Greek that bad?	Είναι τα Ελληνικά μου τόσο άσχημα;	eeneh tah ehleeneekah moo tosso ahskheemah
Do you mind if I sit here?	Σας ενοχλεί εάν καθήσω εδώ;	sahss ehnokhlee ehahn kahtheeso ehdho
Can I get you a drink?	Μπορώ να σας φέρω ένα ποτό;	borro nah sahss fehro ehnah potto
Are you waiting for someone?	Περιμένετε κάποιον;	pehreemehnehteh kah-peeonn
Are you free this evening?	Είστε ελεύθερος/-η απόψε;	eesteh ehlehfthehross/-ee ahpopseh

Would you like to go out with me tonight?	Θα θέλατε να βγούμε έξω μαζί απόψε;	thah **theh**lahteh nah **vghoo**meh **ehk**so mah**zee** ah**pop**seh
Would you like to go dancing?	Θα θέλατε να πάμε να χορέψουμε;	thah **theh**lahteh nah **pah**meh nah khor**reh**psoomeh
Shall we go to the cinema (movies)?	Πάμε στον κινηματο-γράφο;	**pah**meh stonn keenee-mahto**ghrah**fo
Would you like to go for a drive?	Θα θέλατε να πάμε βόλτα με το αυτοκίνητο;	thah **theh**lahteh nah **pah**meh **volt**ah meh to ahfto**kkee**neeto
Where shall we meet?	Που θα συναντηθούμε;	poo thah seenahndee-**thoo**meh
I'll pick you up at your hotel.	Θα σας πάρω από το ξενοδοχείο σας.	thah sahss **pah**ro ahpo to ksehnodho**khee**o sahss
I'll call for you at 8.	Θα περάσω να σας πάρω στις 8.	thah peh**rah**sso nah sahss **pah**ro steess 8
May I take you home?	Μπορώ να σας πάω στο σπίτι σας;	bor**ro** nah sahss **pah**o sto **spee**teh sahss
Can I see you again tomorrow?	Μπορώ να σας ξαναδώ αύριο;	bor**ro** nah sahss ksah-nah**dho** **ahv**reeo
I hope we'll meet again.	Ελπίζω να ξανά-συναντηθούμε.	ehl**pee**zo nah ksahnah-seenahndee**thoo**meh

... and you might answer:

I'd love to, thank you.	Θα μου άρεσε πολύ, ευχαριστώ.	thah moo **ah**rehsseh pol**lee** ehfkhah**ree**sto
Thank you, but I'm busy.	Ευχαριστώ, αλλά είμαι πολύ απασχολημένος/-η.	ehfkhah**ree**sto ahl**lah** **ee**meh pol**lee** ahpah-skholleeme**hnoss**/-ee
No, I'm not interested, thank you.	Όχι, δεν με ενδιαφέρει, ευχαριστώ.	**o**khee dhehn meh ehndheeah**feh**ree ehfkhah**ree**sto
Thank you, it's been a wonderful evening.	Ευχαριστώ, ήταν μια υπέροχη βραδιά.	ehfkhah**ree**sto **ee**tahn **mee**ah ee**peh**rokhee vrah**dhee**ah
I've enjoyed myself.	Διασκέδασα πολύ.	dheeah**skeh**dhahssah pol**lee**

Shopping Guide

This shopping guide is designed to help you find what you want with ease, accuracy and speed. It features:

1. A list of all major shops, stores and services (p. 98).
2. Some general expressions required when shopping to allow you to be specific and selective (p. 100).
3. Full details of the shops and services most likely to concern you. Here you'll find advice, alphabetical lists of items and conversion charts listed under the headings below.

Οδηγός για ψώνια

LAUNDRY, see page 29/HAIRDRESSER'S, see page 30

Shops, stores and services   Μαγαζιά και εξυπηρέτηση

Opening times vary from place to place, and are particularly erratic on the islands. Many shops open from 7.30 or 8 a.m. until 2.30 p.m. on Mondays and Wednesdays, and 1.30 p.m. on Saturdays. On the other days they close for a long siesta until 5 p.m., opening afterwards until 8 or 8.30 p.m.

Where's the nearest...?	Που είναι ο κοντινό-τερος/η κοντινότερη/ το κοντινότερο...;	poo eeneh o kondeeno-ttehross/ee kondee-nottehree/to kondee-nottehro
antique shop	το κατάστημα για αντίκες*	to kahtahsteemah yeeah ahndeekehss
art gallery	η γκαλερί τέχνης	ee gahlehree tehkhneess
baker's	το αρτοποιείο (ο φούρνος)	to ahrtoppeeeeo (o foornoss)
bank	η τράπεζα	ee trahpehzah
barber's	το κουρείο	to kooreeo
beauty salon	το ινστιτούτο καλλονής	to eensteetooto kahlon-nneess
bookshop	το βιβλιοπωλείο	to veevleeoppolleeo
butcher's	το κρεοπωλείο	to krehoppolleeo
cake shop	το ζαχαροπλαστείο	to zahkhahroplahsteeo
camera shop	το φωτογραφείο	to fottoghrahfeeo
chemist's	το φαρμακείο	to fahrmahkeeo
dairy shop	το γαλακτοπωλείο	to ghahlahktoppolleeo
delicatessen	το μπακάλικο	to bahkahleeko
dentist	ο οδοντίατρος	o odhondeeahtross
department store	το μεγάλο εμπορικό κατάστημα	to mehghahlo ehmborreeko kahtahsteemah
drugstore	το φαρμακείο	to fahrmahkeeo
dry cleaner's	το καθαριστήριο	to kahthahreesteereeo
electrician	ο ηλεκτρολόγος	o eelehktrolloghoss
fishmonger's	το ιχθυοπωλείο	to eekhtheeoppolleeo
florist's	το ανθοπωλείο	to ahnthoppolleeo
furrier's	το γουναράδικο	to ghoonahrahdheeko
greengrocer's	το μανάβικο	to mahnahveeko
grocery	το παντοπωλείο	to pahndoppolleeo

* The article before each noun should only be used as a guide to the correct gender and not be pronounced; e.g. Where is the nearest bank? Που είναι η κοντινότερη τράπεζα; – poo eeneh ee kondeenottehree trahpehzah

hairdresser's (ladies/men)	το κομμωτήριο	to kommotteereeo
health food shop	το κατάστημα δίαιτας	to kahtahsteemah dheeehtahss
hospital	το νοσοκομείο	to nossokkommeeo
jeweller's	το κοσμηματοπωλείο	to kozmeemahtoppolleeo
launderette	το αυτόματο πλυντήριο	to ahftommahto pleendeereeo
laundry	το πλυντήριο	to pleendeereeo
library	η βιβλιοθήκη	ee veevleeotheekee
market	η αγορά	ee aghorrah
newsagent's	το πρακτορείο	to prahktorreeo
newsstand	το περίπτερο	to pehreeptehro
optician	ο οπτικός	o opteekoss
pastry shop	το ζαχαροπλαστείο	to zahkharoplahsteeo
photographer's	ο φωτογράφος	o fottoghrahfoss
police station	το αστυνομικό τμήμα	to ahsteenommeeko tmeemah
post office	το ταχυδρομείο	to tahkheedhrommeeo
shoemaker's (repairs)	ο τσαγκάρης	o tsahnggahreess
shoe shop	το υποδηματοποιείο	to eepodheemahtoppeeeeo
shopping centre	τα κεντρικά καταστήματα	tah kehndreekah kahtahsteemahtah
souvenir shop	το κατάστημα σουβενίρ	to kahtahsteemah soovehneer
sporting goods shop	το κατάστημα αθλητικών ειδών	to kahtahsteemah ahthleeteekonn eedhonn
stationer's	το χαρτοπωλείο	to khahrtoppolleeo
supermarket	το σούπερ μάρκετ	to "supermarket"
tailor's	το ραφείο	to rahfeeo
telegraph office	το τηλεγραφείο	to teelehghrahfeeo
tobacconist's	το καπνοπωλείο	to kahpnoppolleeo
toy shop	το κατάστημα παιχνιδιών	to kahtahsteemah pehkhneedheeonn
travel agency	το πρακτορείο ταξιδίων	to prahktorreeo tahkseedheeonn
vegetable store	το μανάβικο	to mahnahveeko
veterinarian	ο κτηνίατρος	o kteeneeahtross
watchmaker's	το ωρολογοποιείο	to orrolloghoppeeeeo
wine merchant	το οινοπωλείο	to eenoppolleeo

ΕΙΣΟΔΟΣ	ENTRANCE
ΕΞΟΔΟΣ	EXIT
ΕΞΟΔΟΣ ΚΙΝΔΥΝΟΥ	EMERGENCY EXIT

General expressions   Γενικές εκφράσεις

Where?   Που;

Where's there a good ...?	Που υπάρχει ένα καλό...;	poo ee**pahr**kee **eh**nah kah**lo**
Where can I find a ...?	Που μπορώ να βρω ένα...;	poo bo**rro** nah vro **eh**nah
Where's the shopping area?	Που είναι η περιοχή για ψώνια;	poo **ee**neh ee pehreeo**khee** yeeah psonneeah
Is it far from here?	Είναι μακρυά από εδώ;	**ee**neh mahk**ree**ah ahpo eh**dho**
How do I get there?	Πως μπορώ να πάω εκεί;	poss bo**rro** nah **pa**ho eh**kee**

Service   Εξυπηρέτηση

Can you help me?	Μπορείτε να με βοηθήσετε;	bo**rree**teh nah meh vo-ee-**thee**ssehteh
I'm just looking.	Απλώς κοιτάζω.	ah**ploss** kee**tah**zo
Do you sell...?	Πωλείτε...;	po**llee**teh
I want...	Θέλω...	**theh**lo
Can you show me some...?	Μπορείτε να μου δείξετε μερικά...;	bo**rree**teh nah moo **dhee**ksehteh mehree**kah**
Do you have any...?	Έχετε μερικά...;	**eh**khehteh mehree**kah**
Where's the ... department?	Που είναι το τμήμα...;	poo **ee**neh to **tmee**mah
Where is the lift (elevator)/escalator?	Που είναι το ασανσέρ (ο αναβατήρας)/ η κινητή σκάλα;	poo **ee**neh to ahssahn-**ssehr** (o ahnah-vah**tee**rahss)/ee keenee**tee** **skah**lah

That one   Εκείνο

Can you show me...?	Μπορείτε να μου δείξετε...;	bo**rree**teh nah moo **dhee**ksehteh
this/that	αυτό/εκείνο	ah**fto**/eh**kee**no
the one in the window/in the display case	αυτό εκεί στη βιτρίνα/στο ράφι	ah**fto** eh**kee** stee veet**ree**nah/sto **rah**fee

Defining the article   *Περιγραφή του είδους*

I'd like a ... one.	θα ήθελα ένα/μια...	thah **ee**thehlah **eh**nah/**mee**ah
big	μεγάλο/-λη	meh**ghah**lo/-lee
cheap	φθηνό/-νή	ftheeno/-**nee**
dark	σκούρο/-ρα	**skoo**ro/-rah
good	καλό/-λή	kahlo/-**lee**
heavy	βαρύ/-ριά	vah**ree**/-reeah
large	φαρδύ/-διά	fahr**dhee**/-dheeah
light (weight)	ελαφρό/-ριά	ehlah**fro**/-reeah
light (colour)	ανοιχτό/-ή	ahneekh**to**/-ee
oval	οβάλ	ovvahl
rectangular	μακρόστενο/-νη	mahk**ro**stehno/-nee
round	στρογγυλό/-λή	stronggeelo/-**lee**
small	μικρό/-κρή	meekro/-**kree**
square	τετράγωνο/-νη	teh**trah**ghonno/-nee
sturdy	ανθεκτικό/-κή	ahnthehk**teeko**/-**kee**
I don't want anything too expensive.	Δεν θέλω κάτι πολύ ακριβό.	dhehn **theh**lo **kah**tee pollee ahkreevo

Preference   *Προτίμηση*

Can you show me some more?	Μπορείτε να μου δείξετε κι' άλλα;	bor**ree**teh nah moo **dheek**sehteh kee' **ah**lah
Haven't you anything...?	Δεν έχετε κάτι...;	dhehn **eh**khehteh **kah**tee
cheaper/better	φτηνότερο/καλύτερο	fteeno**tteh**ro/kah**lee**tehro
larger/smaller	μεγαλύτερο/μικρότερο	mehghah**lee**tehro/meekro**tteh**ro

How much?   *Πόσο κάνει;*

How much is this?	Πόσο κάνει αυτό;	posso **kah**nee ahfto
How much are they?	Πόσο κάνουν αυτά;	posso **kah**noon ahftah
I don't understand.	Δεν καταλαβαίνω.	dhehn kahtahlah**veh**no
Please write it down.	Παρακαλώ, γράψτε το.	pahrahkahlo **ghrahps**teh to
I don't want to spend more than... drachmas.	Δεν θέλω να ξοδέψω περισσότερο από... δραχμές.	dhehn **theh**lo nah kso-**dheh**pso pehree**ssot**tehro ahpo... dhrahkh**mehss**

ΕΚΠΤΩΣΕΙΣ SALE

COLOURS, see page 113

Οδηγός για ψώνια

Decision *Απόφαση*

It's not quite what I want.	Δεν είναι ακριβώς αυτό που θέλω.	dhehn **ee**neh ahkree**voss** **ahf**to poo **the**hlo
No, I don't like it.	Όχι, δεν μου αρέσει.	**o**khee dhehn moo ah**reh**ssee

Ordering *Παραγγελεία*

Can you order it for me?	Μπορείτε να μου το παραγγείλετε;	bor**ree**teh nah moo to pahrahng**gee**leteh
How long will it take?	Πόσο καιρό χρειάζεται;	**poss**o keh**ro** khree**ah**zehteh

Delivery *Παράδοση*

I'll take it with me.	Θα το πάρω μαζί μου.	thah to **pah**ro mah**zee** moo
Deliver it to the ...Hotel.	Στείλτε το στο ξενοδοχείο...	**steel**teh to sto ksehnodho**khee**o
Please send it to this address.	Παρακαλώ, στείλτε το σ'αυτή τη διεύθυνση.	pahrahkah**lo** **steel**teh to sahf**tee** tee dhee**ehf**theensee
Will I have any difficulty with the customs?	Θα έχω καμμιά δυσκολία στο τελωνείο;	thah **ehk**ho kah**mee**ah dheeskol**lee**ah sto tehlon**nee**o

Paying *Πληρωμή*

How much is it?	Πόσο κάνει;	**poss**o **kah**nee
Can I pay by traveller's cheque?	Μπορώ να πληρώσω με τράβελερς τσεκ;	bor**ro** nah plee**rosso** meh **trah**vehlehrs tsehk
Do you accept...?	Δέχεστε...;	**dheh**khehsteh
dollars	δολλάρια	dhol**lah**reeah
pounds	Αγγλικές λίρες	ahnggleek**ehss** **lee**rehss
credit cards	πιστωτικές κάρτες	peestotteek**ehss** **kah**rtehss
Do I have to pay the VAT (sales tax)?	Πρέπει να πληρώσω φόρο;	**preh**pee nah plee**rosso** **fo**rro
I think there's a mistake in the bill.	Νομίζω κάνατε λάθος στον λογαριασμό.	nom**mee**zo **kah**nahteh **lah**thoss stonn loghahree**ah**zmo

Anything else?   *Τίποτα άλλο;*

No, thanks, that's all.	Όχι, ευχαριστώ, τίποτε άλλο.	okhee ehfkhahreesto teepotteh ahlo
Yes, I want ...	Ναι, θέλω ...	neh thehlo
Show me ...	Δείξτε μου ...	dheeksteh moo
May I have a bag, please?	Μπορώ να έχω μια τσάντα παρακαλώ;	borro nah ehkho meeah tsahndah pahrahkahlo
Could you wrap it up for me, please?	Μου το τυλίγετε, παρακαλώ;	moo to teeleeyehteh pahrahkahlo

Dissatisfied?   *Δυσαρεστημένος;*

Can you exchange this, please?	Μπορείτε να το αλλάξετε παρακαλώ;	borreeteh nah to ahlahksehteh pahrahkahlo
I want to return this.	Θέλω να επιστρέψω αυτό.	thehlo nah ehpeestrehpso ahfto
I'd like a refund. Here's the receipt.	Θα ήθελα να μου επι-στρέψετε τα χρήματα. Να η απόδειξη.	thah eethehlah nah moo ehpeestrehpsehteh tah khreemahtah. nah ee ahpodheeksee

Μπορώ να σας βοηθήσω;	Can I help you?
Τι θα θέλατε;	What would you like?
Τι ... θα θέλατε;	What ... would you like?
χρώμα/σχήμα ποιότητα/ποσότητα	colour/shape quality/quantity
Λυπούμαι, δεν έχομε άλλο.	I'm sorry, we don't have any.
Μας έχει εξαντληθή.	We're out of stock.
Να σας το παραγγείλουμε;	Shall we order it for you?
Θα το πάρετε ή να σας το στείλουμε;	Will you take it with you or shall we send it?
Τίποτα άλλο;	Anything else?
... δραχμές, παρακαλώ.	That's ... drachmas, please.
Το ταμείο είναι προς τα εκεί.	The cash desk is over there.

Bookshop – Stationer's Βιβλιοπωλείο – Χαρτοπωλείο

In Greece, bookshops and stationer's are the same shop. Newspapers and magazines are sold at kiosks and newsstands.

Where's the nearest...?	Που είναι το κοντινό- τερο...;	poo **ee**neh to kondee- **no**ttehro
bookshop	βιβλιοπωλείο	veevleeoppolleeo
stationer's	χαρτοπωλείο	khahrtoppolleeo
newsstand	περίπτερο	pehreeptehro
Where can I buy an English-language newspaper?	Που μπορώ να αγοράσω μια εφημερίδα στα Αγγλικά;	poo borro nah aghorrah- sso meeah ehfeemehree- dhah stah ahnggleekah
Where's the guide- book section?	Που είναι το τμήμα των τουριστικών οδηγών;	poo **ee**neh to **tmee**mah tonn tooreesteekonn odhee**ghonn**
Where do you keep the English books?	Που έχετε τα Αγγλικά βιβλία;	poo **eh**khehteh tah ahng- gleekah veevleeah
Do you have any of ...'s books in English?	Έχετε βιβλία του... στα Αγγλικά;	**eh**khehteh veevleeah too ... stah ahnggleekah
Do you have second- hand books?	Έχετε μεταχειρισμένα βιβλία;	**eh**khehteh mehtahkhee- reezmehnah veevleeah
I want to buy a/an/ some...	Θέλω να αγοράσω...	**the**hlo nah aghorrahsso
ball-point pen	ένα στυλό διαρκείας	ehnah steelo dheeahr- **kee**ahss
book	ένα βιβλίο	ehnah veevleeo
calendar	ένα ημερολόγειο	ehnah eemehrolloyeeo
cellophane tape	σελοτέϊπ	"Sellotape"
crayons	χρωματιστά μολύβια	khrommahteestah mollee- veeah
dictionary	ένα λεξικό	ehnah lehkseeko
Greek-English	Ελληνοαγγλικό	ehleeno–ahnggleeko
pocket	τσέπης	tsehpeess
drawing paper	χαρτί σχεδίου	khahrtee skhehdheeoo
envelopes	μερικούς φακέλλους	mehreekooss fahkehlooss
eraser	μια γομολάστιχα	meeah ghommollah- steekhah
exercise book	ένα τετράδιο ασκήσεων	ehnah tehtrahdheeo ahskeessehonn
felt-tip pen	ένα μαρκαδόρο	ehnah mahrkahdhorro
fountain pen	ένα πενοφόρο	ehnah pehnofforro

glue	κόλλα	kollah
grammar book	ένα βιβλίο γραμματικής	ehnah veevleeo ghrahmahteekeess
guide book	ένα τουριστικό οδηγό	ehnah tooreesteeko odheegho
ink	μελάνι	mehlahnee
black/red/blue	μαύρο/κόκκινο/μπλε	mahvro/kokkeeno/bleh
(adhesive) labels	(αυτοκόλλητες) ετικέττες	(ahftokkolleeteess) ehteekehtehss
magazine	ένα περιοδικό	ehnah pehreeodheeko
map	ένα χάρτη	ehnah khahrtee
map of the town	ένα χάρτη της πόλης	ehnah khahrtee teess polleess
road map of ...	ένα οδηκό χάρτη της...	ehnah odheeko khahrtee teess
newspaper	μια εφημερίδα	meeah ehfeemehreedhah
American/English	Αμερικανική/Αγγλική	ahmehreekahneekee/ ahnggleekee
notebook	ένα τετράδιο	ehnah tehtrahdheeo
note paper	ένα μπλοκ	ehnah blok
paintbox	ένα κουτί μπογιές	ehnah kootee boyeeehss
paper	μερικές κόλλες χαρτί	mehreekehss kollehss khahrtee
paperback	ένα φτηνό βιβλίο	ehnah fteeno veevleeo
paperclips	συνδετήρες	seendhehteerehss
paper napkins	χαρτοπετσέτες	khahrtoppehtsehtehss
paste	μια κόλλα	meeah kollah
pen	ένα στυλό	ehnah steelo
pencil	ένα μολύβι	ehnah molleevee
playing cards	μια τράπουλα	meeah trahpoolah
pocket calculator	μια υπολογιστική μηχανή τσέπης	meeah eepolloyeesteekee meekhahnee tsehpeess
postcard	μια καρτ-ποστάλ	meeah kahrt postahl
refill (for a pen)	ένα ανταλλακτικό για στυλό	ehnah ahndahlahkteeko yeeah steelo
rubber	μια γομολάστιχα	meeah ghommollah- steekhah
ruler	ένα χάρακα	ehnah khahrahkah
string	σπάγγο	spahnggo
travel guide	ένα ταξιδιωτικό οδηγό	ehnah tahkseedheeotteeko odheegho
typing paper	χαρτί γραφομηχανής	khahrtee ghrahfommee- khahneess
writing pad	ένα μπλοκ αλληλογραφίας	ehnah blok ahleeloghrahfeeahss

Camping equipment *Εφοδιασμός για κατασκήνωση*

I'd like a/an/some...	Θα ήθελα...	thah eethehlah
bottle opener	ένα ανοιχτήρι για μπουκάλια	ehnah ahneekhteeree yeeah bookahleeah
butane gas	μια φιάλη υγραερίου	meeah feeahlee eeghrah-ehreeoo
campbed	ένα κρεββάτι εκστρατείας	ehnah krehvahtee ehkstrahteeahss
can opener	ένα ανοιχτήρι κονσέρβας	ehnah ahneekhteeree konsehrvahss
candles	μερικά κεριά	mehreekah kehreeah
(folding) chair	μια (πτυσσόμενη) καρέκλα	meeah (pteessommehnee) kahrehklah
charcoal	μερικά κάρβουνα	mehreekah kahrvoonah
clothes pegs	μερικά μανδαλάκια	mehreekah mahndhahlahkeeah
compass	μια πυξίδα	meeah peekseedhah
cool box	ένα ψυγείο	ehnah pseeyeeo
corkscrew	ένα τιρ-μπουσόν	ehnah teerboossonn
deck chair	μια πολυθρόνα	meeah polleethronnah
dishwashing detergent	ένα απολυμαντικό πιάτων	ehnah ahpolleemahndeeko peeahtonn
first-aid kit	ένα φαρμακείο για πρώτες βοήθειες	ehnah fahrmahkeeo yeeah protehss voeethee-ehss
fishing tackle	ένα εξοπλισμό για ψάρεμα	ehnah ehksopleezmo yeeah psahrehmah
flashlight	ένα φακό	ehnah fahko
food box	ένα δοχείο για τρόφιμα	ehnah dhokheeoo yeeah troffeemah
frying pan	ένα τηγάνι	ehnah teeghahnee
groundsheet	ένα χαλί τέντας	ehnah khahlee tehndahss
hammock	μια κούνια	meeah kooneeah
haversack	ένα οδοιπορικό σάκο	ehnah odheeporeeko sahko
ice pack	μια παγοτιέρα	meeah pahghotteeeehrah
kerosene	φωτιστικό πετρέλαιο	fotteesteeko pehtrehleho
knapsack	ένα οδοιπορικό σάκο	ehnah odheeporeeko sahko
lamp	μια λάμπα	meeah lahmbah
lantern	ένα φανάρι	ehnah fahnahree
matches	μερικά σπίρτα	mehreekah speertah
mattress	ένα στρώμα	ehnah strommah
methylated spirits	πράσινο οινόπνευμα	prahsseeno eenopnehvmah
mosquito net	μια κουνουπιέρα	meeah koonoopeeeehrah

CAMPING, see page 32

paraffin	φωτιστικό πετρέλαιο	fotteesteeko pehtrehleho
penknife	ένα σουγιά	ehnah sooyeeah
picnic basket	ένα καλάθι για	ehnah kahlahthee yeeah
	πικ-νικ	"picnic"
plastic bag	μια πλαστική τσάντα	meeah plahsteekee tsahndah
rope	ένα σχοινί	ehnah skheenee
rucksack	ένα ταξιδιωτικό σάκκο	ehnah tahkseedheeotteeko sahko
saucepan	μια κατσαρόλα	meeah kahtsahrollah
scissors	ένα ψαλίδι	ehnah psahleedhee
screwdriver	ένα κατσαβίδι	ehnah kahtsahvveedhee
sleeping bag	ένα σάκο ύπνου	ehnah sahko eepnoo
(folding) table	ένα (πτυσσόμενο)	ehnah (pteessommehno)
	τραπέζι	trahpehzee
tent	μια σκηνή	meeah skeenee
tent peg	ένα πάσσαλο	ehnah pahssahlo
tent pole	ένα κοντάρι	ehnah kondahree
tinfoil	αλλουμινόχαρτο	ahloomeenokhahrto
tin opener	ένα ανοιχτήρι	ehnah ahneekhteeree
	κονσέρβας	konsehrvahss
tongs	μια τσιμπίδα	meeah tseembeedhah
torch	ένα φακό	ehnah fahko
vacuum flask	ένα θερμός	ehnah thehrmoss
washing powder	σκόνη πλυσίματος	skonnee pleesseemahtoss
water flask	ένα παγούρι	ehnah pahghooree
wood alcohol	οινόπευμα	eenopnehvmah

Crockery Πιατικά

cups	φλυτζάνια	fleedzahneeah
mugs	κύπελλα	keepehlah
plates	πιάτα	peeahtah
saucers	πιατάκια	peeahtahkeeah
tumblers	ποτήρια	potteereeah

Cutlery Μαχαιροπήρουνα

forks	πηρούνια	peerooneeah
knives	μαχαίρια	mahkhehreeah
spoons	κουτάλια	kootahleeah
teaspoons	κουταλάκια	kootahlahkeeah
(made of) plastic	από πλαστικό	ahpo plahsteeko
(made of) stainless steel	από ανοξείδωτο ατσάλι	ahpo ahnokseedhotto ahtsahlee

Chemist's (drugstore) *Φαρμακείο*

You will recognize a chemist's by the sign outside—a red or green cross, which is lit at night. In the window you'll see a notice telling you where the nearest all-night chemist's is.

Go to a κατάστημα καλλυντικών (kah**tah**steemah kahleendee-**konn**) for perfume and cosmetics.

This section is divided into two parts:

1. Pharmaceutical—medicine, first-aid, etc.
2. Toiletry—toilet articles, cosmetics

General *Γενικά*

Where's the nearest (all-night) chemist's?	Που είναι το κοντι-νότερο (διανυκτε-ρεύον) φαρμακείο;	poo **ee**neh to kondeeno-ttehro (dheeahneekteh-rehvonn) fahrmah**kee**o
What time does the chemist's open/close?	Τι ώρα ανοίγει/κλείνει το φαρμακείο;	tee orrah ah**nee**yee/**klee**nee to fahrmah**kee**o

Part 1 – Pharmaceutical *Φαρμακευτικά*

I want something for...	Θέλω κάτι για...	**theh**lo **kah**tee yeeah
a cold	το κρυολόγημα	to kreeo**llo**yeemah
a cough	το βήχα	to **vee**khah
hay fever	το αλλεργικό συνάχι	to ahlehry**ee**ko seenah**khee**
insect bites	τα κεντρίσματα	tah kehn**dree**zmahtah
a headache	τον πονοκέφαλο	tonn ponno**keh**fahlo
sunburn	το ηλιακό έγκαυμα	to eelee**ah**ko **ehn**gahvmah
travel sickness	τη ναυτία	tee nahf**tee**ah
an upset stomach	την στομαχική ανωμαλία	teen stommahkhee**kee** ahnom**mahlee**ah
Can you make up this prescription for me?	Μπορείτε να μου ετοιμάσετε αυτή τη συνταγή;	bo**ree**teh nah moo ehtee-**mahs**sehteh ahf**tee** tee seendah**yee**e
Can I get it without a prescription?	Μπορώ να το πάρω χωρίς συνταγή;	bo**rro** nah to **pah**ro kho**rreess** seendah**yee**
Shall I wait?	Πρέπει να περιμένω;	**preh**pee nah pehree**meh**hno

DOCTOR, see page 136

Can I have a/an/ some...?	Μπορώ να έχω...;	borro nah ehkho
analgesic	μερικά παυσίπονα	mehreekah pahfseeponnah
antiseptic cream	αντισηπτική κρέμα	ahndeesseepteekee krehmah
aspirin	ασπιρίνη	ahspeereenee
(elastic) bandage	ένα (ελαστικό) επίδεσμο	ehnah (ehlahsteeko) ehpeedhehzmo
Band-Aids	λευκοπλάστη	lehfkoplahstee
contraceptives	αντισυλληπτικά	ahndeesseeleepteekah
corn plasters	έμπλαστρα για κάλλους	ehmblahstrah yeeah kahlooss
cotton wool (absorbent cotton)	μπαμπάκι	bahmbahkee
cough drops	παστίλλιες για το βήχα	pahsteelee-ehss yeeah to veekhah
disinfectant	απολυμαντικό	ahpolleemahndeeko
Elastoplast	ένα λευκοπλάστη	ehnah lehfkoplahstee
eye drops	κολλύριο	kolleereeo
gauze	γάζα αντισηπτική	ghahzah ahndeesseepteekee
insect repellent/ spray	εντομοκτόνο/ένα εντομοκτόνο σπρέι	ehndommoktonno/ehnah ehndommoktonno "spray"
iodine	ιώδιο	eeodheeo
laxative	καθαρκτικό	kahtharkteeko
mouthwash	υγρό για την πλύση του στόματος	eeghro yeeah teen pleessee too stommahtoss
nose drops	σταγόνες για τη μύτη	stahghonnehss yeeah tee meetee
sanitary towels (napkins)	σερβιέττες υγείας	sehrveeehtehss eeyeeahss
suppositories	ένα υπόθετο	ehnah eepothehto
... tablets	...χάπια	...khahpeeah
tampons	μερικά ταμπόν	mehreekah tahmbonn
thermometer	ένα θερμόμετρο	ehnah thehrmommehtro
throat lozenges	παστίλλιες για το λαιμό	pahsteeleeehss yeeah to lehmo
vitamin pills	βιταμίνες	veetahmeenehss

ΔΗΛΗΤΗΡΙΟ	POISON
ΓΙΑ ΕΞΩΤΕΡΙΚΗ ΧΡΗΣΗ ΜΟΝΟ	FOR EXTERNAL USE ONLY

Part 2—Toiletry *Καλλυντικά*

I'd like a/an/some...	Θα ήθελα...	thah **ee**thehlah
after-shave lotion	μια λοσιόν για μετά το ξύρισμα	**mee**ah lossee**onn** yeeah meh**tah** to ks**ee**reezmah
astringent	μια στυπτική λοσιόν	**mee**ah steep**tee**kee lossee**onn**
blusher	ρουζ	rooz
bubble bath	ένα αφρόλουτρο	**eh**nah ahfro**loo**tro
cream	μια κρέμα	**mee**ah **kreh**mah
cleansing cream	ένα γαλάκτωμα	**eh**nah ghah**lah**ktommah
foundation cream	μια βάση	**mee**ah **vah**ssee
moisturizing cream	μια κρέμα υδατική	**mee**ah **kreh**mah eedhahtee**kee**
night cream	μια κρέμα νύκτας	**mee**ah **kreh**mah **neek**tahss
deodorant	ένα αποσμητικό	**eh**nah ahpozmee**tee**ko
emery board	ένα γυαλόχαρτο για τα νύχια	**eh**nah yeeah**lo**khahrto yeeah tah **neek**heeah
eye liner	μια γραμμή για τα μάτια	**mee**ah ghrah**mee** yeeah tah **mah**teeah
eyebrow pencil	ένα μολύβι για τα μάτια	**eh**nah mo**lee**vee yeeah tah **mah**teeah
eye shadow	μια σκιά για τα μάτια	**mee**ah ski**ah** yeeah tah **mah**teeah
face powder	μια πούδρα για το πρόσωπο	**mee**ah **poo**dhrah yeeah to **pross**oppo
foot/hand cream	κρέμα γιά τα πόδια/ χέρια	**kreh**mah yeeah tah **podh**eeah/**kheh**reeah
lipsalve	μια κρέμα για τα χείλια	**mee**ah **kreh**mah yeeah tah **khee**leeah
lipstick	ένα κραγιόν για τα χείλια	**eh**nah krahyee**onn** yeeah tah **khee**leeah
nail brush	μια βούρτσα για τα νύχια	**mee**ah **voort**sah yeeah tah **neek**heeah
nail clippers/scissors	ένα νυχοκόπτη	**eh**nah neekho**kkop**tee
nail file	μια λίμα για τα νύχια	**mee**ah **lee**mah yeeah tah **neek**heeah
nail polish	ένα βερνίκι για τα νύχια	**eh**nah veh**rnee**kee yeeah tah **neek**heeah
nail polish remover	ένα ασετόν για τα νύχια	**eh**nah ahsseh**tonn** yeeah tah **neek**heeah
perfume	ένα άρωμα	**eh**nah **ah**rommah
powder	μια πούδρα	**mee**ah **poo**dhrah
razor	μια ξυριστική μηχανή	**mee**ah kseereestee**kee** meek**hah**nee

razor blades	ξυραφάκια για το ξύρισμα	kseerahfahkeeah yeeah to kseereezmah
safety pins	παραμάνες	pahrahmahnehss
shaving cream	μια κρέμα ξυρίσματος	meeah krehmah kseereezmahtoss
soap	ένα σαπούνι	ehnah sahpoonee
sponge	ένα σφουγγάρι	ehnah sfoonggahree
sun-tan cream	μια κρέμα για τον ήλιο	meeah krehmah yeeah tonn eeleeo
sun-tan oil	ένα λάδι για τον ήλιο	ehnah lahdhee yeeah tonn eeleeo
talcum powder	ταλκ	tahlk
tissues	μερικά χαρτομάντηλα	mehreekah khahrtommahndeelah
toilet paper	χαρτί υγείας	khahrtee eeyeeahss
toilet water	ω ντε τουαλέτ	o deh tooahleht
toothbrush	μια οδοντόβουρτσα	meeah odhondovoortsah
toothpaste	μια οδοντόπαστα	meeah odhondoppahstah
towel	μια πετσέτα	meeah pehtsehtah
tweezers	ένα τσιμπίδι για τα φρύδια	ehnah tseembeedhee yeeah tah freedheeah

For your hair   *Για τα μαλλιά σας*

bobby pins	τσιμπιδάκια	tseembeedhahkeeah
comb	μια χτένα	meeah khtehnah
dry shampoo	ένα στεγνό σαμπουάν	ehnah stehghno sahmbooahn
hairbrush	μια βούρτσα	meeah voortsah
hairgrips	τσιμπιδάκια	tseembeedhahkeeah
hair lotion	μια λοσιόν για τα μαλλιά	meeah losseeonn yeeah tah mahleeah
hair slide	κοκκαλάκια για τα μαλλιά	kokkahlahkeeah yeeah tah mahleeah
shampoo	σαμπουάν	sahmbooahn
for dry/greasy (oily) hair	για ξηρά/ λιπαρά μαλλιά	yeeah kseerah/ leepahrah mahleeah
tint	μια ελαφριά βαφή	meeah ehlahfreeah vahfee
wig	μια περούκα	meeah pehrookah

For the baby   *Για το παιδί*

baby food	παιδική τροφή	pehdheekee troffee
dummy (pacifier)	μια κούκλα	meeah kooklah
feeding bottle	ένα πιπερό	ehnah peepehro
nappies (diapers)	πάννες	pahnehss

Clothing *Ενδύματα*

If you want to buy something specific, prepare yourself in advance. Look at the list of clothing on page 116. Get some idea of the colour, material and size you want. They're all listed on the next few pages.

General *Γενικά*

I'd like ...	Θα ήθελα...	thah **ee**thehlah
I want ... for a 10-year-old boy/girl.	Θέλω ... για ένα αγόρι/κορίτσι 10 ετών.	**theh**lo ... yeeah **eh**nah ahg**horree**/korr**eet**see 10 eht**onn**
I want something like this.	Θέλω κάτι σαν κι'αυτό.	**theh**lo **kah**tee sahn kee**ahf**to
I like the one in the window.	Μου αρέσει αυτό στη βιτρίνα.	moo ahr**ehs**see ahf**to** stee veet**ree**nah
How much is that per metre?	Πόσο κάνει το μέτρο;	**pos**so **kah**nee to **meh**tro

1 centimetre (cm.) = 0.39 in.	1 inch = 2.54 cm.
1 metre (m.) = 39.37 in.	1 foot = 30.5 cm.
10 metres = 32.81 ft.	1 yard = 0.91 m.

Colour *Χρώμα*

I want something in ...	Θέλω κάτι σε...	**theh**lo **kah**tee seh
I want a darker/lighter shade.	Θέλω μια ποιο σκοτεινή/πιο ανοικτή απόχρωση	**theh**lo **mee**ah **peo** skott**eenee**/peeo ahn**eek**tee ahp**ok**hrossee
I want something to match this.	Θέλω κάτι να ταιριάζει με αυτό.	**theh**lo **kah**tee nah tehree-**ah**zee meh ahf**to**
I don't like the colour.	Δεν μου αρέσει το χρώμα.	dhehn moo ahr**ehs**see to **khrom**mah

μονόχρωμο (monnokhrommo) ριγέ (reeyeh) πουά (pooah) καρρώ (kahro) εμπριμέ (ehmbreemeh)

beige	μπεζ	behz
black	μαύρο	**mahv**ro
blue	μπλε	bleh
brown	καφέ	kah**feh**
fawn	μπεζ σκούρο	behz **skoo**ro
golden	χρυσαφένιο	khreessah**feh**neeo
green	πράσινο	**prah**sseeno
grey	γκρίζο	**gree**zo
mauve	μωβ	movv
orange	πορτοκαλί	portokkah**lee**
pink	ροζ	rozz
purple	πορφυρό	por**fee**ro
red	κόκκινο	**kok**keeno
scarlet	κόκκινο της φωτιάς	**kok**keeno teess fotteeahss
silver	ασημένιο	ahsseemehneeo
turquoise	τουρκουάζ	teerkoo**ahz**
white	άσπρο	**ahs**pro
yellow	κίτρινο	**kee**treeno
light...	ανοιχτός...	ahneekh**toss**
dark...	σκούρος...	**skoo**ross

Fabric Ύφασμα

Do you have anything in ...?	Έχετε κάτι σε...;	**eh**khehteh **kah**tee seh
Is that ...?	Είναι ...;	**ee**neh
handmade	χειροποίητο	kheerop**pee**-eeto
imported	εισαγώμενο	eessahg**hom**mehno
made in Greece	ελληνικής κατασκευής	ehleenee**keess** kahtahskeh**veess**
pure cotton/wool	βαμβακερό/μάλλινο	vahmvahke**ro**/**mah**leeno
synthetic	συνθετικό	seenthehteeko
colourfast	ύφασμα που δεν ξεβάφει	eefahzmah poo dhen ksehvahfee
wrinkle resistant	ύφασμα που δεν ζαρώνει	eefahzmah poo dhen zahronnee
I want something thinner.	Θέλω κάτι λεπτότερο.	**theh**lo **kah**tee lehptottehro
Do you have anything of better quality?	Έχετε κάτι καλύτερης ποιότητας;	**eh**khehteh **kah**tee kahlee-tehreess peeoteetahss

Is it hand washable/ machine washable?	Πλένεται στα χέρια/ στη μηχανή;	**pleh**nehteh stah **kheh**reeah/stee meekhahnee
Will it shrink?	Μαζεύει;	mahzehvee
What's it made of?	Τι ύφασμα είναι;	tee eefahzmah eeneh

cambric	βατίστα	vahteestah
camel-hair	καμηλό	kahmeelo
chiffon	μουσελίνα μεταξωτή	moossehleenah mehtahksottee
corduroy	βελούδο κοτλέ	vehloodho kotleh
cotton	βαμβακερό	vahmvahkehro
crepe	ύφασμα κρεπ	eefahzmah "crepe"
denim	χονδρό βαμβακερό ύφασμα	khondhro vahmvahkehro eefahzmah
felt	τσόχα	tsokhah
flannel	φανέλλα	fahnehlah
gabardine	καμπαρντίνα	kahbahrdeenah
lace	δαντέλλα	dhahntehlah
leather	δέρμα	dherhmah
linen	λινό	leeno
poplin	ποπλίνα	popleenah
satin	σατέν	sahtehn
silk	μεταξωτό	mehtahksotto
suede	σουέτ	sooeht
towelling	πετσετέ	pehtsehteh
velvet	βελούδο	vehloodho
velveteen	βελούδο βαμβακερό	vehloodho vahmvahkehro
wool	μαλλί	mahlee
worsted	μάλλινο υφαντό	mahleeno eefahndo

Size Μέγεθος

Sizes can vary from one manufacturer to another, so be sure to try on shoes and clothing before you buy.

| Could you measure me? | Θέλετε να μου πάρετε μέτρα; | **theh**lehteh nah moo **pah**rehteh **meh**trah |
| I don't know the Greek sizes. | Δεν ξέρω τα Ελληνικά μεγέθη. | dhehn **kseh**ro tah ehleeneekah mehyehthee |

A good fit? *Ταιριάζει;*

Can I try it on?	Μπορώ να το δοκιμάσω;	borro nah to dhokkeemahsso
Where's the fitting room?	Που είναι το δοκιμαστήριο;	poo eeneh to dhokkeemahsteereeo
Is there a mirror?	Υπάρχει καθρέφτης;	eepahrkhee kahthrehfteess
It fits very well.	Μου ταιριάζει πολύ καλά.	moo tehreeahzee pollee kahlah
It doesn't fit.	Δεν μου ταιριάζει.	dhehn moo tehreeahzee
It's too ...	Είναι πολύ ...	eeneh pollee
short/long	κοντό/μακρύ	kondo/mahkree
tight/loose	στενό/φαρδύ	stehno/fahrdhee
How long will it take to alter?	Σε πόσες μέρες μπορείτε να μου το διορθώσετε;	seh possehss mehrehss borreeteh nah moo to dheeorthossehteh

Women *Γυναίκες*

	Dresses/suits					
American	8	10	12	14	16	18
British	10	12	14	16	18	20
Greek	42	44	46	48	50	52

	Stockings						Shoes			
American British	8	8½	9	9½	10	10½	5½ 4	6½ 5	7½ 6	8½ 7
Greek	0	1		2		3	37	38	39	40

Men *Άνδρες*

	Suits/overcoats						Shirts			
American British	36	38	40	42	44	46	15	16	17	18
Greek	46	48	50	52	54	56	38	40	42	44

	Shoes									
American British	5	6	7	8	8½	9	9½	10	11	
Greek	38	39	40	41	41½	42	42½	43	44	

NUMBERS, see page 146

Clothes and accessories *Ρούχα και αξεσουάρ*

I'd like a/an/ some ...	Θα ήθελα...	thah eethehlah
anorak	ένα αδιάβροχο τζάκετ	ehnah ahdheeahvrokho dzahkeht
bathing cap	μια σκούφια για το μπάνιο	meeah skoofeeah yeeah to bahneeo
bathrobe	ένα μπουρνούζι	ehnah boornoozee
blouse	μια μπλούζα	meeah bloozah
bow tie	ένα παπιγιόν	ehnah pahpeeyeeonn
bra	ένα σουτιέν	ehnah sooteeehn
braces	τιράντες	teerahndehss
briefs	κυλότες	keelottehss
cap	μια κασκέτα	meeah kahskehtah
cardigan	μια πλεκτή ζακέττα	meeah plehktee zahkehtah
coat	ένα παλτό	ehnah pahlto
dress	ένα φόρεμα	ehnah forrehmah
evening dress (woman's)	ένα βραδυνό φόρεμα	ehnah vrahdheeno forrehmah
girdle	ένα λαστέξ	ehnah lahstehkss
gloves	γάντια	ghahndeeah
handbag	μια τσάντα	meeah tsahndah
handkerchief	ένα μαντήλι	ehnah mahndeelee
hat	ένα καπέλλο	ehnah kahpehlo
jacket	μια ζακέττα	meeah zahkehtah
jeans	μπλου-τζήν	bloodzeen
kneesocks	κάλτσες μέχρι τα γόνατα	kahltsehss mehkhree tah ghonnahtah
nightdress	ένα νυκτικό	ehnah neekteeko
pair of ...	ένα ζευγάρι...	ehnah zehvghahree
panties	κυλότες	keelottehss
pants (Am.)	ένα παντελόνι	ehnah pahndehlonnee
panty-girdle	ένα λαστέξ	ehnah lahstehks
panty hose	ένα καλτσόν	ehnah kahltsonn
pullover	ένα πουλόβερ	ehnah poolovehr
roll-neck (turtle-neck)	με ζιβάγκο	meh zeevahnggo
round neck	με λαιμόκοψη	meh lehmokkopsee
V-neck	με ανοιχτό λαιμό	meh ahneekhto lehmo
with long/short	με μακρυά/κοντά	meh mahkreeah/ kondah
sleeves	μανίκια	mahneekeeah
sleeveless	χωρίς μανίκια	khorreess mahneekeeah

pyjamas	μια πυτζάμα	meeah peedzahmah
raincoat	ένα αδιάβροχο	ehnah ahdheeahvrokho
scarf	ένα κασκόλ	ehnah kahskoll
shirt	ένα πουκάμισο	ehnah pookahmeesso
shorts	ένα σορτς	ehnah sorts
skirt	μια φούστα	meeah foostah
slip	ένα κομπιναιζόν	ehnah kombeenehzonn
socks	κάλτσες	kahltsehss
sports jacket	ένα σακκάκι σπόρ	ehnah sahkahkee spor
stockings	κάλτσες γυναικείες	kahltsehss yeenehkeeehss
suit (man's)	ένα κοστούμι	ehnah kostoomee
suit (woman's)	ένα ταγιέρ	ehnah tahyeeehr
suspenders (Am.)	τιράντες	teerahndehss
sweater	ένα πουλόβερ	ehnah poolovvehr
sweatshirt	ένα φανελάκι σπορ	ehnah fahnehlahkee spor
swimming trunks	ένα μαγιό	ehnah mahyeeo
swimsuit	ένα μαγιό	ehnah mahyeeo
T-shirt	ένα τι-σερτ	ehnah teessehrt
tie	μια γραβάτα	meeah ghrahvahtah
tights	ένα καλσόν	ehnah kahlsonn
tracksuit	μια φόρμα	meeah formah
trousers	ένα παντελόνι	ehnah pahndehlonnee
umbrella	μια ομπρέλα	meeah ombrehlah
underpants (men)	ένα σώβρακο	ehnah sovrahko
undershirt	μια φανέλλα εσώρουχο	meeah fahnehlah ehssorrookho
vest (Am.)	ένα γιλέκο	ehnah yeelehko
vest (Br.)	μια φανέλλα εσώρουχο	meeah fahnehlah ehssorrookho
waistcoat	ένα γιλέκο	ehnah yeelehko

belt	μια ζώνη	meeah zonnee
buckle	μια εγγράφα ζώνης	meeah ehnggrahfah zonneess
button	ένα κουμπί	ehnah koombee
collar	ένα γιακά	ehnah yeeahkah
pocket	μια τσέπη	meeah tsehpee
press stud (snap fastener)	μια σούστα	meeah soostah
zip (zipper)	ένα φερμουάρ	ehnah fehrmooahr

Shoes *Παπούτσια*

I'd like a pair of ...	Θα ήθελα ένα ζευγάρι...	thah eethehlah ehnah zehvghahree
boots	μπότες	bottehss
moccasins	μοκασίν	mokkasseen
plimsolls (sneakers)	αθλητικά παπούτσια	ahthleeteekah pahpootseeah
sandals	σάνδαλα	sahndhahlah
shoes	παπούτσια	pahpootseeah
flat/with a heel	ίσια/με τακούνι	eesseeah/meh tahkoonee
slippers	παντόφλες	pahndoflehss
These are too ...	Είναι πολύ ...	eeneh pollee
narrow/wide	στενά/φαρδιά	stehnah/fahrdheeah
large/small	μεγάλα/μικρά	mehghahlah/meekrah
Do you have a larger/ smaller size?	Έχετε ένα μέγεθος μεγαλήτερο/μικρότερο;	ehkhehteh ehnah mehyehthoss mehghahleetehro/meekrotehro
Do you have the same in black?	Έχετε το ίδιο σε μαύρο;	ehkhehteh to eedheeo seh mahvro
cloth	ύφασμα	eefahzmah
leather	δέρμα	dhehrmah
rubber	λάστικο	lahsteeko
suede	σουέτ	sooeht
Is it genuine leather?	Είναι από γνήσιο δέρμα;	eeneh ahpo ghneesseeo dhehrmah
I need some shoe polish/shoelaces.	Χρειάζομαι μια μπογιά/ κορδόνια υποδημάτων.	khreeahzommeh meeah boyeeah/kordhoneeah eepodheemahtonn

Shoes worn out? Here's the key to getting them fixed again:

Can you repair these shoes?	Μπορείτε να επιδιορθώσετε αυτά τα παπούτσια;	borreeteh nah ehpeedheeorthossehteh ahftah tah pahpootseeah
Can you stitch this?	Μπορείτε να το ράψετε;	borreeteh nah to rahpsehteh
I want new soles and heels.	Θέλω νέες σόλες και τακούνια.	thehlo nehehss sollehss keh tahkooneeah
When will they be ready?	Πότε θα είναι έτοιμα;	potteh thah eeneh ehteemah

Electrical appliances   *Ηλεκτρικές συσκευές*

The general rule in Greece is 220-volt, 50-cycle AC current.

What's the voltage?	Πόσα βολτ είναι το ρεύμα;	possah volt eeneh to rehvmah
Do you have a battery for this?	Έχετε μια μπαταρία γι'αυτό;	ehkhehteh meeah bahtahreeah yeeahfto
This is broken. Can you repair it?	Έχει σπάσει. Μπορείτε να το διορθώσετε;	ehkhee spahssee. borreeteh nah to dheeorthossehteh
Can you show me how it works?	Μπορείτε να μου δείξετε πως λειτουργεί;	borreeteh nah moo dheeksehteh poss leetooryee
I'd like a/an/some...	Θα ήθελα...	thah eethehlah
adaptor	ένα μετασχηματιστή πρίζας	ehnah mehtahskheemahteestee preezahss
amplifier	ένα ενισχυτή	ehnah ehneeskheetee
clock-radio	ένα ραδιοξυπνητήρι	ehnah rahdheeookseepneeteeree
electric toothbrush	μια ηλεκτρική οδοντόβουρτσα	meeah eelehktreekee odhondovoortsah
extension lead (cord)	μια μπαλαντέζα	meeah bahlahndehzah
hair dryer	ένα στεγνωτήρα μαλλιών	ehnah stehghnotteerah mahleeonn
headphones	ακουστικά	ahkoosteekah
(travelling) iron	ένα σίδερο (για ταξίδι)	ehnah seedhehro (yeeah tahkseedhee)
lamp	μια λάμπα	meeah lahmbah
plug	μια πρίζα	meeah preezah
portable ...	ένα φορητό ...	ehnah forreeto
radio	ράδιο	rahdheeo
record player	ένα πικ-απ	ehnah peek-ahp
shaver	μια ξυριστική μηχανή	meeah kseereesteekee meekhahnee
speakers	μεγάφωνα	mehghahfonnah
(cassette) tape recorder	ένα κασεττόφωνο	ehnah kahssehtoffonno
(colour) television	μια (έγχρωμη) τηλεόραση	meeah (ehngkhrommee) teelehorrahssee
transformer	ένα μετασχηματιστή	ehnah mehtahskheemahteestee
video cassette	μια βίντεο-κασέττα	meeah veedehokahssehtah
video recorder	ένα βίντεο	ehnah veedeho

Grocery *Παντοπωλείον*

I'd like some bread, please.	Θα ήθελα λίγο ψωμί, παρακαλώ.	thah **ee**thehlah **lee**gho psom**mee** pahrahkah**lo**
What sort of cheese do you have?	Τι είδους τυριά έχετε;	tee **ee**dhooss teeree**ah** **eh**khehteh
A piece of ...	Ένα κομμάτι από...	**eh**nah kom**mah**tee ah**po**
that one	αυτό	ahf**to**
the one on the shelf	αυτό στο ράφι	ahf**to** sto **rah**fee
I'll have one of those, please.	Θα πάρω ένα από αυτά, παρακαλώ.	thah **pah**ro **eh**nah ah**po** ahf**tah** pahrahkah**lo**
May I help myself?	Μπορώ να εξυπηρετηθώ μόνος/-η μου;	bor**ro** nah ehkseepeereh-**tee**tho **mon**noss/-ee moo
I'd like ...	Θα ήθελα...	thah **ee**thehlah
a kilo of apples	ένα κιλό μήλα	**eh**nah **kee**lo **mee**lah
half a kilo of tomatoes	μισό κιλό ντομάτες	mee**sso** **kee**lo dom**mah**tehss
100 grams of butter	100 γραμμάρια βούτυρο	100 ghrah**mah**reeah **voo**teero
a litre of milk	ένα λίτρο γάλα	**eh**nah **lee**tro **ghah**lah
4 slices of ham	4 φέτες ζαμπόν	4 **feh**tehss zahm**bonn**
a packet of tea	ένα κουτί τσάι	**eh**nah koo**tee** **tsah**hee
a jar of jam	ένα κουτί μαρμελάδα	**eh**nah koo**tee** mahrmeh**lah**dhah
a tin (can) of peaches	μια κονσέρβα ροδάκινα	mee**ah** kon**sehr**vah ro**dhah**keenah
a box of chocolates	ένα κουτί σοκολάτες	**eh**nah koo**tee** sok**kol**lah**tehss
a tube of mustard	μια μουστάρδα σε σωληνάριο	mee**ah** moos**tahr**dhah seh solleenah**ree**o

1 kilogram or kilo (kg.) = 1000 grams (g.)	
100 g. = 3.5 oz.	½ kg. = 1.1 lb.
200 g. = 7.0 oz.	1 kg. = 2.2 lb.
1 oz. = 28.35 g.	
1 lb. = 453.60 g.	

1 litre (l.) = 0.88 imp. quarts = 1.06 U.S. quarts	
1 imp. quart = 1.14 l.	1 U.S. quart = 0.95 l.
1 imp. gallon = 4.55 l.	1 U.S. gallon = 3.8 l.

FOOD, see also page 63

Jeweller's – Watchmaker's   *Κοσμηματοπωλείο – Ωρολογοποιείον*

Could I see that, please?	Μπορώ να δω εκείνο παρακαλώ;	borro nah dho ehkeeno pahrahkahlo
Do you have anything in gold?	Έχετε κάτι σε χρυσό;	ehkhehteh kahtee seh khreesso
How many carats is this?	Πόσων καρατίων είναι αυτό;	possonn kahrahteeonn eeneh ahfto
Is this real silver?	Αυτό είναι αληθινό ασήμι;	ahfto eeneh ahleetheeno ahsseemee
Can you repair this watch?	Μπορείτε να επιδιορθώσετε αυτό το ρολόι;	borreeteh nah ehpeedheeorthossehteh ahfto to rolloee
I'd like a/an/some...	Θα ήθελα...	thah eethehlah
alarm clock	ένα ξυπνητήρι	ehnah kseepneeteeree
bangle	ένα βραχιόλι	ehnah vrahkheeollee
battery	μια μπαταρία	meeah bahtahreeah
bracelet	ένα βραχιόλι	ehnah vrahkheeollee
chain bracelet	μια αλυσίδα του χεριού	meeah ahleesseedhah too khehreeoo
charm bracelet	ένα μπρελόκ βραχιόλι	ehnah brehlok vrahkheeollee
brooch	μια καρφίτσα	meeah kahrfeetsah
chain	μια αλυσίδα	meeah ahleesseedhah
charm	ένα μπρελόκ	ehnah brehlok
cigarette case	μια τσιγαροθήκη	meeah tseeghahrotheekee
cigarette lighter	έναν αναπτήρα	ehnan ahnahpteerah
clip	ένα κλιπς	ehnah kleeps
clock	ένα ρολόι	ehnah rolloee
cross	ένα σταυρό	ehnah stahvro
cuff-links	ένα ζευγάρι μανικετόκουμπα	ehnah zehvghahree mahneekehtokoombah
cutlery	μαχαιροπήρουνα	mahkhehroppeeroonah
earrings	ένα ζευγάρι σκουλαρίκια	ehnah zehvghahree skoolahreekeeah
gem	ένα πολύτιμο λίθο	ehnah polleeteemo leetho
jewel box	μια μπιζουτιέρα	meeah beezooteeehrah
necklace	ένα κολλιέ	ehnah kolleeeh
pendant	ένα παντατίφ	ehnah pahndahteef
pin	μια καρφίτσα	meeah kahrfeetsah
pocket watch	ένα ρολόι τσέπης	ehnah rolloee tsehpeess
powder compact	μια πουδριέρα	meeah poodhreeehrah

ring	ένα δακτυλίδι	ehnah dhahkteeleedhee
engagement ring	ένα δακτυλίδι αρραβώνα	ehnah dhahkteeleedhee ahrahvonnah
signet ring	ένα δακτυλίδι με οικόσημο	ehnah dhahkteeleedhee meh eekosseemo
wedding ring	μια βέρα	meeah vehrah
rosary	ένα κομπολόι για προσευχές	ehnah kombolloee yeeah prossehfkhehss
silverware	μερικά ασημικά	mehreekah ahsseemeekah
watch	ένα ρολόι	ehnah rolloee
automatic	αυτόματο	ahftommahto
digital	ψηφιακό	pseefeeahko
quartz	χαλαζία	khahlahzeeah
with a second hand	με δείκτη για δευτερόλεπτα	meh dheektee yeeah dhehftehrollehptah
waterproof	αδιάβροχο	ahdheeahvrokho
watchstrap	ένα μπρασελέ για ρολόι	ehnah brahsehleh yeeah rolloee
wristwatch	ένα ρολόι χεριού	ehnah rolloee khehreeoo

amber	κεχριμπάρι	kehkhreembahree
amethyst	αμέθυστος	ahmehtheestoss
chromium	χρώμιο	khrommeeo
copper	χαλκός	khahlkoss
coral	κοράλι	korrahlee
crystal	κρύσταλλο	kreestahlo
cut glass	κρύσταλλο ταγιέ	kreestahlo tahyeeeh
diamond	διαμάντι	dheeahmahndee
emerald	σμαράγδι	zmahrahghdhee
enamel	σμάλτο	zmahlto
gold	χρυσός	khreessoss
gold plated	επίχρυσο	ehpeekhreesso
ivory	ελεφαντόδοντο	ehlehfahndodhondo
jade	ζαντ	zahnd
onyx	όνυχας	onneekhahss
pearl	μαργαριτάρι	mahrghahreetahree
pewter	κασσίτερος	kahsseetehross
platinum	πλατίνα	plahteenah
ruby	ρουμπίνι	roombeenee
sapphire	σαφείρι	zahfeeree
silver	ασήμι	ahsseemee
silver plated	επάργυρο	ehpahryeero
topaz	τοπάζι	tohpahzee
turquoise	τουρκουάζ	teerkooahz

Optician   Οπτικός

I've broken my glasses.	Έσπασα τα γυαλιά μου.	ehspahssah tah yeeahleeah moo
Can you repair them for me?	Μπορείτε να μου τα επιδιορθώσετε;	borreeteh nah moo tah ehpeedheeorthossehteh
Can you change the lenses?	Μπορείτε να αλλάξετε τους φακούς;	borreeteh nah ahlahksehteh tooss fahkooss
I want tinted lenses.	Θέλω φακούς φιμέ.	thehlo fahkooss feemeh
The frame is broken.	Έσπασε ο σκελετός.	ehspahsseh o skehlehtoss
I'd like a spectacle case.	Θα ήθελα μια θήκη για τα γυαλιά.	thah eethehlah meeah theekee yeeah tah yeeahleeah
I'd like to have my eyesight checked.	Θα ήθελα να κάνω ένα τεστ για τα μάτια μου.	thah eethehlah nah kahno ehnah tehsst yeeah tah mahteeah moo
I'm short-sighted/long-sighted.	Είμαι μύωπας/πρεσβύωπας.	eemeh meeoppahss/prehzveeoppahss
I want some contact lenses.	Θέλω φακού επαφής.	thehlo fahkooss ehpahfeess
I've lost one of my contact lenses.	Έχασα ένα από τους φακούς επαφής μου.	ehkhahssah ehnah ahpo tooss fahkooss ehpahfeess moo
Could you give me another one?	Μπορείτε να μου δώσετε έναν άλλο;	borreeteh nah moo dhossehteh ehnahn ahlo
I have hard/soft lenses.	Έχω σκληρούς/μαλακούς φακούς.	ehkho skleerooss/mahlahkooss fahkooss
Do you have any contact-lens fluid?	Έχετε υγρό για τους φακούς επαφής;	ehkhehteh eeghro yeeah tooss fahkooss ehpahfeess
I'd like to buy a pair of sunglasses.	Θα ήθελα να αγοράσω ένα ζευγάρι γυαλιά ήλιου.	thah eethehlah nah aghorrahsso ehnah zehvghahree yeeahleeah eeleeoo
May I look in a mirror?	Μπορώ να κοιτάξω στον καθρέφτη;	borro nah keetahkso stonn kahthrehftee
I'd like to buy a pair of binoculars.	Θα ήθελα να αγοράσω ένα ζευγάρι κυάλια.	thah eethehlah nah aghorrahsso ehnah zehvghahree keeahleeah

Photography   Φωτογραφείο

I want a(n) ... camera.	Θέλω μια ... φωτο- γραφική μηχανή.	**thehlo meeah ... fotto- ghrahfeekee meekahhnee**
automatic	αυτόματη	ahftommahtee
inexpensive	φθηνή	ftheenee
simple	απλή	ahplee
Show me some cine (movie) cameras, please.	Δείξτε μου μερικές κινηματογραφικές μηχανές, παρακαλώ.	**dhee**ksteh moo mehree**kehss** keenee- mahtoghrahfee**kehss** meekahh**nehss** pahrahkahlo
I'd like to have some passport photos taken.	Θα ήθελα να βγάλω μερικές φωτογραφίες για το διαβατήριο.	thah **ee**thehlah nah **vgha**hlo mehree**kehss** fottoghrahf**eee**hss yeeah to dheeahvaht**ee**reeo

Film   Φιλμ

I'd like a film for this camera.	Θα ήθελα ένα φιλμ γι'αυτή τη μηχανή.	thah **ee**thehlah **eh**nah feelm yeeahf**tee** tee meekahh**nee**
black and white	ασπρόμαυρο	ahsprommahvro
colour	έγχρωμο	**ehng**khrommo
colour negative	έγχρωμο αρνητικό	**ehng**khrommo ahrneeteeko
colour slide	έγχρωμο σλάιντς	**ehng**khrommo ''slides''
cartridge	ένα φιλμ κασέττα	**eh**nah feelm kahs**seh**tah
disc film	μια ντισκέττα	meeah dees**keh**tah
roll film	ένα φιλμ ρολό	**eh**nah feelm rollo
video cassette	ένα βίντεο-κασέττα	**eh**nah **vee**deho- kahs**seh**tah
24/36 exposures	ένα εικοσιτεσσάρι τριανταεξάρι φιλμ	**eh**nah eekosseeteehss**sah**ree treeahndahehk**sah**ree feelm
this size	αυτό το μέγεθος	ahfto to **meh**yehthoss
this ASA/DIN number	αυτό τον αριθμό ASA/DIN	ahfto tonn ahreeth**mo** ''ASA/DIN''
artificial light type	για τεχνητό φως	yeeah tehkhneeto foss
daylight type	για φως της μέρας	yeeah foss teess mehrahss
fast (high-speed)	υψηλής ταχύτητας	eepsee**leess** tahkhee**tee**tahss
fine grain	λεπτού κόκου	lehptoo kokkoo

Processing *Εμφάνιση*

How much do you charge for developing?	Πόσο κοστίζει η εμφάνιση;	posso kosteezee ee ehmfahneessee
I want ... prints of each negative.	Θέλω ... φωτογραφίες από κάθε αρνητικό.	thehlo ... fottoghrah- feeehss ahpo kahtheh ahrneeteeko
with a mat finish	ματ	maht
with a glossy finish	γυαλιστερές	yeeahleestehrehss
Will you enlarge this, please?	Μπορείτε να μου μεγενθύνετε αυτό παρακαλώ;	borreeteh nah moo mehyehntheenehteh ahfto pahrahkahlo
When will the photos be ready?	Πότε θα είναι έτοιμες οι φωτογραφίες;	potteh thah eeneh ee ehteemehss ee fottoghrahfeeehss

Accessories and repairs *Αξεσουάρ και επισκευές*

I want a/an/some...	Θέλω ...	thehlo
battery	μια μπαταρία	meeah bahtahreeah
(electronic) flash	ένα (ηλεκτρονικό) φλας	ehnah (eelehktronneeko) flahss
filter	ένα φίλτρο	ehnah feeltro
for black and white	για ασπρόμαυρο	yeeah ahsprommahvro
for colour	για έχρωμο	yeeah ehkrommo
lens	ένα φακό	ehnah fahko
telephoto lens	ένα τηλεφακό	ehnah teelehfahko
wide-angle lens	ένα ευρυγώνιο φακό	ehnah ehvreeghonneeo fahko
Can you repair this camera?	Μπορείτε να διορθώσετε αυτή την φωτογραφική μηχανή;	borreeteh nah dheeortho- ssehteh ahftee teen fotto- ghrahfeekee meekhahnee
The film is jammed.	Το φιλμ έχει μπλεχτεί.	to feelm ehkhee blehkhtee
There's something wrong with the ...	Κάτι δεν λειτουργεί καλά στο ...	kahtee dhehn leetooryee kahlah sto
exposure counter	μετρητή των φωτο- γραφιών	mehtreetee tonn fottoghrahfeeonn
film winder	γύρισμα του φιλμ	yeereezmah too feelm
flash attachment	μια υποδοχή για φλας	meeah eepodhokhee yeeah flahss fahko
light meter	φωτόμετρο	fottomehtro
rangefinder	αποστασιόμετρο	ahpostahsseeommehtro
shutter	διάφραγμα	dheeahfrahghmah

NUMBERS, see page 146

Tobacconist's *Καπνοπωλείον*

Greek tobacco products, of good quality and generally mild, are far cheaper than the few foreign brands (manufactured under licence) available.

A packet of cigarettes, please.	Ένα κουτί τσιγάρα, παρακαλώ.	ehnah kootee tseeghahrah pahrahkahlo
Do you have any American/English cigarettes?	Έχετε Αμερικάνικα/ Αγγλικά τσιγάρα;	ehkhehteh ahmehreekah- neekah/ahnggleekah tseeghahrah
I'd like a carton.	Θα ήθελα μια κούτα.	thah eethehlah meeah kootah
Give me a/some ... please.	Δώστε μου ... παρακαλώ.	dhosteh moo ... pahrahkahlo
candy	καραμέλες	kahrahmehlehss
chewing gum	μια τσίχλα	meeah tseekhlah
chocolate	μια σοκολάτα	meeah sokkollahtah
cigarette case	μια τσιγαροθήκη	meeah tseeghahrotheekee
cigarette holder	μια πίπα για στιγάρα	meeah peepah yeeah tseeghahrah
cigarettes	τσιγάρα	tseeghahrah
filter-tipped	με φίλτρο	meh feeltro
without filter	χωρίς φίλτρο	khorreess feeltro
light/dark tobacco	ξανθό/μαύρο καπνό	ksahntho/**mah**vro kahpno
mild/strong	ελαφρυά/βαρυά	ehlahfreeah/vahreeah
menthol	μεντόλ	mehndoll
king-size	κιγκ-σάιζ	"king-size"
cigars	πούρα	poorah
lighter	ένα αναπτήρα	ehnah ahnahpteerah
lighter fluid/gas	υγραέριο/αέριο για αναπτήρα	eeghrahehreeo/ ahehreeo yeeah ahnahpteerah
matches	σπίρτα	speertah
pipe	μια πίπα	meeah peepah
pipe cleaners	καθαριστήρες πίπας	kahthahreesteerehss peepahss
pipe tobacco	καπνό πίπας	kahpno peepahss
pipe tool	πανί πίπας	pahnee peepahss
postcard	μια καρτ-ποστάλ	meeah kahrt-postahl
stamps	γραμματόσημα	ghrahmahtoseemah
sweets	καραμέλες	kahrahmehlehss
wick	ένα φιτίλι	ehnah feeteelee

Miscellaneous   Διάφορα

Souvenirs   Σουβενίρς (Ενθύμια)

Greece offers a wide range of handicrafts, particularly hand-woven textiles, costumed dolls and embroidered blouses and tablecloths. Ceramics and costume jewellery are most often designed in classic Greek styles. The flea markets offer countless antiques, including all sorts of copper, brass, bronze and other metallic objects. However, the exportation of ancient artifacts is strictly controlled, and it's virtually impossible to take any out of the country.

For those who like fine furs, Greece is noted for its marten—and especially stone marten—pelts.

alabaster objects	αλάβαστρο	ahlahvahstro
backgammon	τάβλι	tahvlee
bed rug	κάλυμμα κρεβατιού	kahleemah krehvahteeoo
brass	μπρούντζινα είδη	broondzeenah eedhee
ceramics	κεραμικά	kehrahmeekah
copper bells	χάλκινα κουδούνια	khahlkeenah koodhoo-neeah
dolls in national costumes (evzon)	κούκλες με εθνικές στολές (εύζωνος)	kooklehss meh ehthnee-kehss stollehss (ehvzonnoss)
embroidery	κέντημα	kehndeemah
floor rug	χαλί	khahlee
fur	γούνα	ghoonah
hand-knotted carpet	κιλίμι (χειροποίητο χαλί)	keeleemee (kheeropeeeeto khahlee)
honey	μέλι	mehlee
icon	εικόνα	eekonnah
long-fleeced woollen rug	φλοκάτη	flokkahtee
olive oil	ελαιόλαδο	ehlehollahdho
pottery	είδη αγγειοπλαστικής	eedhee ahnggeeoplah-steekeess
shepherd's coat	κάπα	kahpah
silverware	ασημικά	ahsseemeekah
tote bag	ταγάρι	tahghahree
wine	κρασί	krahssee
worry-beads	κομπολόι	kombolloee

Records – Cassettes   Δίσκοι – Κασέττες

Do you have any records by ...?	Έχετε δίσκους του...;	ehkhehteh dheeskooss too
I'd like a ...	Θα ήθελα ...	thah eethehlah
cassette	μια κασέττα	meeah kahssehtah
compact disc	ένα δίσκο για πικ-απ λέιζερ	ehnah dheesko yeeah "pick-up laser"
Do you have any songs by ...?	Έχετε τραγούδια του...;	ehkhehteh trahghoodheeah too
Can I listen to this record?	Μπορώ να ακούσω αυτό το δίσκο;	borro nah ahkoosso ahfto to dheesko
chamber music	μουσική δωματίου	moosseekee dhommahteeoo
classical music	κλασσική μουσική	klahsseekee moosseekee
folk music	λαϊκή μουσική	laheekee moosseekee
instrumental music	ενορχήστρωση	ehnorkheestrossee
jazz	τζαζ	dzahz
light music	ελαφρά μουσική	ehlahfrah moosseekee
orchestral music	μουσική ορχήστρας	moosseekee orkheestrahss
pop music	μουσική ποπ	moosseekee pop

Toys   Παιχνίδια

I'd like a toy/ game ...	Θα ήθελα ένα παιχνίδι ...	thah eethehlah ehnah pehkhneedhee
for a boy	για ένα αγόρι	yeeah ehnah ahghorree
for a five-year-old girl	για ένα πεντάχρονο κοριτσάκι	yeeah ehnah pehndah-khronno koreetsahkee
(beach) ball	μια μπάλα (της παραλίας)	meeah bahlah (teess pahrahleeahs)
bucket and spade (pail and shovel)	ένα κουβαδάκι και φτυαράκι	ehnah koovahdhahkee keh fteeahrahkee
building blocks (bricks)	ένα παιχνίδι ξύλοκατασκευή	ehnah pehkhneedhee kseelokkahtahskehvee
card game	μια τράπουλα	meeah trahpoolah
chess set	ένα σκάκι	ehnah skahkee
doll	μια κούκλα	meeah kooklah
electronic game	ένα ηλεκτρονικό παιχνίδι	ehnah eelehktronneeko pehkhneedhee
flippers	βατραχοπέδιλα	vahtrahkhopehdheelah
snorkel	ένα αναπνευστήρα	ehnah ahnahpnehfsteerah

Your money: banks—currency

At larger banks there will probably be someone who speaks English, and in most tourist centres you'll find small currency exchange offices — especially during the summer season. Exchange rates shouldn't vary much from office to office, and you'll normally get a slightly better rate for traveller's cheques and Eurocheques than for cash. If possible, change money in a bank rather than a hotel, it's better value for money. Always take your passport and look out for the *change* sign in Latin letters.

Banks are open from Monday to Friday between 8 a.m. and 1 or 2 p.m. However, currency exchange offices within banks may stay open until 7 or 8 in the evening, some on Saturdays and Sundays.

The Greek monetary system is based on the drachma (abbreviated drs. — in Greek Δρχ). There are coins of 1, 2, 5, 10, 20 and 50 drachmas, and bank notes of 50, 100, 500, 1000 and 5000 drachmas.

Where's the nearest bank?	Που είναι η κοντινό-τερη τράπεζα;	poo **ee**neh ee kondeeno-ttehree **trah**pehzah
Where's the nearest currency exchange office?	Που είναι το κοντινότερο γραφείο αλλαγής συναλλάγματος;	poo **ee**neh to kondeenottehro ghrah**fee**o ahlah**yeess** seenahlah**ghm**ahtoss
What time does the bank open/close?	Τι ώρα ανοίγει/κλείνει η τράπεζα;	tee orrah ahn**ee**yee/**klee**nee ee **trah**pehzah

At the bank Στη τράπεζα

I want to change some dollars/pounds.	Θέλω να αλλάξω μερικά δολλάρια/μερικές Αγγλικές λίρες.	**theh**lo nah ahl**lah**kso mehree**kah** dhol**lah**reeah/mehree**kehss** ahnnngglee-**kehss lee**rehss

I want to cash a traveller's cheque.	Θέλω να εξαργυρώσω ένα τράβελερς τσεκ.	the**hlo** nah ehksahryee-rosso **eh**nah "traveller's" tsehk
What's the exchange rate?	Ποια είναι η τιμή συναλλάγματος;	peeah **ee**neh ee tee**mee** seenahl**lahgh**mahtoss
How much commission do you charge?	Πόση προμήθεια χρεώνετε;	**pos**see prom**mee**theeah khreh**on**nehteh
Can you cash a personal cheque?	Μπορείτε να εξαργυρώσετε ένα προσωπικό τσεκ;	bor**ree**teh nah ehksahryee**ros**sehteh **eh**nah pros**sop**peeko tsehk
Can you telex my bank in London?	Μπορείτε να στήλετε ένα τέλεξ στη τράπεζα μου στο Λονδίνο;	bor**ree**teh nah **stee**lehteh **eh**nah "telex" stee **trah**pehzah moo sto lon**dhee**no
I have a/an/some ...	Έχω ...	**eh**kho
bank card	μια τραπεζιτική κάρτα	**mee**ah trahpehzeetee**kee kahr**tah
credit card	μια πιστωτική κάρτα	**mee**ah peestottee**kee kahr**tah
Eurocheques	Eurocheques	"eurocheques"
introduction from ...	μια σύσταση από ...	**mee**ah **see**stahssee ah**po**
letter of credit	μια πιστωτική επιστολή	**mee**ah peestottee**kee** ehpeesto**lee**
I'm expecting some money from New York. Has it arrived?	Περιμένω μερικά λεφτά από τη Νέα Υόρκη. Μήπως έχουν φθάση;	pehree**meh**no mehree**kah** leh**ftah** ah**po** tee **neh**ah ee**or**kee. **mee**poss **eh**khoon **ftah**ssee
Please give me ... notes (bills) and some small change.	Παρακαλώ δώστε μου ... χαρτονομίσματα και μερικά ψιλά.	pahrahkah**lo dhos**teh moo.. khahrtonnom**mee**zmahtah keh mehree**kah** psee**lah**

Deposits—Withdrawals   *Κατάθεση – Ανάληψη*

I want to ...	Θέλω να ...	the**hlo** nah
open an account	ανοίξω λογαριασμό	ah**neek**so loghahree**ahz**mo
withdraw ... drachmas	σηκώσω ... δραχμές	see**kos**so... drahk**hmehss**
Where should I sign?	Που να υπογράψω;	poo ah eepo**ghrah**pso
I want to deposit this in my account.	Θέλω να καταθέσω αυτό στο λογαριασμό μου.	the**hlo** nah kahtah**thehs**so ah**fto** sto loghahree**ahz**mo moo

NUMBERS, see page 146

Business terms   *Εμπορικές εκφράσεις*

My name is ...	Το όνομα μου είναι ...	to onnommah moo eeneh
Here's my card.	Ορίστε η κάρτα μου.	orreesteh ee kahrtah moo
I have an appointment with ...	Έχω ραντεβού με τον/την ...	ehkho rahndehvoo meh tonn/teen
Can you give me an estimate of the cost?	Μπορείτε να μου δώσετε μια εκτίμηση των εξόδων;	borreeteh nah moo dhossehteh meeah ehkteemeessee tonn ehksodhonn
What's the rate of inflation?	Πόσο ψηλός είναι ο πληθωρισμός;	posso psseeloss eeneh o pleethorreezmoss
Can you provide me with an interpreter/ a secretary?	Μπορείτε να μου βρείτε ένα/μια διερμηνέα/ γραμματέα;	borreeteh nah moo vreeteh ehnah/meeah dhee-ehrmeenehah/ ghrahmahtehah
Where can I make photocopies?	Που μπορώ να κάνω φωτοτυπίες;	poo borro nah kahno fottotteepeeehss

amount	το ποσόν	to possonn
balance	το ισοζύγιο	to eessozeeyeeo
capital	το κεφάλαιο	to kehfahleho
cheque	η επιταγή	ee ehpeetahyee
contract	το συμβόλαιο	to seemvolleho
discount	η έκπτωση	ee ehkptossee
expenses	η δαπάνη	ee dhahpahnee
interest	ο τόκος	o tokkoss
investment	η επένδυση κεφαλαίου	ee ehpehndheessee kehfahlehoo
invoice	το τιμολόγιο	to teemolloyeeo
loss	η ζημιά	ee zeemeeah
mortgage	η υποθήκη	ee eepotheekee
payment	η πληρωμή	ee pleerommee
percentage	το επί τις εκατόν	to ehpee teess ehkahtonn
profit	το κέρδος	to kehrdhoss
purchase	η αγορά	ee aghorrah
sale	η πώληση	ee polleessee
share	η μετοχή	ee mehtokhee
transfer	η μεταβίβαση	ee mehtahveevahssee
value	η τιμή	ee teemee

At the post office

Post offices handle letters, stamp sales, parcels and money orders, but not telegrams and phone calls. They can be recognised by a sign reading ΕΛ.ΤΑ. Hours vary, but main post offices are usually open from 8 a.m. to 8 p.m., Monday to Friday. But you can also buy stamps at newsstands and souvenir shops — with a 10 per cent surcharge. Post boxes are painted yellow, and if you want to send letters by registered post or parcels to foreign destinations, don't seal them until they have been checked at the post office by an official.

Where's the nearest post office?	Που είναι το κοντινότερο ταχυδρομείο;	poo eeneh to kondeenotehro tahkheedhrommeeo
What time does the post office open/close?	Τι ώρα ανοίγει/ κλείνει το ταχυδρομείο;	tee orrah ahneeyee/ kleenee to tahkheedhrommeeo
A stamp for this letter/postcard, please.	Γραμματόσημα για αυτό το γράμμα/ αυτή τη κάρτα, παρακαλώ.	ghrahmahtosseemah yeeah ahfto to ghrahmah/ ahftee tee kahrtah pahrahkahlo
A ...-drachma stamp, please.	Γραμματόσημα των... δραχμών, παρακαλώ.	ghrahmahtosseemah tonn... dhrahkhmonn pahrahkahlo
What's the postage for a letter to London?	Πόσο κοστίζει ένα γράμμα για το Λονδίνο;	posso kosteezee ehnah ghrahmah yeeah to londheeno
Where's the letter-box (mailbox)?	Που είναι το γραμματοκιβώτιο;	poo eeneh to ghrahmahtokkeevotteeo
I want to send this parcel.	Θέλω να στείλω αυτό το δέμα.	thehlo nah steelo ahfto to dhehmah
I want to send this by...	Θέλω να στείλω αυτό...	thehlo nah steelo ahfto
air mail	αεροπορικώς	ahehropporreekoss
express (special delivery)	εξπρές	"express"
registered mail	συστημένο	seesteemehno

At which counter can I cash an international money order?	Σε ποιο γκισέ μπορώ να εξαργυρώσω μια διεθνή ταχυδρομική επιταγή;	seh peeo geesseh borro nah ehksahryeerosso meeah dheeehthnee tahkheedhrommeekee ehpeetahyee
Where's the poste restante (general delivery)?	Που είναι η ποστ-ρεστάντ;	poo eeneh ee post-rehstahnd
Is there any post for me? My name is...	Υπάρχει ταχυδρομείο για μένα; Ονομάζομαι...	eepahrkhee tahkheedhro- mmeeo yeeah mehnah. onnommahzommeh

ΓΡΑΜΜΑΤΟΣΗΜΑ	STAMPS
ΔΕΜΑΤΑ	PARCELS
ΕΠΙΤΑΓΕΣ	MONEY ORDERS

Telecommunications *Τηλεπικοινωνίες*

Every town of any size has an office of the Greek Telecommunications Organization OTE and this is where to go to telephone or send telegrams — if, that is, your hotel is too small to be able to cope.

Public telephone booths are scattered around the towns. Blue ones are for local calls only, while orange ones permit direct dialling to other towns in Greece and to countries abroad connected to the international network. You'll find directions for use clearly written in English.

Telegrams *Τηλεγραφήματα*

I want to send a telegram/telex.	Θέλω να στείλω ένα τηλεγράφημα/τέλεξ.	thehlo nah steelo ehnah teelehghrahfeemah/"telex"
May I have a form, please?	Μου δείνετε ένα έντυπο, παρακαλώ;	moo dheenehteh ehnah ehndeepo pahrahkahlo
How much is it per word?	Πόσο κοστίζει η λέξη;	posso kosteezee ee lehksee
How much will this telex cost?	Πόσο θα κοστίση αυτό το τέλεξ;	posso thah kosteessee ahfto to "telex"

Ταχυδρομείο

Τηλέφωνο

Telephoning *Τηλεφωνῶ*

Where's the telephone?	Που είναι το τηλέφωνο;	poo eeneh to teelehfonno
Where's the nearest telephone booth?	Που είναι ο κοντινότερος τηλεφωνικός θάλαμος;	poo eeneh o kondeenotehross teelehfonneekoss thahlahmoss
May I use your phone?	Μπορώ να χρησιμοποιήσω το τηλέφωνό σας;	borro nah khreesseemoppeeeesso to teelehfonno sahss
Do you have a telephone directory for Athens?	Έχετε ένα τηλεφωνικό κατάλογο της Αθήνας;	ehkhehteh ehnah teelehfonneeko kahtahlogho teess ahtheenahss
I want to telephone to England.	Θέλω να τηλεφωνήσω στην Αγγλία.	thehlo nah teelehfonneesso steen ahnggleeah
What's the dialling (area) code for ...?	Ποιος είναι ο τηλεφωνικός κωδικός αριθμός για...;	peeoss eeneh o teelehfonneekoss kodheekoss ahreethmoss yeeah
How do I get the international operator?	Ποιον αριθμό πρέπει να πάρω για τις διεθνείς πληροφορίες;	peeon ahreethmo prehpee nah pahro yeeah teess dheeehthneess pleerofforreeehss

Operator *Χειριστής*

Good morning. I want Patras 123456.	Καλημέρα σας. Θέλω Πάτρα 123456.	kahleemehrah sahss thehlo pahtrah 123456
Can you help me get this number?	Μπορείτε να με βοηθήσετε να πάρω αυτό τον αριθμό;	borreeteh nah meh voeetheessehteh nah pahro ahfto tonn ahreethmo
I want to place a personal (person-to-person) call.	Θέλω να τηλεφωνήσω με προσωπική κλήση.	thehlo nah teelehfonneesso meh prossoppeekee kleessee
I want to reverse the charges (call collect).	Θέλω μια κλήση πληρωτέα από τον παραλήπτη.	thehlo meeah kleessee pleerottehah ahpo ton pahrahleeptee

Speaking *Στο τηλέφωνο*

| Hello, this is ... speaking. | Παρακαλώ, εδώ ... | pahrahkahlo ehdho |

NUMBERS, see page 146

I want to speak to ...	Θέλω να μιλήσω με ...	**theh**lo nah meel**ee**sso meh
I want extension ...	Θέλω εσωτερικό ...	**theh**lo ehssottehree**ko**
Is that ...?	Είναι το ...;	**ee**neh to
Speak louder/more slowly, please.	Μιλάτε πιο δυνατά/ πιο αργά, παρακαλώ.	mee**lah**teh peeo dheen**ah**tah/peeo ahr**ghah** pahrahkah**lo**

Bad luck *Κακή τύχη*

Would you try again later, please?	Μπορείτε να δοκι- μάσετε πάλι αργότερα, παρακαλώ;	borr**ee**teh nah dhokkee- **mahss**ehteh pahlee ahr- **ghot**tehrah pahrahkah**lo**
Operator, you gave me the wrong number.	Κύριε/Κυρία, μου δώσατε λάθος αριθμό.	**kee**reeeh/kee**ree**ah moo **dhoss**ahteh **lah**thoss ahree**thmo**
Operator, we were cut off.	Κύριε/Κυρία, μας κόπηκε η γραμμή.	**kee**reeeh/kee**ree**ah mahss **kopp**eekeh ee ghrah**mee**

Not there *Δεν είναι εδώ*

When will he/she be back?	Πότε θα επιστρέψει;	**pott**eh thah ehpee- **streh**psee
Will you tell him/ her I called? My name is ...	Μπορείτε να του/της πείτε ότι τηλεφώνησα; Το όνομα μου είναι ...	borr**ee**teh nah too/teess **pee**teh ottee teelehfonn- **ees**sah to onnommah moo **ee**neh
Would you ask him/ her to call me?	Μπορείτε να του/της πείτε να μου τηλεφωνήσει;	borr**ee**teh nah too/ teess **pee**teh nah moo teelehfonn**ees**see
Would you take a message, please?	Μπορώ να αφήσω μια παραγγελία, παρα- καλώ;	bor**ro** nah ah**fee**sso meeah pahrahnggeh**lee**ah pahrahkah**lo**

Charges *Κόστος*

| What was the cost of that call? | Πόσο κόστισε αυτό το τηλεφώνημα; | **poss**o **kost**eesseh ah**fto** to teeleh- **fonn**eemah |
| I want to pay for the call. | Θέλω να πληρώσω για το τηλεφώνημα. | **theh**lo nah plee**ross**o **yee**ah to teeleh**fonn**eemah |

Doctor

Make sure your health insurance policy covers any illness or accident while on holiday. If it doesn't, ask your insurance representative, automobile association or travel agent for details of special health insurance.

General *Γενικά*

Can you get me a doctor?	Μπορείτε να μου βρήτε ένα ιατρό;	borreeteh nah moo vreeteh ehnah eeahtro
Is there a doctor here?	Υπάρχει εδώ κοντά ένας ιατρός;	eepahrkhee ehdho kondah ehnahss eeahtross
I need a doctor — quickly.	Χρειάζομαι ένα ιατρό γρήγορα.	khreeahzommeh ehnah eeahtro ghreeghorrah
Where can I find a doctor who speaks English?	Που μπορώ να βρω ένα ιατρό που να μιλάει Αγγλικά;	poo borro nah vro ehnah eeahtro poo nah meelahee ahnggleekah
Where's the surgery (doctor's office)?	Που είναι το ιατρείο;	poo eeneh to eeahtreeo
What are the surgery (office) hours?	Ποιες είναι οι ώρες επισκέψεων;	peeehss eeneh ee orrehss ehpeeskehpsehonn
Could the doctor come to see me here?	Θα μπορούσε ο ιατρός να έλθη να με δη εδώ;	thah borroosseh o eeahtross nah ehlthee nah meh dhee ehdho
What time can the doctor come?	Τι ώρα μπορεί να έλθη ο ιατρός;	tee orrah borree nah ehlthee o eeahtross
Can you recommend a/an ...?	Μπορείτε να μου συστήσετε ...	borreeteh nah moo seesteessehteh
general practitioner	ένα παθολόγο/ πρακτικό	ehnah pahthollogho/ prahkteeko
children's doctor	ένα παιδίατρο	ehnah pehdheeahtro
eye specialist	ένα οφθαλμίατρο	ehnah ofthahlmeeahtro
gynaecologist	ένα γυναικολόγο	ehnah yeenehkollogho
Can I have an appointment ...?	Μπορώ να κλείσω ραντεβού ...;	borro nah kleesso rahndehvoo
tomorrow	για αύριο	yeeah ahvreeo
as soon as possible	όσο το δυνατό συντομώτερα	osso to dheenahto seendommottehrah

CHEMIST'S, see page 108

Parts of the body   *Τα μέρη του σώματος*

arm	το χέρι	to **kheh**ree
back	η πλάτη	ee **plah**tee
bladder	η ουροδόχος κύστη	ee oorod**hok**hoss **kees**tee
bone	το κόκκαλο	to **kok**kahlo
bowel	το έντερο	to **ehn**dehro
breast	το στήθος	to **stee**thoss
chest	ο θώρακας	o **thor**rahkahss
ear	το αυτί	to ah**ftee**
eye	το μάτι	to **mah**tee
eyes	τα μάτια	tah **mah**teeah
face	το πρόσωπο	to **pros**soppo
finger	το δάκτυλο	to **dhahk**teelo
foot	το πόδι	to **pod**hee
genitals	τα γεννητικά όργανα	tah yehnee**tee**kah **or**ghahnah
gland	ο αδένας	o ahd**heh**nahss
hand	το χέρι	to **kheh**ree
head	το κεφάλι	to keh**fah**lee
heart	η καρδιά	ee kahrd**hee**ah
jaw	το σαγόνι	to sah**ghon**nee
kidney	το νεφρό	to neh**fro**
knee	το γόνατο	to **ghon**nahto
leg	το πόδι	to **pod**hee
lip	το χείλος	to **khee**loss
liver	το συκώτι	to see**kot**tee
lung	ο πνεύμονας	o **pnehv**monnahss
mouth	το στόμα	to **stom**mah
muscle	ο μυς	o meess
neck	ο σβέρκος	o **zvehr**koss
nerve	το νεύρο	to **nehv**ro
nervous system	το νευρικό σύστημα	to nehv**ree**ko **sees**teemah
nose	η μύτη	ee **mee**tee
rib	το πλευρό	to pleh**vro**
shoulder	ο ώμος	o **om**moss
skin	το δέρμα	to **dhehr**mah
spine	η σπονδυλική στήλη	ee spondheelee**kee** **stee**lee
stomach	το στομάχι	to stom**mah**khee
tendon	ο τένοντας	o **teh**nondahss
thigh	ο μηρός	o mee**ross**
throat	ο λαιμός	o leh**moss**
tongue	η γλώσσα	ee **ghlos**sah
tonsils	οι αμυγδαλές	ee ahmeeghdhah**lehss**
vein	η φλέβα	ee **fleh**vah

Accident – Injury   Δυστύχημα – Τραυματισμός

There has been an accident.	Έγινε ένα δυστύχημα.	ehyeeneh ehnah dheesteekheemah
My child has had a fall.	Το παιδί μου έπεσε κάτω.	to pehdhee moo ehpehsseh kahto
He/She has hurt his/her head.	Αυτός/Αυτή χτύπησε στο κεφάλι του/της.	ahftoss/ahftee khteepeesseh sto kehfahlee too/teess
He's/She's unconscious.	Έχασε τις αισθήσεις του/της.	ehkhahsseh teess ehstheesseess too/teess
He's/She's bleeding (heavily).	Αυτός/Αυτή αιμορραγεί (πάρα πολύ).	ahftoss/ahftee ehmorrahyee (pahrah pollee)
He's/She's (seriously) injured.	Είναι (σοβαρά) τραυματισμένος/-η.	eeneh (sovvahrah) trahvmahteezmehnoss/-ee
His/Her arm is broken.	Έσπασε το χέρι του/της.	ehspahseh to khehree too/teess
His/Her ankle is swollen.	Πρήστηκε ο αστράγαλος του/της.	preesteekeh o ahstrahghahloss too/teess
I've been stung.	Κεντρίστηκα.	kehndreesteekah
I've got something in my eye.	Έχω κάτι στο μάτι μου.	ehkho kahtee sto mahtee moo
I've got a/an ...	Έχω ...	ehkho
blister	μια φουσκάλα	meeah fooskahlah
boil	ένα σπυρί	ehnah speeree
bruise	μια μελανιά	meeah mehlahneeah
burn	ένα έγκαυμα	ehnah ehnggahvmah
cut	ένα κόψιμο	ehnah kopseemo
graze	ένα γδάρσιμο	ehnah ghdhahrseemo
insect bite	ένα τσίμπημα απο έντομο	ehnah tseembeemah ahpo ehndommo
lump	ένα εξόγκωμα	ehnah ehksonggommah
rash	ένα εξάνθημα	ehnah ehksahntheemah
sting	ένα κέντρισμα	ehnah kehndreezmah
swelling	ένα πρήξιμο	ehnah preekseemo
wound	μια πληγή	meeah pleeyee
Could you have a look at it?	Μπορείτε να το εξετάσετε;	borreeteh nah to ehksehtahssehteh
I can't move my...	Δεν μπορώ να κουνήσω το ... μου.	dhehn borro nah kooneesso to ... moo

Που σας πονάει;	Where does it hurt?
Τι είδους πόνους έχετε;	What kind of pain is it?
υπόκοφους/οξείς/περιοδικούς διαρκείς/που έρχονται και φεύγουν	dull/sharp/throbbing constant/on and off
Είναι ...	It's ...
σπασμένο/στραμπουλιγμένο εξαρθρωμένο/σχισμένο	broken/sprained dislocated/torn
Θέλω να κάνετε μια ακτινο-γραφία.	I want you to have an X-ray.
Θα βάλετε γύψο.	You'll get a plaster.
Είναι μολυσμένο.	It's infected.
Έχετε κάνει τα εμβόλια για τον τέτανο;	Have you been vaccinated against tetanus?
Θα σας δώσω ένα αντισηπτικό/παυσίπονο.	I'll give you an antiseptic/a painkiller.

Illness *Αρρώστια*

I'm not feeling well.	Δεν αισθάνομαι καλά.	dhehn ehsthahnommeh kahlah
I'm ill.	Είμαι άρρωστος.	eemeh ahrostoss
I feel ...	Αισθάνομαι ...	ehsthahnommeh
dizzy	ζαλάδες	zahlahdhehss
nauseous	ναυτία	nahfteeah
shivery	ρίγη	reeyee
I've got a fever.	Έχω πυρετό.	ehkho peerehto
My temperature is 38 degrees.	Έχω 38 βαθμούς πυρετό.	ehkho 38 vahthmooss peerehto
I've been vomiting.	Έκανα εμετό.	ehkahnah ehmehto
I'm constipated/I've got diarrhoea.	Είμαι δυσκοίλιος/Έχω διάρροια.	eemeh dheeskeeleeoss/ehkho dheeahrreeah
I'm allergic to ...	Είμαι αλλεργικός στο ...	eemeh ahlehryeekoss sto
I'm diabetic.	Είμαι διαβητικός/-ή.	eemeh dheeahveeteekoss/-ee

I've got (a/an) ...	Έχω ...	ehkho
asthma	άσθμα	ahsthmah
backache	πόνο στη πλάτη	ponno stee plahtee
cold	κρυολόγημα	kreeoloyeemah
cough	βήχα	veekhah
cramps	κράμπες	krahmbehss
earache	πόνο στο αυτί	ponno sto ahftee
hay fever	συνάχι	seenahkhee
headache	πονοκέφαλο	ponnokehfahlo
indigestion	χαλασμένο στομάχι	khahlahzmehno stommahkhee
nosebleed	αιμορραγία στη μύτη	ehmorrahyeeah stee meetee
palpitations	ταχυπαλμία	tahkheepahlmeeah
rheumatism	ρευματισμούς	rehvmahteezmooss
sore throat	λαιμόπονους	lehmopponnooss
stiff neck	στραβολαιμιάσει	strahvollehmeeahssee
stomach ache	πόνο στο στομάχι	ponno sto stommahkhee
sunstroke	ηλίαση	eeleeahssee

I have difficulties breathing.	Έχω δυσκολίες στην αναπνοή.	ehkho dheeskoleeehss steen ahnahpnoee
I have a pain in my chest.	Έχω πόνους στο στήθος μου.	ehkho ponnooss sto steethoss moo
I had a heart attack ... years ago.	Έχω πάθει καρδιακή προσβολή πριν από ... χρόνια.	ehkho pahthee kahrdheeahkee prosvollee preen ahpo ... khronneeah
My blood pressure is too high/too low.	Η πίεση μου είναι πολύ ψηλή/πολύ χαμηλή.	ee peeehssee moo eeneh pollee pseelee/pollee khahmeelee

Women's section *Γυναικείο παράρτημα*

I have period pains.	Έχω πόνους από τη περίοδο.	ehkho ponnooss ahpo tee pehreeodho
I have a vaginal infection.	Έχω μια φλεγμονή της μήτρας.	ehkho meeah flehghmonnee teess meetrahss
I'm on the pill.	Παίρνω αντισυλληπτικά χάπια.	pehrno ahndeessee- leepteekah khahpeeah
I haven't had my period for 2 months.	Δεν έχω περίοδο εδώ και 2 μήνες.	dhehn ehkho pehreeodho ehdho keh 2 meenehss
I'm (3 months) pregnant.	Είμαι (3 μηνών) έγκυος.	eemeh (3 meenonn) ehnggeeoss

Από πότε αισθάνεστε έτσι;	How long have you been feeling like this?
Είναι η πρώτη φορά που το έχετε αυτό;	Is it the first time you've had this?
Θα σας μετρήσω την θερμοκρασία/πίεση σας.	I'll take your temperature/ blood pressure.
Σηκώστε το μανήκι σας, παρακαλώ.	Roll up your sleeve, please.
Παρακαλώ, γδυθείτε (μέχρι τη μέση).	Please undress (down to the waist).
Παρακαλώ, ξαπλώστε εκεί.	Please lie down over here.
Ανοίξτε το στόμα σας.	Open your mouth.
Αναπνέετε βαθειά.	Breathe deeply.
Βήξτε, παρακαλώ.	Cough, please.
Που έχετε πόνους;	Where do you feel the pain?
Έχετε ...	You've got (a/an) ...
αφροδισιακό νόσημα	venereal disease
γαστρίτιδα	gastritis
γρίππη	flu
ίκτερος	jaundice
ιλαρά	measles
κυστίτιδα	cystitis
πνευμονία	pneumonia
σκωληκοειδίτιδα	appendicitis
τροφική δηλητηρίαση	food poisoning
φλέγμοση από ...	inflammation of ...
(Δεν) Είναι μεταδοτική.	It's (not) contagious.
Θα σας κάνω μια ένεση.	I'll give you an injection.
Θέλω δείγμα από το αίμα/κόπρανα/ούρα σας.	I want a specimen of your blood/stools/urine.
Πρέπει να μείνετε στο κρεββάτι για ... μέρες.	You must stay in bed for ... days.
Θα ήθελα να δείτε ένα ειδικό.	I want you to see a specialist.
Θα ήθελα να πάτε στο νοσοκομείο για μια γενική εξέταση.	I want you to go to the hospital for a general checkup.

Prescription – Treatment   Συνταγή – Θεραπεία

This is my usual medicine.	Αυτό είναι το συνηθι- σμένο φάρμακο μου.	ahfto **ee**neh to seeneetheez**meh**no **fahr**mahko moo
Can you give me a prescription for this?	Μπορείτε να μου δώσετε μια συνταγή για αυτό;	bor**ree**teh nah moo **dhoss**ehteh mee**ah** seendah**hyee yee**ah ahfto
Can you prescribe a/an/some ...	Μπορείτε να μου γράψετε ...	bor**ree**teh nah moo **ghrahp**sehteh
antidepressant	ένα μέσο κατά της μελαγχολίας	**eh**nah **meh**sso kah**tah** teess mehlahnkhol**lee**ahss
sleeping pills	μερικά υπνωτικά	mehree**kah** eepnot**tee**kah
tranquillizer	μερικά ηρεμιστικά	mehree**kah** eerehmees**tee**kah
I'm allergic to antibiotics/penicillin.	Είμαι αλλεργικός στα αντιβιοτικά/στη πενικιλλίνη.	**ee**meh ahlehryee**koss** stah ahndeeveeot**tee**kah/stee pehneekee**lee**nee
Must I swallow them whole?	Πρέπει να τα καταπίνω ολόκληρα;	**preh**pee nah tah kahtah**pee**no ol**lok**leerah

Τι θεραπεία κάνετε;	What treatment are you having?
Τι φάρμακα παίρνετε;	What medicine are you taking?
Σαν ένεση ή χάπια;	By injection or orally?
Να παίρνετε... κουταλιές από αυτό το φάρμακο...	Take ... teaspoons of this medicine ...
Να παίρνετε ένα χάπι με ένα ποτήρι νερό...	Take one pill with a glass of water...
κάθε ... ώρες	every ... hours
... φορές την ημέρα	... times a day
πριν/μετά από κάθε γεύμα	before/after each meal
το πρωί/το βράδυ	in the morning/at night
εάν αισθάνεστε πόνους	if there is any pain
για ... μέρες	for ... days

CHEMIST'S, see page 108

Fee *Αμοιβή*

How much do I owe you?	Τι σας οφείλω;	tee sahss offeelo
May I have a receipt for my health insurance?	Μπορώ να έχω μια απόδειξη για την ασφάλεια υγείας;	borro nah ehkho meeah ahpodheeksee yeeah teen ahsfahleeah eeyeeahss
Can I have a medical certificate?	Μπορώ να έχω μια ιατρική βεβαίωση;	borro nah ehkho meeah eeahtreekee vehvehossee
Would you fill in this health insurance form, please?	Μπορείτε να συμπληρώσετε αυτή την ασφαλιστική αίτηση, παρακαλώ;	borreeteh nah seemblee-rossehteh ahftee teen ahsfahleesteekee ehteessee pahrahkahlo

Hospital *Νοσοκομείο*

What are the visiting hours?	Ποιες είναι οι ώρες επισκέψεως;	peeehss eeneh ee orrehss ehpeeskehpsehoss
When can I get up?	Πότε μπορώ να σηκωθώ;	potteh borro nah seekotho
When will the doctor come?	Πότε έρχεται ο γιατός;	potteeh ehrkhehteh o yeeahtross
I'm in pain.	Έχω πόνους.	ehkho ponnooss
I can't eat/sleep.	Δεν μπορώ να φάω/κοιμηθώ.	dhehn borro nah faho/keemeetho
Can I have a painkiller/some sleeping pills?	Μπορώ να έχω ένα παυσίπονο/μερικά υπνωτικά χάπια;	borro nah ehkho ehnah pahvseeponno/mehreekah eepnotteekah khahpeeah
Where is the bell?	Που είναι το κουδούνι;	poo eeneh to koodhoonee

nurse	η νοσοκόμα	ee nossokkommah
patient	ο/η άρρωστος	o/ee ahrostoss
anaesthetic	η νάρκωση	ee nahrkossee
blood transfusion	η μετάγγιση αίματος	ee mehtahnggeessee ehmahtoss
injection	η ένεση	ee ehnehssee
operation	η εγχείρηση	ee ehngkheereessee
bed	το κρεββάτι	to krehvahtee
bedpan	το ουροδοχείο	to oorodhokheeo
thermometer	το θερμόμετρο	to thehrmommehtro

144

Dentist *Οδοντίατρος*

Can you recommend a good dentist?	Μπορείτε να μου συστήσετε ένα καλό οδοντίατρο;	borreeteh nah moo seesteessehteh ehnah kahlo odhondeeahtro
Can I make an (urgent) appointment to see Dr. ....?	Μπορώ να κλείσω ένα (επείγον) ραντεβού για να δω το γιατρό...;	borro nah kleesso ehnah (ehpeeghonn) rahndehvoo yeeah nah dho to yeeahtro
Can't you make it earlier than that?	Μπορείτε να το κάνετε πιο σύντομα;	borreeteh nah to kahnehteh peeo seendommah
I have a broken tooth.	Έχω σπασμένο δόντι.	ehkho spahzmehno dhondee
I have a toothache.	Έχω πονόδοντο.	ehkho ponnodhondo
I have an abscess.	Έχω ένα απόστημα.	ehkho ehnah ahposteemah
This tooth hurts.	Αυτό το δόντι με πονά.	ahfto to dhondee meh ponnah
at the top	στην κορυφή	steen korreefee
at the bottom	στη ρίζα	stee reezah
in the front	εμπρός	ehmbross
at the back	πίσω	peesso
Can you fix it temporarily?	Μπορείτε να το σφραγίσετε προσωρινά;	borreeteh nah to sfrah-yeessehteh prossorreenah
I don't want it taken out.	Δεν θέλω να το βγάλετε.	dhehn thehlo nah to vghahlehteh
Could you give me an anaesthetic?	Μπορείτε να μου κάνετε μια αναισθητική ένεση;	borreeteh nah moo kahnehteh meeah ahnehstheeteekee ehnehssee
I've lost a filling.	Έφυγε ένα σφράγισμα.	ehfeeyeh ehnah sfrah-yeezmah
The gum is ...	Το ούλο ...	to oolo
very sore	είναι ερεθισμένο	eeneh ehrehtheezmehno
bleeding	αιμορραγεί	ehmorrahyee
I have broken this denture.	Έσπασα αυτή την οδοντοστοιχία.	ehspahssah ahftee teen odhondosteekheeah
Can you repair this denture?	Μπορείτε να επιδιορθώσετε αυτή την οδοντοστοιχία;	borreeteh nah ehpeedhee-orthossehteh ahftee teen odhondosteekheeah

Reference section

Where do you come from? *Από που είστε;*

Africa	Αφρική	ahfreekee
Asia	Ασία	ahsseeah
Australia	Αυστραλία	ahfstrahleeah
Europe	Ευρώπη	ehvroppee
North America	Βόρειος Αμερική	vorreeoss ahmehreekee
South America	Νότιος Αμερική	notteeoss ahmehreekee
Albania	Αλβανία	ahlvahneeah
Austria	Αυστρία	ahfstreeah
Belgium	Βέλγιο	vehlyeeo
Bulgaria	Βουλγαρία	voolghahreeah
Canada	Καναδά	kahnahdhah
China	Κίνα	keenah
Cyprus	Κύπρος	keepross
Denmark	Δανία	dhahneeah
England	Αγγλία	ahnggleeah
Finland	Φινλανδία	feenlahndheeah
France	Γαλλία	ghahleeah
Germany	Γερμανία	yehrmahneeah
Great Britain	Μεγάλη Βρεττανία	mehghahlee vrehtahneeah
Greece	Ελλάδα	ehlahdhah
India	Ινδία	eendheeah
Ireland	Ιρλανδία	eerlahndheeah
Israel	Ισραήλ	eesraheel
Italy	Ιταλία	eetahleeah
Japan	Ιαπωνία	eeahponneeah
Luxembourg	Λουξεμβούργο	looksehmvoorgho
Netherlands	Ολλανδία	ollahndheeah
New Zealand	Νέα Ζηλανδία	nehah zeelahndheeah
Norway	Νορβηγία	norveeyeeah
Portugal	Πορτογαλλία	portoghahleeah
Scotland	Σκωτία	skotteeah
South Africa	Νότιος Αφρική	notteeoss ahfreekee
Soviet Union	Σοβιετική Ένωση	sovveeehteekee ehnossee
Spain	Ισπανία	eespahneeah
Sweden	Σουηδία	sooeedheeah
Switzerland	Ελβετία	ehlvehteeah
Turkey	Τουρκία	toorkeeah
United States	Ηνωμένες Πολιτίες	eenommehnehss polleeteeeehss
Wales	Ουαλία	ooahleeah
Yugoslavia	Γιουγκόσλαβία	yeeoogoslahveeah

Numbers *Αριθμοί*

0	μηδέν	meedhehn
1	ένας, μια, ένα	ehnahss, meeah, ehnah
2	δύο	dheeo
3	τρία	treeah
4	τέσσερα	tehssehrah
5	πέντε	pehndeh
6	έξι	ehksee
7	επτά	ehptah
8	οκτώ	okto
9	εννιά	ehneeah
10	δέκα	dhehkah
11	έντεκα	ehndehkah
12	δώδεκα	dhodhehkah
13	δεκατρία	dhehkahtreeah
14	δεκατέσσερα	dhehkahtehssehrah
15	δεκαπέντε	dhehkahpehndeh
16	δεκαέξι	dhehkahehksee
17	δεκαεπτά	dhehkahehptah
18	δεκαοκτώ	dhehkahokto
19	δεκαεννιά	dhehkahehneeah
20	είκοσι	eekossee
21	είκοσι ένα	eekossee ehnah
22	είκοσι δύο	eekossee dheeo
23	είκοσι τρία	eekossee treeah
24	είκοσι τέσσερα	eekossee tehssehrah
25	είκοσι πέντε	eekossee pehndeh
26	είκοσι έξι	eekossee ehksee
27	είκοσι επτά	eekossee ehptah
28	είκοσι οκτώ	eekossee okto
29	είκοσι εννιά	eekossee ehneeah
30	τριάντα	treeahndah
31	τριάντα ένα	treeahndah ehnah
32	τριάντα δύο	treeahndah dheeo
33	τριάντα τρία	treeahndah treeah
40	σαράντα	sahrahndah
41	σαράντα ένα	sahrahndah ehnah
42	σαράντα δύο	sahrahndah dheeo
43	σαράντα τρία	sahrahndah treeah
50	πενήντα	pehneendah
51	πενήντα ένα	pehneendah ehnah
52	πενήντα δύο	pehneendah dheeo
53	πενήντα τρία	pehneendah treeah
60	εξήντα	ehkseendah
61	εξήντα ένα	ehkseendah ehnah

62	εξήντα δύο	ehkseendah dheeo
63	εξήντα τρία	ehkseendah treeah
70	εβδομήντα	ehvdhommeendah
71	εβδομήντα ένα	ehvdhommeendah ehnah
72	εβδομήντα δύο	ehvdhommeendah dheeo
73	εβδομήντα τρία	ehvdhommeendah treeah
80	ογδόντα	oghdhondah
81	ογδόντα ένα	oghdhondah ehnah
82	ογδόντα δύο	oghdhondah dheeo
83	ογδόντα τρία	oghdhondah treeah
90	ενενήντα	ehnehneendah
91	ενενήντα ένα	ehnehneendah ehnah
92	ενενήντα δύο	ehnehneendah dheeo
93	ενενήντα τρία	ehnehneendah treeah
100	εκατό	ehkahto
101	εκατόν ένα	ehkahtonn ehnah
102	εκατόν δύο	ehkahtonn dheeo
110	εκατόν δέκα	ehkahtonn dhehkah
120	εκατόν είκοσι	ehkahtonn eekossee
130	εκατόν τριάντα	ehkahtonn treeahndah
140	εκατόν σαράντα	ehkahtonn sahrahndah
150	εκατόν πενήντα	ehkahtonn pehneendah
160	εκατόν εξήντα	ehkahtonn ehkseendah
170	εκατόν εβδομήντα	ehkahtonn ehvdhomeendah
180	εκατόν ογδόντα	ehkahtonn oghdhondah
190	εκατόν ενενήτα	ehkahtonn ehnehneendah
200	διακόσια	dheeahkosseeah
300	τριακόσια	treeahkosseeah
400	τετρακόσια	tehtrahkosseeah
500	πεντακόσια	pehndahkosseeah
600	εξακόσια	ehksahkosseeah
700	επτακόσια	ehptahkosseeah
800	οκτακόσια	oktahkosseeah
900	εννιακόσια	ehneeahkosseeah
100	χίλια	kheeleeah
1100	χίλια εκατό	kheeleeah ehkahto
1200	χίλια διακόσια	kheeleeah dheeahkosseeah
2000	δύο χιλιάδες	dheeo kheeleeahdhehss
5000	πέντε χιλιάδες	pehndeh kheeleeahdhehss
10,000	δέκα χιλιάδες	dhehkah kheeleeahdhehss
50,000	πενήντα χιλιάδες	pehneendah kheeleeahdhehss
100,000	εκατό χιλιάδες	ehkahto kheeleeahdhehss
1,000,000	ένα εκατομμύριο	ehnah ehkahtommeereeo
1,000,000,000	ένα δισεκατομμύριο	ehnah dheessehkahtomeereeo

first	πρώτος, πρώτη, πρώτο	prottoss prottee protto
second	δεύτερος, -η, -ο	dhehftehross -ee -o
third	τρίτος, -η, -ο	treetoss -ee -o
fourth	τέταρτος, -η, -ο	tehtahrtoss -ee -o
fifth	πέμπτος, -η, -ο	pehmptoss -ee -o
sixth	έκτος, -η, -ο	ehktoss -ee -o
seventh	έβδομος, -η, -ο	ehvdhommoss -ee -o
eighth	όγδοος, -η, -ο	oghdho-oss -ee -o
ninth	ένατος, -η, -ο	ehnahtoss -ee -o
tenth	δέκατος, -η, -ο	dhehkahtoss -ee -o
once	μια φορά	meeah forrah
twice	δύο φορές	dheeo forrehss
three times	τρεις φορές	treess forrehss
a half/half a ...	μισό/μισό ...	meesso/meesso
half of ...	το μισό του...	to meesso too
half (adj.)	μισός, -ή, -ό	meessoss -ee -o
a quarter	ένα τέταρτο	ehnah tehtahrto
one third	ένα τρίτο	ehnah treeto
a pair of	ένα ζευγάρι	ehnah zehvghahree
a dozen	μία δωδεκάδα	meeah dhodhekahdhah
one per cent	ένα τις εκατό	ehnah teess ehkahto
3.4%	3.4 τις εκατό	3 kommah 4 teess ehkahto
1987	χίλια εννιακόσια ογδόντα επτά	kheeleeah ehneeahkos-seeah oghdhondah ehptah
1992	χίλια εννιακόσια ενενήντα δύο	kheeleeah ehneeahkos-seeah ehnehneendah dheeo
2003	δύο χιλιάδες τρία	dheeo kheeleeahdhehss treeah

Year and age *Χρόνια και ηλικία*

year	ο χρόνος	o khronnoss
decade	η δεκαετία	ee dhehkahehteeah
century	ο αιώνας	o ehonnahss
this year	φέτος	fehtoss
last year	πέρσι	pehrsee
next year	ο επόμενος χρόνος	o ehpommehnoss khronnoss
each year	κάθε χρόνο	kahtheh khronno
the 16th century	ο δέκατος έκτος αιώνας	o dhehkahtoss ehktoss ehonnahss
in the 20th century	στον εικοστό αιώνα	stonn eekostonn ehonnah

How old are you?	Πόσο χρονών είστε;	posso khronnonn eesteh
I'm 30 years old.	Είμαι 30 χρονών.	eemeh 30 khronnonn
He/She was born in 1960.	Αυτός/Αυτή γεννήθηκε το χίλια εννιακόσια εξήντα.	ahftoss/ahftee yehneetheekeh to kheeleeah ehneeahkosseeah ehkseendah
What is his/her age?	Πόσο χρονών είναι αυτός/αυτή;	posso khronnonn eeneh ahftoss/ahftee
Children under 16 are not admitted.	Απαγορεύεται η είσοδος κάτω των δεκαέξι χρονών.	ahpahghorrehvehteh ee eessodhoss kahto tonn dhehkahehksee khronnonn

Seasons   Εποχές

spring	η άνοιξη	ee ahneeksee
summer	το καλοκαίρι	to kahlokkehree
autumn	το φθινόπωρο	to ftheenopporro
winter	ο χειμώνας	o kheemonnahss
high season	η σαιζόν	ee sehzonn
low season	έξω από την σαιζόν	ehkso ahpo teen sehzonn

Months   Μήνες

January	Ιανουάριος	eeahnooahreeoss
February	Φεβρουάριος	fehvrooahreeoss
March	Μάρτιος	mahrteeoss
April	Απρίλιος	ahpreeleeoss
May	Μάιος	maheeoss
June	Ιούνιος	eeooneeoss
July	Ιούλιος	eeooleeoss
August	Αύγουστος	ahvghoostoss
September	Σεπτέμβριος	sehptehmvreeoss
October	Οκτώβριος	oktovreeoss
November	Νοέμβριος	noehmvreeoss
December	Δεκέμβριος	dhehkehmvreeoss
in September	το Σεπτέμβριο	to sehptehmvreeo
since October	από τον Οκτώβριο	ahpo tonn oktovreeo
the beginning of January	οι αρχές του Ιανουαρίου	ee ahrkhehss too eeahnooahreeoo
the middle of February	τα μέσα του Φεβρουαρίου	tah mehssah too fehvrooahreeoo
the end of March	τα τέλη του Μαρτίου	tah tehlee too mahrteeoo

Days and date *Μέρες και ημερομηνίες*

What day is it today?	Τι μέρα είναι σήμερα;	tee mehrah eeneh seemehrah
Sunday	Κυριακή	keereeahkee
Monday	Δευτέρα	dhehftehrah
Tuesday	Τρίτη	treetee
Wednesday	Τετάρτη	tehtahrtee
Thursday	Πέμπτη	pehmptee
Friday	Παρασκευή	pahrahskehvee
Saturday	Σάββατο	sahvahto
It's ...	Είναι ...	eeneh
July 1	πρώτη Ιουλίου	prottee eeooleeoo
March 10	δέκα Μαρτίου	dhehkah mahrteeoo
in the morning	το πρωί	to prooee
during the day	κατά την διάρκεια της μέρας	kahtah teen dheeahrkeeah teess mehrahss
in the afternoon	το απόγευμα	to ahpoyehvmah
in the evening	το βράδυ	to vrahdhee
at night	τη νύκτα	tee neektah
yesterday	χθες	khthehss
today	σήμερα	seemehrah
tomorrow	αύριο	ahvreeo
the day after tomorrow	μεθαύριο	mehthahvreeo
the day before	η προηγούμενη μέρα	ee proeeghoomehnee mehrah
the next day	η επόμενη μέρα	ee ehpommehnee mehrah
two days ago	πριν δύο μέρες	preen dheeo mehrehss
in three days' time	σε τρεις μέρες	seh treess mehrehss
last week	η περασμένη βδομάδα	ee pehrahzmehnee vdhommahdhah
next week	η επόμενη βδομάδα	ee ehpommehnee vdhommahdhah
for a fortnight (two weeks)	για δύο βδομάδες	yeeah dheeo vdhommahdhehss
birthday	τα γενέθλια	tah yehnehthleeah
day off	η άδεια	ee ahdheeah
(public) holiday	η αργία	ee ahryeeah
holidays/vacation	οι διακοπές	ee dheeahkoppehss
week	η βδομάδα	ee vdhommahdhah
weekend	το Σαββατοκύριακο	to sahvahtokkeereeahko
working day	η εργάσιμη μέρα	ee ehrghahsseemee mehrah

Public holidays *Δημόσιες αργίες*

Banks, offices and shops are closed on the following days:

Jan. 1	Πρωτοχρονιά	New Year's Day
Jan. 6	Θεοφάνια	Epiphany
March 25	Εικοστή πέμπτη Μαρτίου (Του Ευαγγελισμού)	Greek Independence Day
May 1	Πρωτομαγιά	May Day
Aug. 15	Δεκαπενταύγουστος (Της Παναγίας)	Assumption Day
Oct. 28	Εικοστή ογδόη Οκτωβρίου (Μέρα του ΟΧΙ)	"No" Day commemorating Greek defiance of Italian ultimatum and invasion of 1940
Dec. 25	Χριστούγεννα	Christmas Day
Dec. 26	Δεύτερη μέρα των Χριστουγέννων	St. Stephen's Day
Movable dates:	Καθαρή Δευτέρα	1st day of Lent: Clean Monday
	Μεγάλη Παρασκευή	Good Friday
	Δευτέρα του Πάσχα	Easter Monday
	Αναλήψεως	Ascension
	Αγίου Πνεύματος	Whit Monday ("Holy Spirit")

Merry Christmas!	Καλά Χριστούγεννα!	kahlah khreestooyehnah
Happy New Year!	Ευτυχισμένος ο Καινούργιος Χρόνος!	ehfteekheezmehnoss o kehnooryeeoss khronnoss
Happy Easter!	Καλό Πάσχα!	kahlo pahskhah
Happy birthday!	Χρόνια Πολλά!	khronneeah pollah
Best wishes!	Χαιρετίσματα!	khehrehteezmahtah
Congratulations!	Συγχαρητήρια!	seengkhahreeteereeah
Good luck/All the best!	Καλή τύχη/Με το καλό!	kahlee teekhee/meh to kahlo
Have a good trip!	Καλό ταξίδι!	kahlo tahkseedhee
Have a good holiday!	Καλές διακοπές!	kahlehss dheeahkoppehss
Best regards from ...	Χαιρετισμούς από ...	khehrehteezmooss ahpo
My regards to ...	Τους χαιρετισμούς μου στον/στην...	tooss khehrehteezmooss moo stonn/steen

What time is it?   *Τι ώρα είναι;*

Excuse me. Can you tell me the time?	Με συγχωρείτε. Μπορείτε να μου πείτε τι ώρα είναι;	meh seengkhorreeteh. borreeteh nah moo peeteh tee orrah eeneh
It's ...	Είναι ...	eeneh
five past one	μια και πέντε	meeah keh pehndeh
ten past two	δύο και δέκα	dheeo keh dhehkah
a quarter past three	τρεις και τέταρτο	treess keh tehtahrto
twenty past four	τέσσερις και είκοσι	tehssehreess keh eekossee
twenty-five past five	πέντε και εικοσιπέντε	pehndeh keh eekosseepehndeh
half past six	έξι και μισή	ehksee keh meessee
twenty-five to seven	επτά παρά εικοσιπέντε	ehptah pahrah eekosseepehndeh
twenty to eight	οκτώ παρά είκοσι	okto pahrah eekossee
a quarter to nine	εννιά παρά τέταρτο	ehneeah pahrah tehtahrto
ten to ten	δέκα παρά δέκα	dhehkah pahrah dhehkah
five to eleven	έντεκα παρά πέντε	ehndehkah pahrah pehndeh
twelve o'clock (noon/midnight)	δώδεκα (το μεσημέρι/τα μεσάνυκτα)	dhodhehkah (to mehsseemehree/tah mehssahneektah)
in the morning	το πρωί	to proee
in the afternoon	το απόγευμα	to ahpoyehvmah
in the evening	το βράδυ	to vrahdhee
The train leaves at ...	Το τραίνο φεύγει...	to trehno fehvyee
13.04 (1.04 p.m.)	στις δεκατρείς και τέσσερα λεπτά	steess dhehkahtreess keh tehssehrah lehptah
0.40 (0.40 a.m.)	στις μια παρά είκοσι το πρωί	steess meeah pahrah eekossee to proee
in five minutes	σε πέντε λεπτά	seh pehndeh lehptah
in a quarter of an hour	σε ένα τέταρτο της ώρας	seh ehnah tehtahrto teess orrahss
half an hour ago	πριν μισή ώρα	preen meessee orrah
about two hours	σε δύο ώρες περίπου	seh dheeo orrehss pehreepoo
more than 10 minutes	σε περισσότερο από δέκα λεπτά	seh pehreessottehro ahpo dhehkah lehptah
less than 30 seconds	σε λιγότερο από τριάντα λεπτά	seh leeghottehro ahpo treeahndah lehptah
The clock is fast/ slow.	Το ρολόι πάει μπροστά/ πίσω.	to rolloee pahee brostah/ peesso

Common abbreviations   *Γερικές συντομογραφίες*

Δις. Διδα/Δδα.	Δεσποινίς	Miss
δρχ.	δραχμές	drachmas
Ε.Ε.Σ.	Ελληνικός Ερυθρός Σταυρός	Greek Red Cross
Ε.Λ.Π.Α.	Ελληνική Λέσχη Περιηγή- σεως και Αυτοκινήτου	Automobile and Touring Club of Greece
ΕΛ.ΤΑ.	Ελληνικά Ταχυδρομεία	Greek Post Office
Ε.Ο.Τ.	Ελληνικός Οργανισμός Τουρισμού	Greek Tourist Organization
Η.Π.Α.	Ηνωμένες Πολιτείες Αμερικής	U.S.A.
Κ., κ., Κος.	Κύριος	Mr.
Κα.	Κυρία	Mrs.
μ.μ.	μετά μεσημβρίας	p.m.
Ο.Σ.Ε.	Οργανισμός Σιδηροδρόμων Ελλάδος	Railway Company of Greece
Ο.Τ.Ε.	Οργανισμός Τηλεπικοινωνιών Ελλάδος	Telecommunications Company of Greece
π.μ.	προ μεσημβρίας	a.m.
Τ.Α.	Τουριστική Αστυνομία	Tourist Police
τηλ.	τηλέφωνο	telephone
Φ.Π.Α.	Φόρος Προστιθέμενης Αξίας	VAT, value-added tax
χλμ.	χιλιόμετρα	kilometres

Signs and notices   *Σήματα*

Αναβατήρας	Lift
Ανδρών	Gentlemen
Ανοικτό	Open
Απαγορεύεται...	... forbidden
Απαγορεύεται η είσοδος	No entrance
Απαγορεύεται το κάπνισμα	No smoking
Γυναικών	Ladies
Είσοδος	Entrance
Είσοδος ελευθέρα	No admission charge
Έξοδος	Exit
Έξοδος κινδύνου	Emergency exit
Κατειλημένος	Occupied
Κίνδυνος	Danger
Κίνδυνος - Θάνατος	Danger of death
Κλειστό	Closed
Κρατημένο	Reserved
Πληροφορίες	Information
Πρώτες βοήθειες	First aid
Στάσις λεωφορείων	Bus stop

Emergency Κίνδυνος

Call the police	Καλέστε την αστυνομία	kahlehsteh teen ahsteenomeeah
Consulate	Προξενείο	proksehneeo
DANGER	ΚΙΝΔΥΝΟΣ	keendheenoss
Embassy	Πρεσβεία	prehzveeah
FIRE	ΦΩΤΙΑ	foteeah
Gas	Αέριο	aehreeo
Get a doctor	Καλέστε ένα γιατρό	kahlehsteh ehnah yeeahtro
Go away	Φύγετε	feeyehteh
HELP	ΒΟΗΘΕΙΑ	voeetheeah
Get help quickly	Καλέστε βοήθεια αμέσως	kahlehsteh voeetheeah ahmehssos
I'm ill	Είμαι άρρωστος	eemeh ahrostoss
I'm lost	Έχω χαθεί	eehkho khahthee
Leave me alone	Αφήστε με ήσυχο/-η	ahfeesteh meh eessekho/-ee
LOOK OUT	ΠΡΟΣΟΧΗ	prossokhee
Poison	Δηλητήριο	dheeleeteereeo
POLICE	ΑΣΤΥΝΟΜΙΑ	ahsteenomeeah
Stop that man/woman	Σταματήστε αυτόν τον άνδρα/αυτή την γυναίκα	stahmahteesteh ahftonn tonn ahndrah/ahftee teen yeenehkah
STOP THIEF	ΣΤΑΜΑΤΗΣΤΕ ΤΟΝ ΚΛΕΦΤΗ	stahmahteesteh tonn klehftee

Lost! Απολεσθέντα!

Where's the ...?	Που είναι...;	poo eeneh
lost property (lost and found) office	το γραφείο απολεσθέντων	to grahfeeo ahpollehsthehndonn
police station	το αστυνομικό τμήμα	to ahsteenommeeko tmeemah
I want to report a theft.	Θέλω να καταγγείλω μια κλοπή.	thehlo nah kahtahnggeelo meeah kloppee
My ... has been stolen.	Εκλάπη το ... μου.	ehklahpee to ... moo
I've lost my ...	Έχασα ... μου.	ehkhahssah ... moo
handbag	την τσάντα	teen tsahndah
passport	το διαβατήριο	to dheeahvahteereeo
wallet	το πορτοφόλι	to portoffollee

CAR ACCIDENTS, see page 78

155

Conversion tables

Centimetres and inches

To change centimetres into inches, multiply by .39.

To change inches into centimetres, multiply by 2.54.

	in.	feet	yards
1 mm	0.039	0.003	0.001
1 cm	0.39	0.03	0.01
1 dm	3.94	0.32	0.10
1 m	39.40	3.28	1.09

	mm	cm	m
1 in.	25.4	2.54	0.025
1 ft.	304.8	30.48	0.304
1 yd.	914.4	91.44	0.914

(32 metres = 35 yards)

Temperature

To convert Centigrade into degrees Fahrenheit, multiply Centigrade by 1.8 and add 32.

To convert degrees Fahrenheit into Centigrade, subtract 32 from Fahrenheit and divide by 1.8.

A very basic grammar

Until recently Greek had evolved comparatively little in the two thousand years which followed Pericles, Plato and Alexander the Great. But there are essentially two forms of modern Greek: the first is a purist – nearly classical – language that's almost never spoken; the second is called Demotike or colloquial. It's the latter we're using in this book.

Those who have studied classical Greek have a great advantage, but should be somewhat cautious on certain details. Modern colloquial Greek differs from the ancient language in the number of cases, verb forms and a more common use of prepositions. Accents indicate the stressed syllable, and in modern Greek only one remains. This is written as a vertical or slightly slanting stroke over the vowel (ά).

Below is the briefest possible outline of some essential features of modern, spoken Greek.

Articles

Nouns in Greek are either masculine, feminine or neuter. They agree with and are classified by the article which precedes them. This is true of both definite (**the**) and indefinite (**a/an**) articles.

	Masculine		**Feminine**		**Neuter**	
Singular	Def.	Indef.	Def.	Indef.	Def.	Indef.
Subject	o	ένας	η	μια	το	ένα
Object	το(ν)	ένα(ν)	τη(ν)	μια(ν)	το	ένα
Possessive	του	ενός	της	μιας	του	ενός
Plural	Definite		Definite		Definite	
Subject	οι		οι		τα	
Object	τους		τις		τα	
Possessive	των		των		των	

Nouns

According to their use in the sentence, Greek nouns change their endings. Since articles and modifying adjectives undergo related changes, the table below shows the declension of three parts of speech. A fourth, the vocative, is rarely encountered, being only used for addressing people.

	Masculine singular (the good man)	**Masculine plural** (the good men)
Subject	ο καλός άνθρωπος	οι καλοί άνθρωποι
Object	τον καλόν άνθρωπο	τους καλούς ανθρώπους
Possessive	του καλού ανθρώπου	των καλών ανθρώπων

	Feminine singular (the good woman)	**Feminine plural** (the good women)
Subject	η καλή γυναίκα	οι καλές γυναίκες
Object	την καλή γυναίκα	τις καλές γυναίκες
Possessive	της καλής γυναίκας	των καλών γυναικών

	Neuter singular (the good child)	**Neuter plural** (the good children)
Subject	το καλό παιδί	τα καλά παιδιά
Object	το καλό παιδί	τα καλά παιδιά
Possessive	του καλού παιδιού	των καλών παιδιών

There are, unfortunately, certain exceptions to the declensions, but the chart below outlines the main rules:

	Masculine			**Feminine**		**Neuter**		
	Singular							
Subject	-ος	-ας	-ης	-η	-α	-ο	-ι	-α
Object	-ο	-α	-η	-η	-α	-ο	-ι	-α
Possessive	-ου	-α	-η	-ης	-ας	-ου	-ιου	-ατος
	Plural							
Subject	-οι	-ες	-ες	-ες		-α	-ια	-ατα
Object	-ους	-ες	-ες	-ες		-α	-ια	-ατα
Possessive	-ων			-ων		-ων	-ων	-ατων

Γραμματική

Adjectives

For declension, see preceding page. The comparative is formed by means of the adverb **πιο** ("more"). The person or thing compared to takes the object case and is preceded by the preposition **από** (our conjunction "than").

> Ο Πέτρος είναι πιο πλούσιος από τον Μιχάλη.
> Peter is richer than Michael.

The superlative is formed by placing the definite article before the comparative. It's followed by the possessive form.

> Ο Πέτρος είναι ο πιο πλούσιος της Αθήνας.
> Peter is the richest man in Athens.

A few adjectives have irregular degrees of comparison, like:

καλός	good	καλύτερος	better	ο καλύτερος	best
κακός	bad	χειρότερος	worse	ο χειρότερος	worst

Personal and possessive pronouns

	Subj.	Dir. obj.	Indir. obj.	Possess.
I, me, my	εγώ	με	μου	μου
you, your*	(ε)σύ	σε	σου	σου
he, him, his	αυτός	τον	του	του
she, her	αυτή	την	της	της
it, its	αυτό	το	του	του
we, us, our	εμείς	μας		μας
you, your*	εσείς	σας		σας
they, them, their (m.)	αυτοί	τους		
they, them, their (f.)	αυτές	τις		τους
they, them, their (nt.)	αυτά	τα		

He saw me = Με είδε.
He gave me = Μου έδωσε.

The possessive form of personal pronouns is used as a possessive adjective. It always follows the noun it modifies.

> το όνομά μου my name (lit.: the name of me)

---

* There are two forms for "you" in Greek: (ε)σύ is used when talking to relatives, close friends and children; (ε)σείς is the plural and at the same time the polite or formal form.

Demonstratives

"This" (αυτός) and "that" (εκείνος) preceding a noun are always
followed by the article as well.

αυτός ο άνθρωπος	this man
αυτή η γυναίκα	this woman
αυτό το παιδί	this child

Prepositions

Prepositions are followed by the object form. The preposition
σε ("in", "at", "to") is contracted with the article, e.g., **στον,
στην, στο**.

Verbs

Greek verbs may have two different endings: active (ending in
− ω) and passive (usually ending in **-μαι**). Generally, verbs with
active endings express action done **by** the subject, those with
passive endings express action done **to** the subject. Unfortunately, there are many exceptions such as **έρχομαι** (I come)
which has a passive ending but an active meaning.

Generally, the personal pronoun is not used, since the verb
ending indicates the subject.

Within this basic grammar, it's obviously impossible to examine
the verb system of Greek, which is very different from English.

But here are the active endings in the present:

	Singular	Plural
1st person	-ω	-με
2nd person	-εις	-τε
3rd person	-ει	-ουν

βλέπω   I see (or: I am seeing)

Passive endings present many irregularities.

In most cases, **negatives** are formed by placing δεν before the verb.

> Ο κύριος πεινάει.
> The man is hungry.

> Ο κύριος δεν πεινάει.
> The man isn't hungry.

Questions are simply formed by changing the intonation of your voice. Note the use of the semi-colon in lieu of a question mark.

Auxiliary verbs

Here is the present tense of the two auxiliary verbs είμαι (to be) and έχω (to have).

I am	είμαι	I have	έχω
you are	είσαι	you have	έχεις
he, she, it is	είναι	he, she, it has	έχει
we are	είμαστε	we have	έχουμε
you are	είστε	you have	έχετε
they are	είναι	they have	έχουν

Note

In Greek, as in many languages, the endings of words sometimes differ according to whether the speaker or the person being spoken to is a man or a woman. We have indicated these cases by offering first the masculine version and then the feminine ending.

I'm American.
(man) Είμαι Αμερικάνος
(woman) Είμαι Αμερικανίδα
Shown as Αμερικάνος/-ίδα

Are you single?
(speaking to a man) Είστε ελεύθερος
(to a woman) Είστε ελεύθερη
Shown as ελεύθερος/-η

Dictionary
and alphabetical index

English—Greek

f féminine   m masculine   nt neuter   pl plural

For adjectives where only the masculine -ος ending is given, the feminine and neuter endings are always -η and -ο (see grammar section).

A

a ένας/μια/ένα ehnahss/meeah/ehnah 156

abbey μοναστήρι nt monnah**steeree** 81

abbreviation συντομογραφία f seendommoghrahfeeah 153

about (approximately) περίπου pehreepoo 78, 152

above πάνω pahno 15, 63

abscess απόστημα nt ahposteemah 144

absorbent cotton μπαμπάκι nt bahmbahkee 109

accept, to δέχομαι dehkhommeh 62, 102

accident δυστύχημα nt dheesteekheemah 78, 138

account λογαριασμός m loghahreeahzmoss 130

ache πόνος m ponnoss 141

adaptor μετασχηματιστής πρίζας m mehtahskheemahteesteess preezahss 119

address διεύθυνση f dheeehftheensee 21, 25, 31, 76, 79, 102

adhesive αυτοκόλλητος ahftokkolleetoss 105

admission είσοδος f eessodhoss 82, 89, 153

after μετά mehtah 15, 77

afternoon απόγευμα nt ahpoyehvmah 150, 152

after-shave lotion λοσιόν για μετά το ξύρισμα f losseeonn yeeah mehtah to kseereezmah 110

age ηλικία f eeleekeeah 148

ago πριν preen 148, 150

air conditioning κλιματισμός m kleemahteezmoss 23

airmail αεροπορικώς aehropporreekoss 132

airplane αεροπλάνο nt aehroplahno 65

airport αεροδρόμιο nt aehrodhrommeeo 16, 21, 65

alarm clock ξυπνητήρι nt kseepneeteeree 121

alcohol αλκοόλ nt ahlko-ol 37

alcoholic οινοπνευματώδης/-ης/-ες eenopnehvmahtodheess 59

allergic αλλεργικός ahlehryeekoss 140, 142

allow, to επιτρέπω ehpeetrehpo 82

almond αμύγδαλο nt ahmeeghdhahlo 53, 54

alphabet αλφάβητο nt ahlfahveeto 6

alter, to (garment) διορθώνω dheeorthonno 115

amazing καταπληκτικός kahtahpleekteekoss 84

ambulance ασθενοφόρο nt ahstennofforror 79

American Αμερικάνικος ahmehreekahneekoss 105, 126

American (person) Αμερικάνος/-ίδα m/f ahmehreekahnoss/-eedhah 92, 160

amount τιμή teemee 62; ποσόν nt possonn 131

anaesthetic νάρκωση f nahrkossee 143, 144

analgesic παυσίπονο nt pahfseeponno 109

anchovy αντζούγια f ahndzooyeeah 41, 44

and και keh 15

animal ζώο nt zo-o 85

ankle αστράγαλος m ahstrahghahloss 138

anorak αδιάβροχο τζάκετ nt ahdheeahvrokho tzahkeht 116

antibiotic αντιβιοτικό nt ahndeeveeotteeko 142

DICTIONARY

Λεξικό

antiques αντίκες f/pl ahndeekehss 83

antique shop κατάστημα για αντίκες nt katahsteemah yeeah ahndeekehss 98

antiseptic αντισηπτικός ahndeesseepteekoss 109

any αρκετά ahrkehtah 14

anyone κανείς kahnees 12, 16

anything κάτι kahtee 25, 101

apartment (flat) διαμέρισμα nt dheeahmehreezmah 22

aperitif απεριτίφ nt ahpehreeteef 56

appendicitis σκωληκοειδίτιδα f skolleekooeedheeteedhah 141

appetizer ορεκτικό nt orrehkteeko 41

apple μήλο nt meelo 53, 60, 64, 120

appliance συσκευή f seeskehvee 119

appointment ραντεβού nt rahndehvoo 30, 131, 136, 144

apricot βερύκοκο nt vehreekokko 53

April Απρίλιος m ahpreeleeoss 149

archaeology αρχαιολογία f ahrkheholloyeeah 83

architect αρχιτέκτονας m/f ahrkheetehktonnahss 83

area code υπεραστικός αριθμός m eepehrahsteekoss ahreethmoss 134

arm χέρι nt khehree 137, 138

arrival άφιξη f ahfeeksee 16, 65

arrive, to φθάνω fthahno 65, 69, 130

art τέχνη f tehkhnee 83

artery αρτηρία f ahrteereeah 137

art gallery γκαλερί τέχνης f gahlehree tehkhneess 81, 98

artichoke αγγινάρα f ahnggeenahrah 41, 42, 49

artificial τεχνητός tehkhneetoss 124

artist καλλιτέχνης m kahleetehkhneess 81, 83

ashtray σταχτοδοχείο nt stahkto-dhokheeo 27

ask, to ερωτώ ehrotto 36, 76

asparagus σπαράγγια nt/pl spahrahnggeeah 41, 50

aspirin ασπιρίνη f ahspeereenee 109

asthma άσθμα nt ahsthmah 140

at στο sto 15

at once αμέσως ahmehssoss 31

aubergine μελιτζάνα f mehleedzah-nah 49

August Αύγουστος m ahvghoostoss 149

aunt θεία f theeah 93

automatic αυτόματος ahftommahtoss 20, 122, 124

autumn φθινόπωρο nt ftheenopporro 149

awful τρομερός trommehross 84; απαίσιος ahpehsseeoss 94

B

baby μωρό nt morro 24, 111

baby food παιδική τροφή f pehdheekee troffee 111

babysitter μπέιμπυ σίτερ f "babysitter" 27

back πλάτη f plahtee 137

backache πόνος στην πλάτη m ponnoss steen plahtee 140

backgammon τάβλι nt tahvlee 127

bacon μπέικον nt "bacon" 38, 46

bad κακός kahkoss 14

bag τσάντα f tsahndah 18, 103

baggage αποσκευές f/pl ahposkeh-vehss 17, 18, 26, 31, 70

baggage cart καροτσάκι αποσκευών nt kahrotsahkee ahposkevonn 18, 70

baggage check γραφείο διαφυλάξεως αποσκευών nt ghrahfeeo dheeahfeelahksehoss ahposkehvonn 66, 70

baker's αρτοποιείο nt ahrtopeeeeo 98

balance (account) ισοζύγιο nt eessozeeyeeo 131

balcony μπαλκόνι nt bahlkonnee 23

ball (inflated) μπάλα f bahlah 128

ballet μπαλέτο nt bahlehto 88

ball-point pen στυλό διαρκείας nt steelo dheeahrkeeahss 104

banana μπανάνα f bahnahnah 53, 64

Band-Aid λευκοπλάστης m lehfko-plahsteess 109

bank (finance) τράπεζα f trahpehzah 98, 129, 130

banknote χαρτονόμισμα nt khahrtonnommeezmah 130

barber's κουρείο nt kooreeo 30, 98

basil βασιλικός m vahseeleekoss 51

basketball καλαθόσφαιρα f kahlah-thosfehrah, μπάσκετ f "basket" 89

bath (hotel) μπάνιο nt bahneeo 23, 25, 27

bathing cap σκούφια για το μπάνιο f skoofeeah yeeah to bahneeo 116

DICTIONARY

bathing hut καμπίνα f kahmbeenah 91

bathrobe μπουρνούζι nt boornoozee 116

bathroom μπάνιο nt bahneeo 27

bath towel πετσέτα του μπάνιου f pehtsehtah too bahneeoo 27

battery μπαταρία f bahtahreeah 75, 78, 119, 121, 125

be, to είμαι eemeh 11, 160

beach παραλία f pahrahleeah 90

beach ball μπάλα της παραλίας f bahlah teess pahrahleeahss 128

bean φασολάκι nt fahssollahkee 50

beard γένεια nt/pl yehneeah 31

beautiful ωραίος/-α/-ο orrehoss 14, 84

beauty salon ινστιτούτο καλλονής nt eensteetooto kahlonneess 30, 98

bed κρεββάτι nt krehvahtee 24, 141, 143

bed and breakfast δωμάτιο και πρόγευμα nt dhommahteeo keh proyehvmah 24

bedpan ουροδοχείο oorodhokheeo 143

beef βοδινό nt vodheeno 46

beer μπύρα f beerah 56, 64

before (place) πριν preen 15

begin, to αρχίζω ahrkheezo 87

beginning αρχή f ahrkhee 149

behind πίσω από peesso ahpo 15, 77

bell (electric) κουδούνι nt koodhoonee 127, 143

below κάτω kahto 15, 63

belt ζώνη f zonnee 117

bend (road) στροφή f stroffee 79

berth κρεββάτι nt krehvahtee 68, 69, 70

better καλύτερος kahleetehross 14, 25, 101, 113

between ανάμεσα ahnahmehssah 15

bicycle ποδήλατο nt podheelahto 74

big μεγάλος mehghahloss 13, 25

bill λογαριασμός m loghahreeahzmoss 31, 62, 102; (banknote) χαρτονόμισμα nt khartonnommeezmah 130

billion (Am.) δισεκατομμύριο nt dheessehkahtommeereeo 147

binoculars κυάλια nt/pl keeahleeah 123

bird πουλί nt poolee 85

birthday γενέθλια nt/pl yehnehthleeah 150, 151

biscuit (Br.) μπισκότο nt beeskotto 64

bitter πικρός peekross 61

black μαύρος mahvross 38, 53, 60, 105, 113

bladder ουροδόχος κύστη f oorodhokhoss keestee 137

blade ξυραφάκι nt kseerahfahkee 110

blanket κουβέρτα f koovehrtah 27

bleach ξέβαμμα nt ksehvahmah 30

bleed, to αιμορραγώ ehmorrahgho 138, 144

blind ρολό nt rollo 29

blister φουσκάλα f fooskahlah 138

blood αίμα nt ehmah 141

blood pressure πίεση f peeehssee 140, 141

blood transfusion μετάγγιση αίματος f mehtahnggeessee ehmahtoss 143

blouse μπλούζα f bloozah 116

blow-dry στέγνωμα nt stehghnommah 30

blue μπλε bleh 105, 113

blusher ρουζ nt rooz 110

boarding house πανσιόν f pahnseeonn 19, 22

boat βάρκα f vahrkah 73, 74

bobby pin τσιμπιδάκι nt tseembeedhahkee 111

body σώμα nt sommah 137

boil σπυρί nt speeree 138

boiled egg βραστό αυγό nt vrahsto ahvgho 38

bone κόκκαλο nt kokkahlo 137

book βιβλίο nt veevleeo 12, 104

booking office γραφείο κρατήσεως nt ghrahfeeo krahteessehoss 66

bookshop βιβλιοπωλείο nt veevleeoppolleeo 98, 104

boot μπότα f bottah 118

botanical gardens βοτανικός κήπος nt vottahneekoss keeposs 81

botany βοτανική f vottahneekee 83

bottle μπουκάλι nt bookahlee 17, 58, 59

bottle-opener ανοιχτήρι για μπουκάλια nt ahneekhteeree yeeah bookahleeah 106

bowel έντερο nt ehndehro 137

box κουτί nt kootee 120

boxing πυγμαχία f peeghmahkheeah 89

boy αγόρι nt ahghorree 112, 128

boyfriend φίλος m feeloss 93

bra σουτιέν nt sooteeehnn 116

Λεξικό

bracelet βραχιόλι nt vrahkheeollee 121

braces *(suspenders)* τιράντες f/pl teerahndehss 116

brake φρένο nt frehno 75, 78

brandy κονιάκ nt konneeahk 59

bread ψωμί nt psommee 36, 38, 64

break, to σπάζω spahzo 123, 138

breakdown βλάβη f vlahvee 78

breakdown van ρυμουλκό nt reemoolko 78

breakfast πρόγευμα nt proyehvmah 24, 34, 38

breast στήθος nt steethoss 137

breathe, to αναπνέω ahnahpneho 140, 141

bridge γέφυρα f yehfeerah 85

briefs κυλότες f/pl keelottehss 116

bring, to φέρνω fehrno 13

British Βρεττανός/-ίδα m/f vrehtahnoss/-eedhah 92

broken σπασμένος spahzmehnoss 29, 119, 139, 144

brooch μπρελόκ βραχιόλι nt brehlokk vrahkheeollee 121

brother αδελφός m ahdhehlfoss 93

brown καφέ kahfeh 113

bruise μελανιά f mehlahneeah 138

brush βούρτσα f voortsah 111

bubble bath αφρός μπάνιου m ahfross bahneeoo 110

bucket κουβάς m koovahss 128

buckle εγγράφα ζώνης f ehnggrahfah zonneess 117

build, to κτίζω kteezo 83

building κτίριο nt kteereeo 81, 83

bulb λάμπα m lahmbah 28, 75, 119

burn έγκαυμα nt ehnggahvmah 138

burn out, to καίγομαι kehghommeh 28

bus λεωφορείο nt lehofforreeo 18, 19, 65, 72, 80

business εμπόριο nt ehmborreeo 131

bus stop στάση f stahssee 72, 153

busy απασχολημένος ahpahskholleemehnoss 96

but αλλά ahlah 15

butane gas υγραέριο nt eeghrahehreeo 32, 106

butcher's κρεοπωλείο nt krehoppolleeo 98

butter βούτυρο nt vooteero 36, 38, 64, 120

button κουμπί nt koombee 29, 117

buy, to αγοράζω ahghorrahzo 67, 82, 104

C

cabbage λάχανο nt lahkhahno 49

cabin *(ship)* καμπίνα f kahmbeenah 74

cable car εναέριο βαγκόνι nt ehnahehreeo vahgonnee 74

café καφενείο nt kahfehneeo 33

cake κέικ nt "cake" 54, 64; γλυκό nt ghleeko 37

calculator υπολογιστική μηχανή f eepolloyeesteekee meekhahnee 105

calendar ημερολόγειο nt eemehrollo- yeeo 104

call, to *(summon)* καλώ kahlo 78, 79, 154; *(phone)* τηλεφωνώ teelehfonno 135

calm ήσυχος eesseekhoss 90

camera φωτογραφική μηχανή f fottoghrahfeekee meekhahnee 124, 125

camera shop φωτογραφείο nt fottograhfeeo 98

camp, to κατασκηνώνω kahtah- skeenonno 32

campbed κρεββάτι εκστρατείας nt krehvahtee ehkstrahteeahss 106

camping κατασκήνωση f kahtahskeenossee, κάμπινγκ nt "camping" 32, 106

camp site μέρος για κάμπινγκ nt mehross yeeah "camping" 32

can *(of peaches)* κονσέρβα f konsehrvah 120

can, to *(be able)* μπορώ borro 12

Canadian Καναδός/-έζα m/f kahnahdhoss/-ehzah 92

canal κανάλι nt kahnahlee 85

cancel, to ακυρώνω ahkeeronno 65

candle κερί nt kehree 106

candy καραμέλα f kahrahmehlah 54, 126

can opener ανοιχτήρι κονσέρβας nt ahneekhteeree konsehrvahss 106

cap κασκέτα f kahskehtah 116

capital *(finance)* κεφάλαιο nt kehfahleho 131

car αυτοκίνητο nt ahftokkeeneeto 19, 20, 26, 32, 75, 76, 78

carafe καράφα f kahrahfah 58

carat καράτιον nt kahrahteeonn 121

caravan τροχόσπιτο nt trokhospeeto 32

carbonated αεριούχος/-α/-ο ahehreeookhoss 60

carburettor καρμπυρατέρ *nt* kahrbeerahtehr 78
card κάρτα *f* kahrtah 130; *(playing card)* χαρτί *nt* khahrtee 93
card game τράπουλα *f* trahpoolah 128
cardigan πλεκτή ζακέτα *f* plehktee zahkehtah 116
car hire ενοικίαση αυτοκινήτου *nt* ehneekeeahssee ahftokeeneetoo 19, 20
car park πάρκινγκ *nt* "parking" 77
car rental ενοικίαση αυτοκινήτου *nt* ehneekeeahssee ahftokeeneetoo 19, 20
carrot καρόττο *nt* kahrotto 49
carry, to μεταφέρω mehtahfehro 21
cart καροτσάκι *nt* kahrotsahkee 18, 70
carton *(of cigarettes)* κούτα *f* kootah 17, 126
cartridge *(camera)* φιλμ κασέττα *nt* feelm kahssehtah 124
cash, to εξαργυρώνω ehksahryeeronno 129, 133
cash desk ταμείο *nt* tahmeeo 103, 155
cassette κασέττα *f* kahssehtah 119, 128
castle πύργος *m* peerghoss 81
catalogue κατάλογος *m* kahtahloghoss 82
cathedral μητρόπολη *f* meetroppollee 81
Catholic καθολικός kahtholleekoss 84
cauliflower κουνουπίδι *nt* koonoopeedhee 49
caution κίνδυνος *m* keendheenoss 79, 153, 154
cave σπήλιο *m* speeleho 81
cellophane tape σελοτέιπ *nt* "Sellotape" 104
cemetery νεκροταφείο *nt* nehkrottahfeeo 81
centimetre εκατοστό *nt* ehkahtosto 112
centre κέντρο *nt* kehndro 19, 21, 76
century αιώνας *m* ehonnahss 148
ceramics κεραμική *m* kehrahmeekee 83
certificate βεβαίωση *m* vehvehossee 143
chain *(jewellery)* αλυσίδα *f* ahleesseedhah 121
chair καρέκλα *f* kahrehklah 106

change *(money)* ψιλά *nt/pl* pseelah 62, 77, 130
change, to αλλάξω ahlahkso 18, 65, 68, 123, 129
chapel παρεκκλήσι *nt* pahrehkleessee 81
charcoal κάρβουνα *nt/pl* kahrvoonah 106
charge τιμή *f* teemee 20; λογαριασμός *m* loghahreeahzmoss 28
charge, to κοστίζω kosteezo 32; πληρώνω pleeronno 24
cheap φτηνός fteenoss 14, 24, 25, 101
check τσεκ *nt* tsehk 130; *(restaurant)* λογαριασμός *m* loghahreeahzmoss 62
check to, ελέγχω ehlehngkho 75; *(baggage)* καταγράφω kahtahghrahfo 70
check out, to αναχωρώ ahnahkhorro 31
checkup *(medical)* εξέταση *f* ehksehtahssee 141
cheers! στην υγειά σας steen eeyeeah sahss 56
cheese τυρί *nt* teeree 40, 43, 52
chef μάγειρας *m* mahyeerahss 40
chemist's φαρμακείο *nt* fahrmahkeeo 98, 108
cheque τσεκ *nt* tsehk 130
cherry κεράσι *nt* kehrahssee 53
chess σκάκι *nt* skahkee 93, 128
chest στήθος *nt* steethoss 140
chewing gum τσίχλα *f* tseekhlah 126
chicken κοτόπουλο *nt* kottoppoolo 41, 43, 48, 63
chicory *(Br.)* ραδίκι *nt* rahdheekee 49
child παιδί *nt* pehdhee 24, 61, 82, 138, 149
children's doctor παιδίατρος *m* pehdheeahtross 136
chips πατάτες τηγανιτές *f/pl* pahtahtehss teeghahneetehss 40; *(Am.)* τσιπς (πατατάκια) *nt/pl* tseeps (pahtahtahkeeah) 64
chocolate σοκολάτα *f* sokkollahtah 38, 54, 61, 64, 120, 126
choice προτίμηση *f* protteemeessee 40
chop μπριζόλα *f* breezollah 46
Christmas Χριστούγεννα *nt/pl* khreestooyehnah 151
church εκκλησία *f* ehkleesseeah 81, 84

cigar πούρο nt **pooro** 126
cigarette τσιγάρο nt **tseeghahro** 17, 95, 126
cigarette lighter αναπτήρας m **ahnahpteerahss** 121
cine camera κινηματογραφική μηχανή f **keeneemahtoghrahfeekee meekhahnee** 124
cinema κινηματογράφος m **keeneemahtoghrahfoss** 86, 96
city πόλη f **pollee** 81
clam μύδι nt **meedhee** 44
classical κλασσικός **klahsseekoss** 128
clean καθαρός **kahthahross** 61
clean, to καθαρίζω **kahthahreezo** 29, 76
cleansing cream γαλάκτωμα nt **ghahlahktommah** 110
cliff γκρεμός m **grehmoss** 85
clip κλιπς nt **kleeps** 121
cloakroom γκαρντερόμπα f **gahrndehrombah** 87
clock ρολόι nt **rolloee** 121, 152
clog, to βουλώνω **voolonno** 28
close, to κλείνω **kleeno** 11, 82, 108, 132
closed κλειστός **kleestoss** 153
cloth ύφασμα nt **eefahzmah** 118
clothes ρούχα nt/pl **rookhah** 29, 116
clothes peg μανδαλάκια nt/pl **mahndhahlahkeeah** 106
clothing ένδυμα nt **ehndheemah** 112
cloud σύνεφο nt **seenehfo** 94
coach (bus) λεωφορείο nt **lehofforreeo** 71
coat παλτό nt **pahlto** 116
cod μπακαλιάρος m **bahkahleeahross** 44
coffee καφές m **kahfehss** 38, 60, 64
coin νόμισμα nt **nommeezmah** 83
cold κρύος **kreeoss** 14, 25, 38, 41, 61, 94
cold (illness) κρυολόγημα nt **kreeolloyeemah** 108, 140
collect call κλήση πληρωτέα από τον παραλήπτη f **kleessee pleerottehah ahpo tonn pahrahleeptee** 134
colour χρώμα nt **khrommah** 103, 112, 124
colour chart δειγματολόγειο nt **dheeghmahtolloyeeo** 30
colour negative έγχρωμο αρνητικό nt **ehngkhrommo ahrneeteeko** 124
colour rinse ρενσάζ f **rehnsahz** 30

colour slide έγχρωμο σλάιντ nt **ehngkhrommo ''slide''** 124
comb χτένα f **khtehnah** 111
come, to έρχομαι **ehrkhommeh** 36, 59, 92, 94, 136, 143, 145
commission προμήθεια f **prommeetheeah** 130
common (frequent) χρήσιμος **khreesseemoss** 153
compact disc δίσκο για πικ-απ λέιζερ nt **dheesko yeeah ''pick-up laser''** 128
compartment διαμέρισμα nt **dheeahmehreezmah** 69
compass πυξίδα f **peekseedhah** 106
complaint παράπονο nt **pahrahponno** 61
concert συναυλία f **seenahvleeah** 88
confirm, to επιβεβαιώνω **ehpeevehvehonno** 65
confirmation επιβεβαίωση f **ehpeevehvehossee** 23
congratulations συγχαρητήρια nt/pl **seenghkahreeteereeah** 151
connection (train) ανταπόκριση f **ahndahpokreessee** 65, 67
constipated δυσκοίλιος/-α/-ο **dheeskeelleeoss** 139
consulate προξενείο nt **proksehneeo** 154
contact lens φακός επαφής m **fahkoss ehpahfeess** 123
contagious μεταδοτικός **mehtahdhotteekoss** 141
contain, to περιέχω **pehreeehkho** 37
contraceptive αντισυλληπτικό nt **ahndeesseeleepteeko** 109
control έλεγχος m **ehlehngkhoss** 16
convent μοναστήρι nt **monnah-steeree** 81
cookie μπισκότο nt **beeskotto** 54, 64
copper χαλκός m **khahlkoss** 122, 127
corduroy βελούδο κοτλέ nt **vehloo-dho kotleh** 114
cork φελός m **fehloss** 61
corkscrew τιρ-μπουσόν nt **teerboossonn** 106
corn (Am.) καλαμπόκι nt **kahlahmbokkee** 49
corner γωνία f **ghonneeah** 21, 36, 77
cost έξοδα nt/pl **ehksodhah** 131
cost, to κοστίζω **kosteezo** 11, 80, 134
cot παιδικό κρεββάτι nt **pehdheeko krehvahtee** 24

DICTIONARY

cotton βαμβακερό nt vamvahkehro 113, 114

cotton wool μπαμπάκι nt bahmbahkee 109

cough βήχας m veekhahss 108, 140

cough, to βήχω veekho 141

cough drops παστίλλιες για τον βήχα f/pl pahsteelee-ehss yeeah tonn veekhah 109

counter γκισέ nt geesseh 133

country χώρα f khorrah 92

countryside ύπεθρος f eepehthross 85

cousin ξάδελφος m ksahdhehlfoss, ξαδέλφη f ksahdhehlfee 93

cover charge κουβέρ nt koovehr 62

crab καβούρι nt kahvooree 41, 44

cracker κράκερ nt krahkehr 64

cramp κράμπα f krahmbah, 140

cream κρέμα f krehmah 60, 110

credit πίστωση f peestossee 130

credit card πιστωτική κάρτα f peestotteekee kahrtah 20, 31, 62, 102, 130

crisps τσιπς (πατατάκια) nt/pl tseeps (pahtahtahkeeah) 64

crockery πιατικά nt/pl peeahteekah 107

cross σταυρός m stahvross 121

crossing (by sea) διαδρομή f dheeahdhrommee 74

crossroads σταυροδρόμι nt stahvrodhrommee 77

cruise κρουαζιέρα f krooahzeeehrah 74

crystal κρύσταλλο nt kreestahlo 122

cucumber αγγούρι nt ahnggooree 42, 49

cup φλιτζάνι nt fleedzahnee 36, 60, 107

currency exchange office γραφείο αλλαγής συναλλάγματος nt grahfeeo ahlahyeess seenahlahghmahtoss 18, 129

current ρεύμα nt rehvmah 90

curtain κουρτίνα f koorteenah 28

curve (road) στροφή f stroffee 79

customs τελωνείο nt tehlonneeo 16, 102

cut κόψιμο nt kopseemo 30, 138

cut, to κόβω kovvo 30

cutlery μαχαιροπήρουνα nt/pl mahkhehroppeeroonah 107, 121

cycling ποδηλασία f podheelahsseeah 89

cystitis κυστίτιδα f keesteeteedhah 141

D

dairy γαλακτοπωλείο nt ghahlahktoppolleeo 98

dance, to χορεύω khorrehvo 88, 96

danger κίνδυνος nt keendheenoss 79, 153, 164

dangerous επικίνδυνος ehpeekeendheenoss 90

dark σκοτεινός skotteenoss 25, 112; σκούρος/-α/-ο skooross 101

date ημερομηνία f eemehrommeeneeah 25, 150; (fruit) χουρμάς m khoormahss 53

daughter κόρη f korree 93

day μέρα f mehrah 16, 20, 24, 32, 80, 150

decaffeinated χωρίς καφεΐνη khorreess kahfeheenee 60

December Δεκέμβριος m dhehkehmvreeoss 149

decision απόφαση f ahpoffahssee 25, 102

deck (ship) κατάστρωμα nt kahtah-strommah 74

deck chair πολυθρόνα f polleethronnah 91, 106

declare, to δηλώνω dheelonno 16, 17

delay καθυστέρηση f kahtheestehreessee 68

delicatessen μπακάλικο nt bahkahleeko 98

deliver, to στέλνω stehlno 102

delivery παράδοση f pahrahdhossee 102

dentist οδοντίατρος m/f odhondeeahtross 98, 144

denture οδοντοστοιχία f odhondosteekheeah 144

deodorant αποσμητικό nt ahpozmeeteeko 110

department τμήμα nt tmeemah 83, 100

department store μεγάλο εμπορικό κατάστημα nt meghahlo ehmborreeko kahtahsteemah 98

departure αναχώρηση f ahnahkhorreessee 65

deposit (car hire) εγγύηση f ehnggeeeessee 20

deposit, to (bank) καταθέτω kahtahthehto 130

dessert επιδόρπιο nt ehpeedhorpeeo 37, 40, 54

detour (traffic) αλαγή πορείας f ahlahyee porreeahss 79

Λεξικό

develop, to εμφανίζω ehmfah**nee**zo
125

diabetic διαβητικός dheeahveetee-
koss 37, 140

dialling code υπεραστικός αριθμός m
eepehrahstee**koss** ahreeth**moss**
134

diamond διαμάντι nt dheeaah**mahn**dee
122

diaper πάννα για μωρά f **pahn**nah yeeah
morrah 111

diarrhoea διάρροια f dheeah**rree**ah 139

dictionary λεξικό nt lehk**see**ko 104

diesel πετρέλαιο nt peh**treh**leho 75

diet δίαιτα f dhee**eh**tah 37

difficult δύσκολος dhees**koll**oss 14

difficulty δυσκολία f dheeskoll**ee**ah
28, 102, 140

digital ψηφιακός pseefeeah**koss** 122

dining car βαγόνι εστιατόριο nt
vah**ghonnee** ehsteeah**torreo** 70

dining room τραπεζαρία f
trapehzah**reeah** 27

dinner δείπνος m **dheep**noss 34

direct κατευθείαν kahtehf**thee**ahn 65,
68

direct, to δείχνω **dhee**khno 12

direction κατεύθυνση f
kah**tehf**theensee 76

disabled ανάπηρος m ah**nah**peeross
82

discotheque δισκοθήκη f
dheesko**theekee** 88

disease νόσος f **noss**oss 142

dish πιάτο nt pee**ah**to 37, 40, 42

dishwashing detergent απολυμαντικό πιάτων nt ahpolleemah**ndeeko**
peeah**tonn** 106

disinfectant απολυμαντικό nt
ahpolleemah**ndeeko** 109

dislocate, to εξαρθρώνω
ehksahrth**ronno** 139

dissatisfied δυσαρεστημένος
dheessahrehstee**meh**noss 103

disturb, to ενοχλώ ehno**khlo** 155

diversion (traffic) αλαγή πορείας f
ahlah**yee** porreeahss 79

dizziness ζαλάδες f/pl zah**lah**dhehss
139

doctor ιατρός m/f eeah**tross** 79, 136,
154

dog σκύλος m **skee**loss 155

doll κούκλα f **kook**lah 127, 128

dollar δολλάριο nt dhol**lah**reeo 18,
102, 129

door πόρτα f **por**tah 26

double διπλός dhee**ploss** 23, 74

double bed διπλό κρεββάτι nt dhee**plo**
kreh**vah**tee 23

double room διπλό δωμάτιο nt
dhee**plo** dhommah**teeo** 19

down κάτω **kah**to 15

downtown κέντρο της πόλης nt
kehndro teess **poll**eess 81

dozen δωδεκάδα f dhodheh**kah**dhah
120, 148

drachma δραχμή f drah**khmee** 18, 101

dress φόρεμα nt **forreh**mah 116

drink ποτό nt po**tto** 40, 59, 61, 94

drink, to πίνω **pee**no 35, 36

drinking water πόσιμο νερό nt
posseemo nehro 32, 155

drip, to (tap) στάζω **stah**zo 28

drive, to οδηγώ odhee**gho** 21, 76

driving licence άδεια οδηγήσεως f
ahdheeah odhee**yeessehoss** 20, 79

drugstore φαρμακείο nt fahrmah**keeo**
98, 108

dry ξηρός ksee**ross** 30, 58, 111

dry cleaner's στεγνοκαθαριστήριο nt
stehghnokkahthahree**steereeo** 29,
98

duck πάπια f **pah**peeah 48

dummy κούκλα f **kook**lah 111

during κατά την διάρκεια kah**tah** teen
dhee**ahrkeeah** 15, 150

duty (customs) φόρος m **for**ross 17

duty-free shop κατάστημα
αφορολογήτων nt kah**tah**steemah
ahforrolloy**eetonn** 19

dye βαφή f vah**fee** 30

E

each κάθε **kahtheh** 125, 142, 148

ear αυτί nt ahf**tee** 137

earache πόνος στο αυτί m **ponn**oss
sto ahf**tee** 140

early νωρίς nor**reess** 14, 31

earring σκουλαρίκι nt skoolah**reekee**
121

east ανατολή f ahnah**tollee** 77

Easter Πάσχα nt **pahs**khah 151

easy εύκολος **ehf**kolloss 14

eat, to τρώγω **trogho** 36, 37, 143

eel χέλι nt **khehlee** 41, 44

egg αυγό nt ah**vgho** 38, 41, 62, 64

eggplant μελιτζάνα f mehleed**zah**nah
49

eight οκτώ ok**to** 146

eighteen δεκαοκτώ dehkah**okto** 146

eighth όγδοος **oghdho-oss** 148

eighty ογδόντα **oghdhondah** 146

elastic ελαστικός **ehlahsteekoss** 109

Elastoplast λευκοπλάστης m lehfkoplahsteess 109

electrical ηλεκτρικός **eelehktreekoss** 119

electrician ηλεκτρολόγος m eelehktrolloghoss 98

electricity *(current)* ρεύμα nt **rehv-mah** 32

electronic ηλεκτρονικός eelehktronneekoss 125, 128

elevator ασανσέρ nt **ahssahnsehr** 27, 100; αναβατήρας m ahnahvahteerahss 100, 153

eleven έντεκα **ehndehkah** 146

emerald σμαράγδι nt **smahrahghdhee** 122

emergency κίνδυνος m **keendhee-noss** 154

emergency exit έξοδος κινδύνου f ehksodhoss keendheenoo 27, 99

emery board γυαλόχαρτο για τα νύχια nt γeeahlokhahrto yeeah tah neekheeah 110

empty άδειος/-α/-ο ahdheeoss 14

enamel σμάλτο nt **smahlto** 122

end τέλος nt **tehloss** 149

endive *(Am.)* ραδίκι nt rahdheekee 49

engine *(car)* μηχανή f meekhahnee 78

English Αγγλικός ahnggleekoss 126

English *(language)* Αγγλικά nt/pl ahnggleekah 11, 16, 80, 104; *(person)* Άγγλος/-ίδα m/f ahnggloss/ahnggleedhah 92

enjoy oneself, to διασκεδάζω dheeahskehdhahzo 96

enlarge, to μεγενθύνω mehyehntheeno 125

enough αρκετά ahrkehtah 14

entrance είσοδος f eessodhoss 66, 82, 99, 153

envelope φάκελλος m **fahkehloss** 27, 104

equipment εξάρτηση f ehksahrteessee 91

eraser γομολάστιχα f ghommollahsteekhah 104

escalator κινητή σκάλα f keeneetee skahlah 100

estimate εκτίμηση f ehkteemeessee 131

evening βράδυ nt **vrahdhee** 87, 94, 95, 96, 150, 152

evening dress βραδυνό ρούχο nt vrahdheeno **rookho** 88; *(woman)* βραδυνό φόρεμα nt vrahdheeno **forrehmah** 116

everything τα πάντα tah **pahndah** 31

examine, to εξετάζω ehksehtahzo 138

exchange, to αλλάζω ahlahzo 103

exchange rate τιμή συναλλάγματος f teemee seenahlahghmahtoss 18, 130

excursion εκδρομή f ehkdhrommee 80

excuse, to συγχωρώ seengkhorro 69, 78, 152

exhaust pipe εξάτμιση f ehksahtmeessee 78

exhibition έκθεση f ehkthehssee 81

exit έξοδος f ehksodhoss 66, 79, 99

expect, to περιμένω pehreemehno 130

expensive ακριβός ahkreevoss 14, 19, 24, 101

express εξπρές ''express'' 132

expression έκφραση f ehkfrahssee 10, 100

expressway αυτοκινητόδρομος m ahftokeeneetodhrommoss 76

extension cord/lead μπαλαντέζα f bahlahndehzah 119

external εξωτερικός ehksotehreekoss 109

extra επιπλέον ehpeeplehonn 24, 27

eye μάτι nt **mahtee** 137

eye drops κολλύριο nt kolleereeo 109

eyeliner γραμμή για τα μάτια f ghrahmee yeeah tah **mahteeah** 110

eye pencil μολύβι για τα μάτια nt molleevee yeeah tah **mahteeah** 110

eye shadow σκιά για τα μάτια f skeeah yeeah tah mahteeah 110

eyesight όρασις f orrahsseess 123

eye specialist οφθαλμίατρος m ofthahlmeeahtross 136

F

face πρόσωπο nt **prossoppo** 137

face pack μάσκα για το πρόσωπο f mahskah yeeah to prossoppo 30

face powder πούδρα για το πρόσωπο f poodrah yeeah to prossoppo 110

factory εργοστάσιο nt ehrghostahsseeo 81

fair πανηγύρι nt pahneeyeeree 81

fall *(autumn)* φθινόπωρο nt ftheenopporro 150

family οικογένεια f eekoyehneeah 93
fan ανεμιστήρας m ahnehmeesteerahss 28
fan belt ιμάντας του ανεμιστήρα m eemahndahss too ahnehmeesteerah 75
far μακρυά mahkreeah 100
fare τιμή f teemee 21
farm αγρόκτημα nt aghrokteemah 85
fat (meat) λίπος nt leeposs 37
father πατέρας m pahtehrahss 93
February Φεβρουάριος m fehvrooahreeoss 149
fee (doctor) αμοιβή f ahmeevee 143
feeding bottle πιπερό nt peepehro 111
feel, to (physical state) αισθάνομαι ehsthahnommeh 139, 141
felt τσόχα f tsokhah 114
felt-tip pen μαρκαδόρος m mahrkahdhorross 104
ferry φέρρυ-μποτ nt "ferry boat" 74
fever πυρετός m peerehtoss 139
few λίγα leeghah 14; μερικά mehreekah 14, 16
field χωράφι nt khorrahfee 85
fifteen δεκαπέντε dhekahpehndeh 146
fifth πέμπτος pehmptoss 148
fifty πενήντα pehneendah 146
fig σύκο nt seeko 53
file (tool) λίμα f leemah 110
fill in, to συμπληρώνω seembleeronno 26, 143
filling (tooth) σφράγισμα nt sfrahyeezmah 144
filling station πρατήριο βενζίνης nt prahteereeo vehnzeeneess 75
film φιλμ nt feelm 86, 124, 125
filter φίλτρο nt feeltro 125, 126
find, to βρήσκω vreesko 11, 84, 100
fine (OK) καλά kahlah 10; εντάξει ehndahksee 25
fine arts καλές τέχνες f/pl kahlehss tehkhnehss 83
finger δάκτυλο nt dhahkteelo 137
finish, to τελειώνω tehleeonno 125
fire φωτιά f fotteeah 154
first πρώτος prottoss 67, 68, 72, 74, 148
first-aid kit φαρμακείο για πρώτες βοήθειες nt fahrmahkeeo yeeah prottehss voeethee-ehss 106
first class πρώτη θέση f prottee thehssee 68
first name όνομα nt onnommah 25

fish ψάρι nt psahree 43, 44
fish, to ψαρεύω psahrehvo 90
fishing ψάρεμα nt psahrehmah 90
fishing tackle εξοπλισμός για ψάρεμα nt ehksopleezmoss yeeah psahrehmah 106
fishmonger's ιχθυοπωλείο nt eekhtheeoppolleeo 98
fit, to ταιριάζω tehreeahzo 115
fitting room δοκιμαστήριο nt dhokkeemahsteereeo 115
five πέντε pehndeh 146
fix, to σφραγίζω sfrahyeezo 75, 144
fizzy (mineral water) αεριούχος/-α/-ο ahehreeookhoss 60
flannel φανέλλα f fahnehlah 114
flash (photography) φλας nt flahss 125
flashlight φακός m fahkoss 106
flat ίσιος eesseeoss 118
flat (apartment) διαμέρισμα nt dheeahmehreezmah 22
flea market λαϊκή αγορά f laheekee aghorrah 81
flight πτήση f pteessee 65
flippers βατραχοπέδιλα nt/pl vahtrahkhoppehdheelah 128
floor όροφος m orroffoss 27
florist's ανθοπωλείο nt ahnthoppolleeo 98
flour αλεύρι nt ahlehvree 37
flower λουλούδι nt looloodhee 85
flu γρίππη f ghreepee 141
fluid υγρό nt eeghro 123
fog ομίχλη f ommeekhlee 94
folk music λαϊκή μουσική f laheekee moosseekee 128
food φαγητό nt fahyeeto 37, 61
food poisoning τροφική δηλητηρίαση f troffeekee dheeleeteereeahssee 141
foot πόδι nt podhee 137
football ποδόσφαιρο nt podhosfehro 89
footpath μονοπάτι nt monnoppahtee 85
for για yeeah 15
forbid, to απαγορεύω ahpahghorrehvo 153
forecast πρόβλεψη f provlehpsee 94
forest δάσος nt dhahssoss 85
forget, to ξεχνώ ksehkhno 61
fork πηρούνι nt peeroonee 36, 61, 107
form (document) έντυπο nt ehndeepo 25, 133

fortnight δύο βδομάδες *f/pl* dheeo vdhommahdhess 150

fortress φρούριο *nt* frooreeo 81

forty σαράντα sahrahndhah 146

foundation cream βάση *f* vahssee 110

fountain πηγή *f* peeyee 81

fountain pen πενοφόρος *m* pehnofforross 104

four τέσσερα tehssehrah 146

fourteen δεκατέσσερα dhekahtehsserah 150

fourth τέταρτος tehtahrtoss 148

frame *(glasses)* σκελετός *m* skehlehtoss 123

free ελεύθερος ehlehfthehross 13, 69, 82, 95, 155

french fries πατάτες τηγανιτές *f/pl* pahtahtehss teeghahneetehss 40

fresh φρέσκος/-ια/-ο frehskoss 53, 61

Friday Παρασκευή *f* pahrahskehvee 151

fried egg τηγανιτό αυγό *nt* teeghahneeto ahvgho 38

friend φίλος *m* feeloss 92, 95

from από ahpo 15

front μπροστά brostah 75

frost παγετός *m* pahyehtoss 94

fruit φρούτο *nt* frooto 37, 40, 53

fruit cocktail φρουτοσαλάτα *f* frootosahlahtah 53, 54

fruit juice χυμός φρούτων *m* kheemoss frootonn 37, 38, 60

frying pan τηγάνι *nt* teeghahnee 106

full γεμάτος yehmahtoss 14

furniture έπιπλα *nt/pl* ehpeeplah 83

furrier's γουναράδικο *nt* ghoonahrahdheeko 98

G

gallery γκαλερί *f* gahlehree 81

game παιχνίδι *nt* pehkhneedhee 128; *(food)* κυνήγι *nt* keeneeyee 40

garage γκαράζ *nt* gahrahz 26, 78

garden κήπος *m* keeposs 85

garlic σκόρδο *nt* skordho 51

gas αέριο *nt* ahehreeo 154

gasoline βενζίνη *f* vehnzeenee 75, 78

gastritis γαστρίτιδα *f* ghahstreeteedhah 141

gem πολύτιμος λίθος *m* polleeteemoss leethoss 121

general γενικός yehneekoss 27, 100

general delivery ποστ-ρεστάντ *f* post-rehstahnd 133

general practitioner παθολόγος *m/f* patholloghoss, πρακτικός *m/f* prahkteekoss 136

genitals γεννητικά όργανα *nt/pl* yehneeteekah orghahnah 137

geology γεωλογία *f* yeholloyeeah 83

get, to *(find)* βρίσκω vreesko 19, 21, 31, 32, 136; *(obtain)* πέρνω pehrno 108, 134

get off, to κατεβαίνω kahtehvehno 72

get to, to πηγαίνω peeyehno 19

get up, to σηκώνομαι seekonnommeh 143

gift *(present)* δώρο *nt* dhorro 17

gin τζιν *nt* tzeen 59

gin and tonic τζιν και τόνικ *nt* tzeen keh tonneek 59

girdle λαστέξ *m* lahstehks 116

girl κορίτσι *nt* korreetsee 112, 128

girlfriend φίλη *f* feelee 93, 95

give, to δίνω dheeno 13, 123, 126

give way, to *(traffic)* δίνω πρωτοπορεία dheeno prottopporeeah 79

gland αδένας *m* ahdhehnahss 137

glass ποτήρι *nt* potteeree 36, 58, 59, 61, 142

glasses γυαλιά *nt/pl* yeeahleeah 123

glove γάντι *nt* ghahndee 116

glue κόλλα *f* kollah 105

go, to πηγαίνω peeyehno 96, 163

go away, to φεύγω fehvgho 154

gold χρυσός *m* khreessoss 121, 122

golden χρυσαφένιος/-ια/ο khreessafehneeoss 113

golf γκολφ *nt* "golf" 90

good καλός kahloss 14, 101

goodbye αντίο ahndeeo 10

goods εμπορεύματα *nt/pl* ehmborrehvmahtah 16

goose χήνα *f* kheenah 48

gram γραμμάριο *nt* ghrahmahreeo 120

grammar book βιβλίο γραμματικής *nt* veevleeo ghrahmahteekeess 105

grape σταφύλι *nt* stahfeelee 53, 64

grapefruit γκρέιπφρουτ *nt* "grapefruit" 38, 53, 60

gray γκρίζος greezoss 113

graze γδάρσιμο *nt* ghdhahrseemo 138

greasy λιπαρός leepahross 30, 111

great *(excellent)* υπέροχος eepehrokhoss 95

Greece Ελλάδα *f* ehlahdhah 145

Greek Ελληνικός ehleeneekoss 55, 60, 114

Greek *(language)* Ελληνικά nt/pl
ehleeneekah 11
green πράσινος **prahsseenoss** 113
greengrocer's μανάβικο nt
mahnahveeko 98
greeting χαιρετισμός m
khehrehteezmoss 10, 151
grey γκρίζος **greezoss** 113
grocery παντοπωλείο nt
pahndoppolleeo 98, 120
ground floor ισόγειον nt eessoyeeonn
23
group ομάδα f ommahdhah 82
guide ξεναγός m/f ksehnahghoss 80
guidebook τουριστικός οδηγός m
tooreesteekoss odheeghoss 82,
104, 105
gum *(teeth)* ούλο nt oolo 144
gynaecologist γυναικολόγος m/f
yeenehkolloghoss 136

H
hair μαλλιά nt/pl mahleeah 30, 111
hairbrush βούρτσα f voortsah 111
haircut κούρεμα nt koorehmah 30
hairdresser's κομμωτήριο nt
kommotteereeo 27, 30, 98
hair dryer στεγνωτήρας μαλλιών m
stehghnottееrahss mahleeonn
119
hairgrip τσιμπιδάκι nt
tseembeedhahkee 111
hair lotion λοσιόν για μαλλιά f
losseeonn yeeah mahleeah 111
hairspray λακ f lahk 30
half μισός meessoss 148
half an hour μισή ώρα f meessee
orrah 153
half price *(ticket)* μισή τιμή meessee
teemee 68
hall *(large room)* αίθουσα f ehthoossah
88
ham ζαμπόν nt zahmbonn 38, 41, 42,
46, 64
hammock κούνια f kooneeah 106
hand χέρι nt khehree 137
handbag τσάντα f tsahndah 116,
154
handicrafts χειροτεχνία f
kheerottehkhneeah 83
handkerchief μαντήλι nt mahndeelee
116
handmade χειροποίητος
kheeroppeeeetoss 113
hanger κρεμάστρα f krehmahstrah 27

happy ευτυχισμένος
ehfteekheezmehnoss 151
harbour λιμάνι nt leemahnee 74, 81
hard σκληρός skleeross 123
hat καπέλλο nt kahpehlo 116
have, to έχω ehkho 160
hayfever συνάχι nt seenahkhee 108,
140
hazelnut φουντούκι nt foondookee
53
he αυτός ahftoss 158
head κεφάλι kehfahlee 46, 137, 138
headache πονοκέφαλος m
ponnokehfahloss 108, 140
headphones ακουστικά nt/pl
akhoosteekah 119
head waiter αρχισερβιτόρος m
ahrkheessehrveetorross 61
health υγεία f eeyeeah 56
health food shop κατάστημα δίαιτας
nt kahtahsteemah dheeehtahss 99
health insurance ασφάλεια υγείας f
ahsfahleeah eeyeeahss 143
heart καρδιά f kahrdheeah 46, 137
heart attack καρδιακή προσβολή f
kahrdheeahkee prosvollee 140
heat, to θερμαίνω thehrmehno 90
heating θέρμανση f thehrmahnsee
23
heavy βαρύς/-ιά/-ύ vahreess 14, 101
heel τακούνι nt tahkoonee 118
helicopter ελικόπτερο nt
ehleekoptehro 74
help βοήθεια f voeetheeah 154
help! βοήθεια! voeetheeah 154
help, to βοηθώ voeetho 12, 21, 70,
100, 134; *(oneself)* εξυπηρετώ
ehkseepeerehto 64, 120
her της teess 161
herbs βότανα nt/pl vottahnah 51
herb tea τσάι από βότανα nt tsahee
ahpo vottahnah 60
here εδώ ehdho 13, 21
high ψηλός pseeloss 140
high season σαιζόν f sehzonn 149
high tide πλήμμυρα f pahleerreeah 90
hill λόφος m loffoss 85
hire ενοικίαση f ehneekeeahssee 20,
74
hire, to νοικιάζω neekeeahzo 19, 20,
74, 90, 91
his του too 158
history ιστορία f eestorreeah 83
hitchhike, to κάνω ωτοστόπ kahno
ottostopp 74

hole τρύπα f **treepah** 29
holiday αργία f **ahryeeah** 150, 151
holidays διακοπές f/pl **dheeahkoppehss** 16, 150, 151
honey μέλι nt **mehlee** 38, 127
horse racing ιπποδρομία f **eepodhrommeeah** 89
hospital νοσοκομείο nt **nossokkommeeo** 99, 141, 143
hot ζεστός **zehstoss** 14, 23, 25, 28, 38, 60, 94
hot-water bottle θερμοφόρα f **thermofforrah** 27
hotel ξενοδοχείο nt **ksehnodhokheeo** 19, 21, 22, 26, 80
hour ώρα f **orrah** 89, 152
house σπίτι nt **speetee** 83, 85
how πως **poss** 11
how far πόσο μακρυά **posso mahkreeah** 11, 76, 85
how long σε πόσο χρόνο **seh posso khronno** 11, 24
how many πόσα **possah** 11
how much πόσο **posso** 11, 24
hundred εκατόν **ehkatonn** 147
hungry, to be πεινώ **peeno** 13, 35
hurry (to be in a) είμαι βιαστηκός **eemeh veeahsteekoss** 21, 36
hurt, to πονώ **ponno** 138, 144; (oneself) χτυπώ **khteepo** 138
husband σύζυγος m **seezeeghoss** 93
hydrofoil ιπτάμενο δελφίνι nt **eeptahmehno dhehlfeenee** 74

I
I εγώ **ehgho** 158
ice πάγος m **pahghoss** 94
ice-cream παγωτό nt **pahghotto** 54, 64
ice-cube παγονιέρα f **pahghonneeehrah** 27
ill άρρωστος **ahrostoss** 139, 154
illness αρρώστια f **ahrosteeah** 139
important σοβαρός **sovvahross** 13
imported εισαγόμενος **eessahghommehnoss** 113
in μέσα **mehssah** 15
include, to συμπεριλαμβάνω **seembehreelahmvahno** 20, 24, 31, 32, 62, 80
indigestion χαλασμένο στομάχι nt **khahlahzmehno stommahkhee** 140
inexpensive φθηνός **ftheenoss** 35, 124

infect, to μολύνω **molleeno** 139
inflammation φλέγμοση f **flehghmossee** 141
inflation πληθωρισμός m **pleethorreezmoss** 131
influenza γρίππη **ghreepee** 141
information πληροφορία f **pleerofforreeah** 66, 153
injection ένεση f **ehnehssee** 141, 142, 143
injure, to τραυματίζω **trahvmahteezo** 79, 138
injury τραυματισμός m **trahvmahteezmoss** 138
ink μελάνι nt **mehlahnee** 105
inn πανδοχείο nt **pahndhokheeo** 22
insect bite κέντρισμα nt **kehndreezmah** 108
insect repellent εντομοκτόνο nt **ehndommoktonno** 109
inside μέσα **mehssah** 15
instead αντί **ahndee** 37
insurance ασφάλεια f **ahsfahleeah** 20, 79, 143
interest τόκος m **tokkos** 131
interested, to be ενδιαφέρομαι **ehndheeahfehrommeh** 83, 96
interesting ενδιαφέρον **ehndheeahfehronn** 84
international διεθνής/-ής/-ές **dheeehthneess** 133, 134
interpreter διερμηνέας m/f **dhee-ehrmeenehahss** 131
intersection σταυροδρόμι nt **stahvrodhrommee** 77
introduce, to γνωρίζω **ghnorreezo** 92
introduction σύσταση f **seestahssee** 92, 130
investment επένδυση κεφαλαίου f **ehpehndheessee kehfahlehoo** 131
invitation πρόσκληση f **proskleessee** 94
invite, to προσκαλώ **proskahlo** 94
invoice τιμολόγιο f **teemolloyeeo** 131
iodine ιώδιο nt **eeodheeo** 109
Irish (person) Ιρλανδός/-έζα m/f **eerlahndhoss/-ehzah** 92
iron (laundry) σίδηρο nt **seedheero** 119
iron, to σιδερώνω **seedhehronno** 29
its του **too** 160
ivory ελεφαντόδοντο nt **ehlehfahndodhondo** 122

J

jacket ζακέττα f zahkehtah 116

jam μαρμελάδα f mahrmehlahdhah 38, 120

jam, to μπλέκω blehko 28, 125

January Ιανουάριος m eeahnooahreeoss 149

jar κουτί nt kootee 120

jaundice ίκτερος m eektehross 141

jaw σαγόνι nt sahghonnee 137

jazz τζαζ nt dzahz 128

jeans μπλου-τζήν nt bloodzeen 116

jeweller's κοσμηματοπωλείο nt kosmeemahtoppolleeo 99, 121

joint άρθρωση f ahrthrossee 137

journey ταξίδι nt tahkseedhee 71, 151

juice χυμός m kheemoss 38, 60

July Ιούλιος m eeooleeoss 149

June Ιούνιος m eeooneeoss 149

K

kerosene φωτιστικό πετρέλαιο nt fotteesteeko pehtrehleho 106

key κλειδί nt kleedhee 27

kidney νεφρό nt nehfro 137

kilogram κιλό nt keelo 120

kilometre χιλιόμετρο nt kheeleeommehtro 20, 78

kind ευγενικός ehvyehneekoss 95

kind (type) είδος nt eedhoss 46, 53

knee γόνατο nt ghonnahto 137

knife μαχαίρι nt mahkhehree 36, 61, 107

know, to γνωρίζω ghnorreezo 16, 96, 114

L

label ετικέττα f ehteekehtah 105

lace δαντέλλα f dhahndehlah 114

lake λίμνη f leemnee 23, 85

lamb αρνί nt ahrnee 46

lamp λάμπα f lahmbah 29, 106, 119

landscape φύση f feessee 92

lantern φανάρι nt fahnahree 106

large μεγάλος mehghahloss 20, 101, 118, 130

last τελευταίος tehlehftehoss 11, 67, 72, 149

last name επώνυμο ehponneemo 25

late αργά ahrghah 14

later αργότερα ahrghottehrah 135

laugh, to γελώ yehlo 95

launderette αυτόματο πλυντήριο nt ahftommahto pleendeereeo 99

laundry (place) πλυντήριο nt pleendeereeo 29, 99

laundry service πλυντήριο nt pleendeereeo 23

laxative καθαρτικό nt kahthahrteeko 109

leather δέρμα nt dhehrmah 114

leave, to αφήνω ahfeeno 26, 70, 154; φεύγω fehvgho 31, 68, 71, 73

left αριστερός ahreestehross 21, 63, 68, 77

left-luggage office γραφείο αποσκευών nt ghrahfeeo ahposkehvonn 66, 70

leg πόδι nt podhee 137

lemon λεμόνι nt lehmonnee 37, 38, 53, 60, 64

lemonade λεμονάδα f lehmonnahdhah 60, 64

lens φακός nt fahkoss 123, 125

lentil φακή f fahkee 43, 50

less λιγότερα leeghottehrah 14

lesson μάθημα nt mahtheemah 91

letter γράμμα nt ghrahmah 28, 132

letter box γραμματοκιβώτιο nt ghrahmahtokkeevotteeo 132

lettuce μαρούλι nt mahroolee 42, 49

library βιβλιοθήκη f veevleeotheekee 81, 99

licence (permit) άδεια f ahdheeah 20, 79

lie down, to ξαπλώνω ksahplonno 141

life belt σωσίβιο nt sosseeveeo 74

life boat ναυαγοσωστική λέμβος f nahvahghossosteekee lehmvoss 74

lifeguard ακτοφύλακας m ahktoffeelahkahss 90

lift ασανσέρ nt ahssahnsehr 27, 100; αναβατήρας m ahnahvahteerahss 100, 153

light φως nt foss 28; (cigarette) φωτιά f fotteeah 95

light ελαφρής/-ιά/-ύ ehlahfreess 14, 54, 101; (colour) ανοιχτός ahneekhtoss 101, 112, 113

lighter αναπτήρας m ahnahpteerahss 126

light meter φωτόμετρο nt fottommehtro 125

lightning αστραπή f ahstrahpee 94

like to αρέσω ahrehsso 25, 61, 92, 96, 102; (want) θέλω thehlo 13, 20, 23, 38

lip χείλος nt kheeloss 137

lipsalve κρέμα για τα χείλια *f* **kreh-mah yeeah tah kheeleeah** 110

lipstick κραγιόν για τα χείλια *nt* **krah-yeeonn yeeah tah kheeleeah** 110

liqueur λικέρ *nt* **leekehr** 59

listen, to ακούω **ahkooo** 128

litre λίτρο *nt* **leetro** 58, 75, 120

little *(a)* λίγα **leeghah** 14

live, to ζω **zo** 83

liver συκώτι *nt* **seekottee** 46, 137

lobster αστακός *m* **ahstahkoss** 44

long μακρύς/-ιά/-ύ **mahkreess** 76, 115, 117

long-sighted πρεσβύωπας *m/f* **prehzveeoppahss** 123

look, to κοιτάζω **keetahzo** 100, 123

look for, to ψάχνω **psahkhno** 13

look out! προσοχή! **prossokhee** 154

loose φαρδύς/-ιά/-ύ **fahrdheess** 115

lose, to χάνω **khahno** 13, 123, 154

loss ζημιά *f* **zeemeeah** 131

lost property/lost and found office γραφείο απωλεσθέντων αντικειμένων *nt* **ghrahfeeo ahpollehsthehndonn ahndeekeemehnonn** 66, 154

lot *(a)* πολλά **pollah** 14

lotion λοσιόν *f* **losseeonn** 110

loud δυνατός **dheenahtoss** 135

lovely υπέροχος **eepehrokhoss** 94

low χαμηλός **khahmeeloss** 140

low season έξω από την σαιζόν **ehkso ahpo teen sehzonn** 149

low tide άμπωτη *f* **ahmbottee** 90

lozenge παστίλλια *f* **pahsteeleeah** 109

luck τύχη *f* **teekhee** 151

luggage αποσκευές *f/pl* **ahposkeh-vehss** 17, 18, 21, 31, 70

luggage locker τμήμα αποσκευών *nt* **tmeemah ahposkehvonn** 18, 66, 70

luggage trolley καροτσάκι αποσκευών *nt* **kahrotsahkee ahposkehvonn** 18, 70

lump *(bump)* εξόγκωμα *nt* **ehksonggommah** 138

lunch γεύμα *nt* **yehvmah** 34, 35, 80, 94

lung πνεύμονας *m* **pnehvmonnahss** 137

M

magazine περιοδικό *nt* **pehreeo-dheeko** 105

magnificent μεγαλοπρεπής/-ής/-ές **mehghahloprehpeess** 84

maid καμαριέρα *f* **kahmahreeehrah** 26

mail, to ταχυδρομώ **tahkheedhrommo** 28

mail ταχυδρομείο *nt* **tahkheedhrommeeo** 28, 133

mailbox γραμματοκιβώτιο *nt* **ghrahmahtokkeevotteeo** 132

make, to κάνω **kahno** 131

make up, to ετοιμάζω **ehteemahzo** 28, 108

man άνδρας *m* **ahndrahss** 115

manager διευθυντής *m* **dheeehftheendeess** 26

manicure μανικιούρ *nt* **mahnee-keeoor** 30

many πολλοί **pollee** 14

map χάρτης *m* **khahrteess** 76, 105

March Μάρτιος *m* **mahrteeoss** 149

market αγορά *f* **ahghorrah** 81, 99

marmalade μαρμελάδα πορτοκάλι *f* **mahrmehlahdhah portokkahlee** 38

married παντρεμένος **pahndrehmehnoss** 93

mass *(church)* λειτουργία *f* **leetooryeeah** 84

match σπίρτο *nt* **speerto** 106, 126; *(sport)* αγώνας *m* **ahghonnahss** 89

match, to *(colour)* ταιριάζω **tehreeahzo** 112

material *(cloth)* ύφασμα *nt* **eefahzmah** 113

mattress στρώμα *nt* **strommah** 106

May Μάιος *m* **maheeoss** 149

may *(can)* μπορώ **borro** 12

meadow λιβάδι *nt* **leevahdhee** 85

meal γεύμα *nt* **yehvmah** 24, 62, 142

mean, to σημαίνω **seemehno** 11, 25

measles ιλαρά *f* **eelahrah** 141

measure, to πέρνω μέτρα **pehrno mehtrah** 114

meat κρέας *nt* **krehahss** 40, 46, 61

mechanic μηχανικός *m* **meekhah-neekoss** 78

medical ιατρικός **eeahtreekoss** 143

medicine ιατρική *f* **eeahtreekee** 83; *(drug)* φάρμακο *nt* **fahrmahko** 142

meet, to συναντώ **seenahndo** 96

melon πεπόνι *nt* **pehponnee** 41, 53

mend, to διορθώνω **dheeorthonno** 29, 75

menu μενού *nt* **mehnoo** 36, 37, 40

message παραγγελία *f* **pahrahnggehleeah** 28, 135

metre μέτρο *nt* **mehtro** 112

middle κέντρο *nt* **kehn**dro 68, 87; μέση *f* **meh**see 68
midnight μεσάνυχτα *nt* mehssah**neek**tah 152
milk γάλα *nt* **ghah**lah 38, 60, 64
million εκατομμύριο *nt* ehkahtomm**ee**reeo 147
mineral water μεταλλικό νερό *nt* mehtahlee**ko** ne**ro** 60, 64
mint δυόσμος *m* dhee**oz**moss 51
minute λεπτό *nt* leh**pto** 21, 152
mirror καθρέφτης *m* kah**threhf**teess 115, 123
Miss δεσποινίδα *f* dhehspee**nee**dhah 10, 153
miss, to λείπω **lee**po 18, 29, 61
mistake λάθος *nt* **lah**thoss 31, 61, 62, 102
moccasin μοκασίν *nt* mokkah**sseen** 118
moisturizing cream υδατική κρέμα *f* eedhah**tee**kee **kreh**mah 110
moment στιγμή *f* steeg**mee** 12
Monday Δευτέρα *f* dhehf**teh**rah 150
money λεφτά *nt/pl* leh**ftah** 130
month μήνας *m* **mee**nahss 16, 149
moon φεγγάρι *nt* feh**nggah**ree, σελήνη *f* seh**lee**nee 94
moped μοτοποδήλατο *nt* mottoppodhee**lah**to 74
more περισσότερα pehree**ssot**tehrah 14
morning πρωί *nt* pro**ee** 150, 152
mortgage υποθήκη *f* eepo**thee**kee 131
mosque τζαμί *nt* dzah**mee** 84
mosquito net κουνουπιέρα *f* koonoopee**eh**rah 107
motel μοτέλ *nt* mo**tehl** 22
mother μητέρα *f* mee**teh**rah 93
motorbike μοτοσυκλέτα *f* mottossee**kleh**tah 74
motorboat βάρκα με μηχανή *f* **vahr**kah meh meekhah**nee** 91
motorway αυτοκινητόδρομος *m* ahftokkeenee**toh**drommoss 76
mountain βουνό *nt* voo**no** 23, 85
moustache μουστάκι *nt* moo**stah**kee 31
mouth στόμα *nt* **stom**mah 137
move, to κουνώ koo**no** 138
movie φιλμ *nt* feelm 86
movie camera κινηματογραφική μηχανή *f* keeneemahtoghrahfee**kee** meekhah**nee** 124

movies κινηματογράφος *m* keeneemahtoghrah**foss** 86, 96
Mr. κύριος *m* **kee**reeoss 10, 153
Mrs. κυρία *f* kee**ree**ah 10, 153
much πολύ po**lee** 14
mug κύπελλο *nt* **kee**pehlo 107
muscle μυς *m* meess 137
museum μουσείο moo**sseeo** 81
mushroom μανιτάρι *nt* mahnee**tah**ree 41, 49
music μουσική *f* moossee**kee** 83, 128
mussel μύδι *nt* **mee**dhee 44
must, to πρέπει **preh**pee 23, 31, 95
mustard μουστάρδα *f* moo**stahr**dhah 51, 64, 120
my μου moo 158

N
nail *(human)* νύχι *nt* **nee**khee 110
nail brush βούρτσα για τα νύχια *f* **voort**sah yeeah tah nee**kheeah** 110
nail clippers νυχοκόπτης *m* neekho**kkop**teess 110
nail file λίμα για τα νύχια *f* **lee**mah yeeah tah nee**kheeah** 110
nail polish βερνίκι για τα νύχια *nt* vehr**nee**kee yeeah tah nee**kheeah** 110
name όνομα *nt* **onn**ommah 23, 25, 35, 79, 92, 131
napkin πετσέτα *f* peh**tseh**tah 36
nappy πάννα *f* **pah**nah 111
narrow στενός steh**noss** 118
nationality εθνικότητα *f* ehthnee**kott**eetah 25, 92
natural φυσικός feessee**koss** 83
nausea ναυτία *f* nahf**tee**ah 139
near κοντά kon**dah** 32
nearby εδώ κοντά eh**dho** kon**dah** 77, 84
nearest κοντινότερος kondee**not**tehross 73, 75, 78
neat *(drink)* σκέτος **skeh**toss 59
neck σβέρκος *m* **zvehr**koss 30, 137
need, to χρειάζομαι khree**ah**zomeh 29, 118, 136
needle βελόνι *nt* veh**lonn**ee 27
negative αρνητικό *nt* ahrnee**tee**ko 125
nephew ανεψιός *m* ahnehpsee**oss** 93
nerve νεύρο *nt* **nehv**ro 137
nervous νευρικός nehv**ree**koss 137
nervous system νευρικό σύστημα *nt* nehvree**ko** **sees**teemah 137

never ποτέ **potteh** 15

new κοινούργιος/-ια/-ο kehn**oor**yeeoss 14

newsagent's πρακτορείο *nt* prahk**torreeo** 99

newspaper εφημερίδα *f* ehfeemeh**reedh**ah 104, 105

newsstand περίπτερο *nt* peh**reeptehro** 19, 66, 99, 104

New Year Καινούργιος Χρόνος *m* kehn**oor**yeeoss **khronn**oss 151

next επόμενος eh**pommeh**noss 21, 65, 67, 73, 149, 150

next to δίπλα από **dheeplah ahpo** 15, 77

nice *(beautiful)* ωραίος/-α/-ο or**rehoss** 94

niece ανεψιά *f* ahneh**pseeah** 93

night νύκτα *f* **neekt**ah 10, 150

night-club νυκτερινό κέντρο *nt* neektehreeno **kehn**dro 88

night cream κρέμα νύκτας *f* **krehmah neekt**ahss 110

nightdress νυκτικό *nt* neek**teeko** 116

nine εννιά eh**neeah** 146

nineteen δεκαεννιά dhehkaheh**neeah** 146

ninety ενενήντα ehneh**neend**ah 147

ninth ένατος **ehn**ahtoss 148

no όχι **okhee** 10

noise θόρυβος *m* **thorreevoss** 25

nonalcoholic μη οινοπνευματώδης/ -ης/-ες mee eenopnehv**mahto**- dheess 60

nonsmoker μη καπνιστής *m* mee kahpnee**steess** 36, 69

noodle χιλόπιτα *f* kheelo**peetah** 43

noon μεσημέρι *nt* mehsee**mehree** 31, 152

normal κανονικός kahnonnee**koss** 30

north βορράς *m* vor**rahss** 77

nose μύτη *f* **meetee** 137

nosebleed αιμορραγία στη μύτη *f* eemorrah**yeeah** stee **meetee** 140

nose drops σταγόνες για τη μύτη *f/pl* stah**ghonn**ehss **yeeah** tee **meetee** 109

not δεν dhehn 15, 160

note *(banknote)* χαρτονόμισμα *nt* khartonnom**meezmah** 130

notebook τετράδιο *nt* teh**trahdheeo** 105

nothing τίποτα **teepott**ah 15, 17, 37, 54

notice *(sign)* σήμα *nt* **seemah** 153

November Νοέμβριος *m* noehm**vreeos** 149

now τώρα **torrah** 15

number αριθμός *m* ahreeth**moss** 25, 65, 124, 134, 135, 146

nurse νοσοκόμα *f* nossok**kommah** 143

O

occupied κατειλημένος kahteeleeem**ehn**oss 14, 153

October Οκτώβριος *m* ok**tovreeoss** 149

octopus χταπόδι *nt* khtah**podhee** 44

office γραφείο *nt* ghrah**feeo** 19, 60, 80, 154

oil λάδι *nt* **lahdhee** 37, 75, 111

oily λιπαρός leepah**ross** 30, 111

old παλιός/-ά/ό pah**leeoss** 14; *(person)* γέρος *m* **yehross** 14

old town παλιά πόλη *f* pah**leeah pollee** 81

olive ελιά *f* eh**leeah** 41

olive oil ελαιόλαδο *nt* ehleho**llahdho** 127

omelet ομελέττα *f* ommeh**lehtah** 40, 42, 43

on επάνω eh**pahno** 15

once μια φορά meeah for**rah** 148

one ένας/μια/ένα **ehn**ahss/**meeah**/**ehn**ah 146

one-way *(ticket)* απλό ahplo 65, 68

onion κρεμμύδι *nt* kreh**meedhee** 49

only μόνο **monno** 15, 24, 80

open ανοικτός ahneek**toss** 14, 82, 153

open, to ανοίγω ah**neegho** 11, 17, 108, 130, 132, 141

opera όπερα *f* **oppehrah** 72, 81, 88

operation εγχείρηση *f* ehng**kheereessee** 143

operator τηλεφωνητής *m* teelehfonn**eeteess** 134

opposite αντίθετα ahn**deethehtah** 77

optician οπτικός *m* optee**koss** 99, 123

or ή ee 15

orange πορτοκαλής/-ιά/-ί portokkah**leess** 113

orange πορτοκάλι *nt* portok**kahlee** 38, 53, 64

orange juice χυμός πορτοκαλιού *m* khee**moss** portokkah**leeoo** 38, 60

orangeade πορτοκαλάδα *f* portokkah**lahdhah** 60

orchestra ορχήστρα f orkheestrah 88;
(seats) πλατεία f plahteeah 87
order *(goods, meal)* παραγγελεία f
pahrahnggehleeah 40, 102
order, to *(goods, meal)* παραγγέλω
pahrahnggehlo 36, 61, 102, 103
oregano ρίγανη f reeghahnee 51
ornithology ορνιθολογία f
orneetholloyeeah 83
orthodox ορθόδοξος orthodhoksoss
84
our μας mahss 158
outlet *(electric)* υποδοχή πρίζας f
eepodhokhee preezahss 27
outside έξω ehkso 15, 36
overdone πολύ ψημένος pollee
pseemehnoss 61
overtake, to προσπερνώ prospehrno
79
owe, to οφείλω offeelo 143
oyster στρείδι nt streedhee 44

P
pacifier κούκλα f kooklah 111
packet κουτί nt kootee 120, 126
pail κουβάς m koovahss 128
pain πόνος m ponnoss 140, 143
painkiller παυσίπονο nt pahfseeponno
139, 143
paint, to ζωγραφίζω zoghrahfeezo 83
paintbox κουτί μπογιές nt kootee
boyeeehss 105
painter ζωγράφος m zoghrahfoss 83
painting ζωγραφική f zoghrahfeekee
83
pair ζευγάρι nt zehvghahree 116, 118,
148
pajamas πυτζάμα f peedzahmah 117
palace παλάτι nt pahlahtee 81
palpitation ταχυπαλμία f
tahkheepahlmeeah 140
panties κυλότες f/pl keelottehss 116
pants *(trousers)* παντελόνι nt
pahndehlonnee 116
panty girdle λαστέξ nt lahstehks 116
panty hose καλτσόν nt kahltsonn 116
paper χαρτί nt khahrtee 105
paperback φτηνό βιβλίο nt fteeno
veevleeo 105
paperclip συνδετήρας nt
seendhehteerahss 105
paper napkin χαρτοπετσέτα f
khahrtoppehtsehtah 105
paraffin *(fuel)* φωτιστικό πετρέλαιο nt
fotteesteeko pehtrehleho 107

parcel δέμα nt dhehmah 132, 133
parents γονείς m/pl ghonneess 93
park πάρκο nt pahrko 81
park, to σταθμεύω stahthmehvo 26,
77
parking στάθμευση f stahthmehfsee
77, 79
parking meter παρκόμετρο nt
parkomehtro 77
parliament βουλή f voolee 81
part μέρος nt mehross 137
party *(social gathering)* πάρτυ nt
pahrtee 95
pass *(mountain)* ορεινή διάβαση f
orreenee dheeahvahssee 85
pass, to *(car)* προσπερνώ prospehrno
79
passport διαβατήριο nt dheeahvah-
teereeo 16, 17, 25, 26, 124, 154
pasta παστίτσιο nt pahsteetseeo 40
paste *(glue)* κόλλα f kollah 105
pastry πάστα f pahstah 63, 64
pastry shop ζαχαροπλαστείο nt
zahkhahroplahsteeo 99
patch, to *(clothes)* μπαλώνω bahlonno
29
path μονοπάτι nt monnoppahtee 85
patient άρρωστος/-η m/f
ahrostoss/-ee 143
pay, to πληρώνω pleeronno 31, 62,
102, 135
payment πληρωμή f pleerommee 102,
131
pea μπιζέλι nt beezehlee 49
peach ροδάκινο nt rodhahkeeno 53
peak κορυφή f korreefee 85
pear αχλάδι nt ahkhlahdhee 53
pearl μαργαριτάρι nt
mahrghahreetahree 122
pedestrian πεζός m/f pehzoss 79
pen στυλό f steelo 105
pencil μολύβι nt molleevee 105
penicillin πενικιλλίνη f pehneekee-
leenee 142
penknife σουγιάς m sooyeeahss 107
pensioner συνταξιούχος m/f
seendahkseeookhoss 82
people άνθρωποι m/pl ahnthroppee 92
pepper πιπέρι nt peeperee 37, 64
per cent τις εκατόν teess ehkahtonn
148
percentage επί της εκατόν nt ehpee
teess ehkahtonn 131
per day την μέρα teen mehrah 20,
32, 89

perfume άρωμα nt ahrommah 110
perhaps ίσως eessoss 15
per hour την ώρα teen orrah 77, 89
period *(monthly)* περίοδος f pehreeodhoss 140
period pains πόνοι της περιόδου m/pl ponnee teess pehreeodhoo 140
permanent wave περμανάντ f pehrmahnahnd 30
permit άδεια f ahdheeah 90
per night την νύκτα teen neektah 24
person άτομο nt ahtommo 32
personal προσωπικός prossoppee-koss 17
personal/person-to-person call προσωπική κλήση f prossoppeekee kleessee 134
per week την βδομάδα teen vdhommahdhah 20, 24
petrol βενζίνη f vehnzeenee 75, 78
pewter κασσίτερος m kahsseetehross 122
photo φωτογραφία f fottoghrahfeeah 82, 124, 125
photocopy φωτοτυπία f fottottee-peeah 131
photographer φωτογράφος m fottoghrahfoss 99
photography φωτογραφείο nt fottoghrahfeeo 124
phrase φράση f frahsee 12
pick up, to *(person)* πέρνω pehrno 96
picnic πικ-νικ nt "picnic" 63, 107
picture πίναξ m peenahks 83; *(photo)* φωτογραφία f fottoghrahfeeah 82
piece κομμάτι nt komahtee 120
pigeon περιστέρι nt pehreestehree 48
pill χάπι nt khahpee 140, 142
pillow μαξιλάρι nt mahkseelahree 27
pin καρφίτσα f kahrfeetsah 121
pineapple ανανάς m ahnahnahss 53
pink ροζ rozz 113
pipe πίπα f peepah 126
pipe cleaner καθαριστήρας πίπας m kahthahreesteerahss peepahss 126
pipe tobacco καπνός πίπας m kahpnoss peepahss 126
pipe tool πανί πίπας nt pahnee peepahss 126
place τόπος m topposs 25; μέρος nt mehross 76
plane αεροπλάνο nt ahehroplahno 65

plaster *(cast)* γύψος m yeepsoss 139
plastic πλαστικό nt plahsteeko 107
plastic bag πλαστική τσάντα f plahsteekee tsahndah 107
plate πιάτο nt peeahto 36, 61, 107
platform *(station)* αποβάθρα f ahpovvahthrah 66, 67, 68, 69
platinum πλατίνα f plahteenah 122
play *(theatre)* έργο nt ehrgho 86
play, to παίζω pehzo 86, 88, 89, 93
playground γήπεδο nt gheepehdho 32
playing cards *(pack)* τράπουλα f trahpoolah 105
please παρακαλώ pahrahkahlo 10
plimsolls αθλητικά παπούτσια nt/pl ahthleeteekah pahpootseeah 118
plug *(electric)* πρίζα f preezah 29, 119
pneumonia πνευμονία f pnehvmonneeah 141
poached ποσέ posseh 42, 45
pocket τσέπι f tsehpee 117
pocket calculator υπολογιστική μηχανή τσέπης f eepollogeeestee-kee meekhahnee tsehpeess 105
point, to *(show)* δείχνω dheekhno 12
poison δηλητήριο nt dheeleeteereeo 109, 154
poisoning δηλητηρίαση f dheeleeteereeahssee 142
police αστυνομία f ahsteenommeeah 78, 154
police station αστυνομικό τμήμα nt ahsteenommeeko tmeemah 99, 154
pond μικρή λίμνη f meekree leemnee 85
pop music μουσική ποπ f moossee-kee pop 128
pork χοιρινό nt kheereeno 46
port λιμάνι nt leemahnee 74
portable φορητός forreetoss 119
porter αχθοφόρος m ahkhthofforross 18, 70; *(hotel)* θυρωρός m theerorross 26
portion μερίδα f mehreedhah 37, 54, 61
possible δυνατός dheenahtoss 136
post *(letters)* ταχυδρομείο nt tahkheedhrommeeo 28, 133
post, to ταχυδρομώ tahkheedhrommo 28
postage τιμή f teemee 132
postage stamp γραμματόσημο nt ghrahmahtosseemo 28, 126, 132

postcard καρτ-ποστάλ f kahrt-**postahl** 105, 126, 132

poste restante ποστ-ρεστάντ f post-rehstahnd 133

post office ταχυδρομείο nt tahkheedhrommeeo 99, 132

potato πατάτα f pahtahtah 40, 49

pothole λακούβα f lahkoovah 79

pottery αγγειοπλαστική f ahnggeeoplahsteekee 83, 127

poultry πουλερικά nt/pl poolehreekah 40, 48

pound (money) Αγγλική λίρα f ahngghleekee leerah 18, 102, 129

powder πούδρα f poodhrah 110, 121

prawn γαρίδα f ghahreedhah 41, 44

preference προτίμηση f protteemeessee 101

pregnant έγκυος ehnggeeoss 140

premium (gasoline) σούπερ soopehr 75

prescribe, to γράφω ghrahfo 142

prescription συνταγή f seendahyee 108, 142

present (gift) δώρο nt dhorro 17

press, to (iron) σιδερώνω seedhehronno 29

pressure πίεση f peeehssee 75, 140

pretty όμορφος ommorfoss 84

price τιμή f teemee 68

priest παπάς m pahpahss 84

private ιδιωτικός eedheeotteekoss 23, 80, 91

processing (photo) εμφάνιση f ehmfahneessee 125

profession επάγγελμα nt ehpahngghehlmah 25

profit κέρδος nt kehrdhoss 131

programme πρόγραμμα nt proghrahmah 87

prohibit, to απαγορεύω ahpahghorrehvo 32, 82

Protestant διαμαρτυρόμενος dheeahmahrteerommehnoss 84

provide, to βρίσκω vreesko 131

public holiday δημοσία αργία f dheemosseeah ahryeeah 151

pullover πουλόβερ m poolovvehr 116

purchase αγορά f ahghorrah 131

pure καθαρός kahthahross 114

purple πορφυρός porfeeross 113

put, to βάζω vahzo 24

pyjamas πυτζάμα f peedzahmah 117

Q

quality ποιότητα peeoteetah 103, 113

quantity ποσότητα f possotteetah 14, 103

quarter τέταρτο nt **teh**tahrto 148

quarter of an hour τέταρτο της ώρας nt **teh**tahrto teess orrahss 152

quartz χαλαζίας m khahlahzeeahss 122

question ερώτηση f ehrotteessee 11

quick γρήγορος ghreeghorross 14

quickly γρήγορα **ghree**ghorrah 36, 79, 136

quiet ήσυχος eesseekhoss 23, 25

R

rabbi ραββίνος m rahveenoss 84

rabbit κουνέλι nt koonehlee 48

race course/track ιππόδρομος m eepodhrommoss 90

racket (sport) ρακέτα f rahkehtah 90

radiator (car) ψυγείο nt pseeyeeo 78

radio (set) ράδιο nt rahdheeo 28, 119

railroad/railway station σιδηροδρομικός σταθμός m seedeerodhrommeekoss stathmoss 19, 66

rain, to βρέχω vrehkho 94

raincoat αδιάβροχο nt ahdheeahvrokho 117

raisin σταφίδα f stahfeedhah 53

rangefinder αποστασιόμετρο nt ahpostahsseeommehtro 125

rare (meat) λιγοψημένος leeghopseemehnoss 47

rash εξάνθημα nt ehksahntheemah 138

raspberry βατόμουρο nt vahtommooro 53

rate τιμή teemee f 18, 20, 130

razor ξυριστική μηχανή f kseereesteekee meekhahnee 110

razor blade ξυραφάκι για το ξύρισμα nt kseerahfahkee yeeah to kseereezmah 111

ready έτοιμος ehteemoss 29, 118, 125

real αληθινός ahleetheenoss 121

rear πίσω peesso 75

receipt απόδειξη f ahpodheeksee 103, 143

reception ρεσεπσιόν f rehssehpseeonn 23

receptionist υπάλληλος υποδοχής m/f eepahleeloss eepodhokhees, ρεσεπσιονίστ m/f rehssehpseeonneest 26

DICTIONARY

recommend, to συστήνω seesteeno 22, 35, 36, 41, 49, 136, 144; προτείνω protteeno 80, 86, 88
record *(disc)* δίσκος m dheeskoss 128
record player πικ-απ nt ''pick-up'' 119
rectangular μακρόστενος mahkrostehnoss 101
red κόκκινος kokkeenoss 53, 58, 105, 113
reduction έκπτωση f ehkptossee 24, 82
refund επιστροφή f ehpeestroffee 103
register, to *(luggage)* καταγράφω kahtahghrahfo 70
registered mail συστημένο nt seesteemehno 132
registration καταγραφή f kahtahgrahfee 25
regular *(petrol)* απλή ahplee 75
religion θρησκεία f threeskeeah 83
rent, to *(hire)* νοικιάζω neekeeahzo 19, 20, 74, 90, 91
rental ενοικίαση f ehneekeeahssee 20, 74
repair επισκευή f ehpeeskehvee 125
repair, to επιδιορθώνω ehpeedheeorthonno 29, 118, 121, 123, 144
repeat, to επαναλαμβάνω ehpahnahlahmvahno 12
report, to *(a theft)* καταγγέλω kahtahnggehlo 154
require, to απαιτώ ahpeeto 88
reservation κράτηση f krahteessee 19, 23, 65, 68
reservations office γραφείο κρατήσεως nt ghrahfeeo krahteessehoss 68
reserve, to κρατώ krahto 19, 23, 35, 36, 87, 153
resinated *(wine)* ρετσινομένος rehtseenomehnoss 58
resinated wine ρετσίνα f rehtseenah 58
restaurant εστιατόριο nt ehsteeahtorreeo 19, 32, 35, 66
return *(ticket)* μετ'επιστροφής mehtehpeestroffeess 68
return, to *(give back)* επιστρέφω ehpeestrehfo 103
reversed charge call κλήση πληρωτέα από τον παραλήπτη f kleessee pleerottehah ahpo tonn pahrahleeptee 134

rheumatism ρευματισμός m rehvmahteezmoss 140
rib πλευρό nt plehvro 137
rice ρύζι nt reezee 40, 49
right δεξιός/-ά/-ό dhehkseeoss 21, 63, 77, 79; *(correct)* σωστός sostoss 14, 69, 76
ring *(on finger)* δακτυλίδι nt dhahkteeleedhee 122
river ποταμός m pottahmoss 85
road δρόμος m dhrommoss 76, 85
road assistance οδική βοήθεια f odheekee voeetheeah 78
road map οδικός χάρτης m odheekoss khahrteess 105
road sign σήμα τροχαίας nt seemah trokhehahss 79
roast beef ροσμπίφ nt rozbeef 46
roasted ψητός pseetoss 47
rock βράχος m vrahkhoss 59
roll *(bread)* ψωμάκι nt psommahkee 38, 64
room δωμάτιο nt dhommahteeo 19, 22, 23, 24, 25, 27, 28; *(space)* μέρος mehross 32
room service σέρβις δωματίου nt sehrveess dhommahteeoo 23
rope σχοινί nt skheenee 107
rosé ροζέ rozzeh 58
round στρογγυλός stronggeeloss 101
roundtrip *(ticket)* μετ'επιστροφής mehtehpeestroffeess 65, 68
route διαδρομή f dheeahdhrommee 85
rowing boat βάρκα με κουπιά f vahrkah meh koopeeah 91
royal βασιλικός vahsseeleekoss 81
rubber λάστιχο nt lahsteekho 118; *(eraser)* γομολάστιχα f ghommollahsteekhah 105
ruby ρουμπίνι nt roombeenee 122
rucksack ταξιδιωτικός σάκκος m tahkseedheeotteekoss sahkoss 107
ruin ερείπιο nt ehreepeeo 81
ruler *(for measuring)* χάρακας m khahrahkahss 105
rum ρούμι nt roomee 59

S
saddle σέλλα f sehlah 46
safe *(not dangerous)* ακίνδυνος ahkeendheenoss 90
safe χρηματοκιβώτιο nt khreemahtokkeevotteeo 26

Λεξικό

safety pin παραμάνα f pahrahmahnah 111

sailing ιστιοπλοΐα f eesteeoploeeah 89

sailing boat βάρκα με πανί f vahrkah meh pahnee 91

salad σαλάτα f sahlahtah 41, 42, 63

sale πώληση f polleessee 131; *(bargains)* εκπτώσεις f/pl ehkptossess 101

sales tax φόρος m forross 102

salmon σολομός m sollommoss 41

salt αλάτι nt ahlahtee 37, 64

salty αλμυρός ahlmeeross 61

same ίδιος eedheeoss 118

sand άμμος f ahmoss 90

sandal σάνδαλο nt sahndhahlo 118

sandwich σάντουιτς nt sahndooeetss 63

sanitary towel/napkin σερβιέττα υγείας f sehrveeeehtah eeyeeahss 109

sapphire ζαφείρι nt zahfeeree 122

sardine σαρδέλλα f sahrdhehlah 41, 44

Saturday Σάββατο nt sahvahto 150

sauce σάλτσα f sahltsah 51

saucepan κατσαρόλα f kahtsahrollah 107

saucer πιατάκι nt peeahtahkee 107

sausage λουκάνικο nt lookahneeko 43, 46, 64

scarf κασκόλ nt kahskoll 117

school σχολείο nt skholleeo 79

scissors ψαλίδι nt psahleedhee 107, 110

scooter βέσπα f vehspah 74

Scottish *(person)* Σκωτζέζος/-α m/f skotzehzoss/-ah 92

scrambled egg χτυπητό αυγό khteepeeto ahvgho 38

screwdriver κατσαβίδι nt kahtsahveedhee 107

sculptor γλύπτης m ghleepteess 83

sculpture γλυπτική f ghleepteekee 83

sea θάλασσα f thahlahssah 23, 85, 90

seafood θαλασσινά nt/pl thahlahsseenah 40, 44

season εποχή f ehpokhee 149; *(tourism)* σαιζόν nt sehzonn 149

seasoning καρυκεύματα nt/pl kahreekehvmahtah 37

seat θέση f thehssee 68, 69, 87

second δεύτερος dhehftehross 148

second λεπτό nt lehpto 152

second class δεύτερη θέση f dhehftehree thehssee 68

second-hand μεταχειρισμένος mehtahkheereezmehnoss 104

secretary γραμματέας m/f ghrahmahtehahss 27, 131

see, to βλέπω vlehpo 159

sell, to πωλώ pollo 100

send, to στέλνω stehlno 26, 78, 102, 103, 132, 133

sentence πρόταση f prottahssee 12

separately χωριστά khorreestah 62

September Σεπτέμβριος m sehptehmvreeoss 149

serious σοβαρός sovvahross 138

service ποσοστό υπηρεσίας nt possosto eepeerehsseeahss 24; σερβίρισμα nt sehrveereezmah 62; *(religion)* λειτουργία f leetooryeeah 84

serviette πετσέτα f pehtsehtah 36

setting lotion αφρό-λακ m ahfro-lahk 30

seven επτά ehptah 146

seventeen δεκαεπτά dhehkahehptah 146

seventh έβδομος ehvdhommoss 148

seventy εβδομήντα ehvdhommeendah 147

sew, to ράβω rahvo 29

shampoo σαμπουάν nt sahmbooahn 30, 111

shape σχήμα nt skheemah 103

shape to *(hair)* φορμαρίζω formahreezo 30

share *(finance)* μετοχή f mehtokhee 131

sharp οξύς/-εία/-ύ oksseess 139

shave, to ξυρίζω kseereezo 31

shaver ξυριστική μηχανή f kseereesteekee meekhahnee 27, 119

shaving cream κρέμα ξυρίσματος f krehmah kseereezmahtoss 111

she αυτή ahftee 158

shelf ράφι nt rahfee 120

sherbet γρανίτα f ghrahneetah 54

sherry τσέρι nt tsehree 59

shingle *(on beach)* χαλίκι nt khahleekee 90

ship πλοίο nt pleeo 74

shirt πουκάμισο nt pookahmeesso 117

shivers ρίγος nt reeghoss 139

shoe παπούτσι nt pahpootsee 118

shoelace κορδόνι υποδημάτων nt kordhonnee eepodheemahtonn 118

shoemaker's τσαγκάρης m tsahnggahreess 99

shoe polish μπογιά f boyeeah 118

shoe shop υποδηματοποιείο nt eepodheemahtoppeeeeo 99

shop κατάστημα nt kahtahsteemah 98

shopping ψώνια nt/pl psonneeah 97

shopping centre κεντρικά καταστήματα nt/pl kehndreekah kahtahsteemahtah 99

shop window βιτρίνα f veetreenah 100, 112

short κοντός kondoss 30, 115

shorts σορτς nt sortss 117

short-sighted μύωπας m/f meeopahss 123

shoulder ώμος m ommoss 137

shovel φτυάρι nt fteeahree 128

show παράσταση f pahrahstahssee 86, 87

show, to δείχνω dheekhno 12, 76, 100, 101, 103, 119, 124

shower ντους nt dooss 23, 32

shrimp γαρίδα f ghahreedha 44

shrink, to μαζεύω mahzehvo 29, 114

shut κλειστός kleestoss 14

shutter (window) εξώφυλλο nt ehksofeelo 29; (camera) διάφραγμα nt dheeahfrahghmah 125

sick (ill) άρρωστος ahrostoss 139, 154

sickness (illness) αρρώστια f ahrosteeah 139

side πλάγι nt plahyee 30

sideboards/burns φαβορίτες f/pl fahvorreetehss 31

sightseeing αξιοθέατα nt/pl ahkseeothehahtah 80

sightseeing tour περιοδία στα αξιοθέατα f pehreeodheeah stah ahkseeothehahtah 80

sign (notice) σήμα nt seemah 77, 79, 153

sign, to υπογράφω eepoghrahfo 26, 130

signature υπογραφή f eepoghrahfee 25

silk μεταξωτό nt mehtahksotto 114

silver (colour) ασημένιος/-α/-ο ahseemehneeoss 113

silver ασήμι nt ahsseeemee 121, 122

silverware ασημικά nt/pl ahseemeekah 122, 127

simple απλός ahploss 124

since από ahpo 15, 149

sing, to τραγουδώ trahghoodho 88

single (ticket) απλό ahplo 68, 74

single (not married) ελεύθερος/-η m/f ehlehfthehross/-ee 93

single room μονό δωμάτιο nt monno dhommahteeo 19, 23

sister αδελφή f ahdhehlfee 93

sit, to κάθομαι kahthommeh 95

six έξι ehksee 146

sixteen δεκαέξι dhehkahehksee 146

sixth έκτος ehktoss 148

sixty εξήντα ehkseendah 146

size μέγεθος nt mehyehthoss 114, 115, 118, 124

skiing χιονοδρομία f kheeonnodhrommeeah 89

skin δέρμα nt dhehrmah 137

skin-diving υποβρήχιο ψάρεμα nt eepovreekheeo psahrehmah 91

skirt φούστα f foostah 117

sky ουρανός m oorahnoss 94

sleep, to κοιμάμαι keemahmeh 143

sleeping bag σάκος ύπνου m sahkoss eepnoo 107

sleeping car βαγκόν-λι nt vahgonn lee 68, 69

sleeping pill υπνωτικό χάπι nt eepnoteeko khahpee 143

sleeve μανίκι nt mahneekee 116

slice φέτα f fehtah 120

slide (photo) σλάιντ nt "slide" 124

slip κομπινεζόν nt kombeenehzonn 117

slipper παντόφλα f pahndoflah 118

slow αργός ahrghoss 14

slowly αργά ahrghah 11, 21, 135

small μικρός meekross 14, 20, 25, 37, 54, 101, 118, 130

small change ψιλά nt/pl pseelah 130

smoke, to καπνίζω kahpneezo 95

smoked καπνιστός kahpneestoss 41, 45

smoker καπνιστής m kahpneesteess 69

snack σνακ nt "snack" 35, 63

snack bar σνακ μπαρ nt "snack bar" 66

snap fastener σούστα f soostah 117

sneakers αθλητικά παπούτσια nt/pl ahthleeteekah pahpootseeah 118

snow χιόνι nt kheeonnee 94
snow, to χιονίζω kheeonneezo 94
soap σαπούνι nt sahpoonee 27, 111
soccer ποδόσφαιρο nt podhosfehro 89
sock κάλτσα f kahltsah 117
socket υποδοχή πρίζας f eepodhokhee preezahss 27
soft drink αναψυκτικό nt ahnahpseekteeko 40, 64
sole σόλα f sollah 118; (fish) γλώσσα f ghlossah 44
some μερικά mehreekah 14
someone κάποιος/-α/ο kahpeeoss 95
something κάτι kahtee 29, 36, 54, 108, 112, 113, 125, 138
somewhere κάπου kahpoo 87
son γιός m yeeoss 93
song τραγούδι nt trahghoodhee 128
soon σύντομα seendommah 15
sore (painful) ερεθισμένος ehrehtheezmehnoss 144
sore throat λαιμόπονος m lehmopponnoss 140
sorry (I'm) συγγνώμη seenghnommee 10, 16
sort (kind) είδος nt eedhoss 86, 120
soup σούπα f soopah 43
souvenir σουβενίρ nt soovehneer, ενθύμιο nt ehntheemeeo 127
souvenir shop κατάστημα σουβενίρ nt kahtahsteemah soovehneer 99
spade φτυαράκι nt fteeahrahkee 128
spare tyre ρεζέρβα f rehzehrvah 75
spark(ing) plug μπουζί nt boozee 76
speak, to μιλώ meelo 11, 135
special ειδικός eedheekoss 20, 37
special delivery εξπρές "express" 132
specialist ειδικός m/f eedheekoss 141
speciality σπεσιαλιτέ f spehsseeahleeteh 40, 59
specimen (medical) δείγμα nt dheeghmah 141
spell, to συλλαβίζω seelahveezo 12
spend, to ξοδεύω ksodhehvo 101
spice μπαχαρικό nt bahkhahreeko 51
spinach σπανάκι nt spahnahkee 50
spine σπονδυλική στήλη f spondheeleekee steelee 137
sponge σφουγγάρι nt sfoonggahree 111
spoon κουτάλι nt kootahlee 36, 61, 107

sport αθλητισμός m ahthleeteezmoss 89
sporting goods shop κατάστημα αθλητικών ειδών nt kahtahsteemah ahthleeteekonn eedhonn 99
sprain, to στραμπουλίζω strahmbooleezo 139
spring (season) άνοιξη f ahneeksee 149; (water) πηγή f peeyee 85
square τετράγωνος tehtrahghonnoss 101
square (open space) πλατεία f plahteeah 82
squid καλαμάρι nt kahlahmahree 44
stadium στάδιο nt stahdheeo 82
stain λεκές m lehkehss 29
stamp (postage) γραμματόσημο nt ghrahmahtosseemo 28, 126, 132
star αστέρι nt ahstehree, άστρο nt ahstro 94
start, to αρχίζω ahrkheezo 80, 87, 88; (car) ξεκινώ ksehkeeno 78
starter (appetizer) ορεκτικό nt orehkteeko 41
station σταθμός m stahthmoss 19, 21, 66, 73
stationer's χαρτοπωλείο nt khahrtoppolleeo 99, 104
statue άγαλμα nt ahghahlmah 82
stay διαμονή f dheeahmonnee 31, 92
stay, to μένω mehno 16, 24, 26, 93
steak μπιφτέκι m beeftehkee 46
steal, to κλέπτω klehpto 154
stiff neck στραβολαίμιαση f strahvollehmeeahssee 140
sting κέντρισμα nt kehndreezmah 138
sting, to κεντρίζω kehndreezo 138
stitch, to ράβω rahvo 29, 118
stock exchange χρηματιστήριο nt khreemahteesteereeo 82
stocking κάλτσα γυναικεία f kahltsah yeenehkeeah 117
stomach στομάχι nt stommahkhee 137
stomach ache πόνος στο στομάχι m ponnoss sto stommahkhee 144
stools κόπρανα nt/pl koprahnah 141
stop (bus) στάση f stahssee 72
stop! σταμάτα! stahmahtah 154
stop, to σταματώ stahmahto 21, 69, 71, 72, 73, 154
store κατάστημα nt kahtahsteemah 98
straight (drink) σκέτος skehtoss 59

straight ahead ίσια eesseeah 21, 77
strange παράξενος pahrahksehnoss
84
straw *(drinking)* καλαμάκι nt
kahlahmahkee 63
strawberry φράουλα f frahoolah 53
street οδός f odhoss 25
street map οδηκός χάρτης m
odheekoss khahrteess 19, 105
string σπάγγος m spahnggoss 105
student φοιτητής/φοιτήτρια m/f
feeteeteess/feeteetreeah 82, 93
study, to σπουδάζω spoodhahzo 93
stuffed γεμιστός yehmeestoss 41,
47

subway *(rail)* Ηλεκτρικός m
eelehktreekoss 73
sufficient αρκετός ahrkehtoss 67
sugar ζάχαρη f zahkhahree 37, 64
suit κουστούμι nt koostoomee 117;
(woman) ταγιέρ nt tahyeeehr 117
suitcase βαλίτσα f vahleetsah 18
summer καλοκαίρι nt kahlokkehree
149
sun ήλιος m eeleeoss 94
sunburn ηλιακό έγκαυμα nt eeleeahko
ehnggahvmah 108
Sunday Κυριακή f keereeahkee 150
sunglasses γυαλιά ηλίου nt/pl
yeeahleeah eeleeoo 123
sunshade *(beach)* τέντα για τον ήλιο f
tehndah yeeah tonn eeleeo 91
sunstroke ηλίαση f eeleeahssee 140
sun-tan cream κρέμα για τον ήλιο f
krehmah yeeah tonn eeleeo 111
sun-tan oil λάδι για τον ήλιο nt
lahdhee yeeah tonn eeleeo 111
super *(petrol)* σούπερ soopehr 75
supermarket σούπερ μάρκετ nt
"supermarket" 99
suppository υπόθετο nt eepothehto
109
surfboard κανώ nt kahno 91
surname επώνυμο nt ehponneemo 25
suspenders *(Am.)* τιράντες f/pl
teerahndehss 117
swallow, to καταπίνω kahtahpeeno
142
sweater πουλόβερ nt poolovvehr 117
sweatshirt φανελάκι σπορ nt
fahnehlahkee sporr 117
sweet *(food)* γλυκός ghleekoss 55,
58, 61
sweet *(candy)* καραμέλα f
kahrahmehlah 126

sweet corn καλαμπόκι nt
kahlahmbokkee 49
sweetener ζαχαρίνη f zahkhahreenee
37
swell, to πρήζω preezo 138
swelling πρήξιμο nt preekseemo
138
swim, to κολυμπώ kolleembo 90
swimming κολύμπηση f
kolleembeessee 89
swimming pool πισίνα f peesseenah
32, 90
swimming trunks μαγιό nt mahyeeo
117
swimsuit μαγιό nt mahyeeo 117
switch διακόπτης m dheeahkopteess
29
synagogue συναγωγή f seenahgho-
yee 84
synthetic συνθετικός seenthehteekoss
113
system σύστημα nt seesteemah 137

T
table τραπέζι nt trahpehzee 36, 107
tablet χάπι nt khahpee 109
tailor's ραφείο nt rahfeeo 99
take, to πέρνω pehrno 18, 25, 63,
72, 102
talcum powder ταλκ nt tahlk 111
tampon τάμπο nt tahmbo 109
tangerine μανταρίνι nt
mahndahreenee 53
tap *(water)* βρύση f vreessee 28
tape recorder κασσετόφωνο nt
kahssehtoffonno 119
tart πάστα f pahstah 54
tax φόρος m forross 32, 102
taxi ταξί nt tahksee 19, 21, 31
tea τσάι nt tsahee 38, 60, 64
team ομάδα f ommahdhah 89
tear, to σχίζω skheezo 139
teaspoon κουταλάκι f kootahlahkee
107, 142
telegram τηλεγράφημα nt
teelehghrahfeemah 133
telephone τηλέφωνο nt teelehfonno
28, 78, 79, 134
telephone, to τηλεφωνώ teelehfonno
134
telephone booth τηλεφωνικός
θάλαμος m teelehfonneekoss
thahlahmoss 134
telephone call τηλεφώνημα nt
teelehfonneemah 136

telephone directory τηλεφωνικός κατάλογος m teelehfonneekoss kahtahloghoss 134

telephone number αριθμός τηλεφώνου m ahreethmoss teelehfonnoo 134, 135

telephoto lens τηλεφακός m teelehfahkoss 125

television (set) τηλεόραση f teelehorrahssee 28, 119

telex τέλεξ nt ''telex'' 130, 133

tell, to λέγω lehgho 12, 72, 76, 135, 152

temperature θερμοκρασία f thehrmokrahsseeah 90, 141; (fever) πυρετός m peerehtoss 139

ten δέκα dhehkah 146

tendon τένοντας m tehnondahss 137

tennis τέννις nt ''tennis'' 89

tennis court γήπεδο του τέννις nt yeepehdho too ''tennis''

tennis racket ρακέτα του τέννις f rahkehtah too ''tennis'' 90

tent σκηνή f skeenee 32, 107

tenth δέκατος dhehkahtoss 148

tent peg πάσσαλος m pahssahloss 107

tent pole κοντάρι nt kondahree 107

term (word) έκφραση f ehkfrahssee 131

terrace ταράτσα f tahrahtsah 36

tetanus τέτανος m tehtahnoss 139

than από ahpo 15

thanks ευχαριστώ ehfkhahreesto 10

that εκείνος ehkeenoss 159

the o, η, το o, ee, to 156

theatre θέατρο nt thehahtro 82, 86

theft κλοπή f kloppee 154

their τους tooss 159

then τότε totteh 15

there εκεί ehkee 13

thermometer θερμόμετρο nt thermommehtro 109, 143

these αυτοί/-ές/-ά ahftee 159

they αυτοί/-ές/-ά ahftee 158

thief κλέφτης m klehfteess 154

thigh μηρός m meeross 137

thin λεπτός lehptoss 113

think, to (believe) νομίζω nommeezo 31, 62

third τρίτος treetoss 148

third τρίτο nt treeto 148

thirsty, to be διψώ dheepso 13, 35

thirteen δεκατρία dhehkahtreeah 146

thirty τριάντα treeahndah 146

this αυτός ahftoss 159

those εκείνοι/-αι/-α ehkeenee 159

thousand χίλια kheeleeah 147

thread κλωστή f klostee 27

three τρία treeah 146

throat λαιμός m lehmoss 137, 140

throat lozenge παστίλλια για το λαιμό f pahsteeleeah yeeah to lehmo 109

through δια μέσου dheeah mehssoo 15

thunder βροντή f vrondee 94

thunderstorm θύελλα f theeehlah 94

Thursday Πέμπτη f pehmptee 150

ticket εισιτήριο nt eesseeteereeo 68, 87, 89

ticket office γραφείο εισιτηρίων nt ghrahfeeo eesseeteereeonn 67

tide (high) παλίρροια f pahleerreeah 90; (low) άμπωτη f ahmbottee 90

tie γραβάτα f ghrahvahtah 117

tight (clothes) στενός stehnoss 115

tights καλτσόν nt kahltsonn 117

time (clock) ώρα f orrah 34, 67, 80, 136, 152; (occasion) φορά f forrah 142, 148

timetable ωράριο nt orrahreeo 67

tin (can) κουτί nt kootee 120

tinfoil αλλουμινόχαρτο nt ahloomeenokhahrto 107

tin opener ανοιχτήρι κονσέρβας nt ahneekhteeree konsehrvahss 107

tint ελαφρυά βαφή f ehlahfreeah vahfee 111

tinted φιμέ feemeh 123

tire λάστιχο nt lahsteekho 75, 76

tired κουρασμένος koorahzmehnoss 13

tissue (handkerchief) χαρτομάντηλο nt khartommahndeelo 111

to (direction) προς pross 15

toast τοστ nt tost 38

tobacco καπνός m kahpnoss 126

tobacconist's καπνοπωλείο nt kahpnoppolleeo 99, 126

today σήμερα seemehrah 29, 150

toilet (lavatory) τουαλέττα f tooahlehtah 23

toilet paper χαρτί υγείας nt khahrtee eeyeeahss 111

toiletry καλλυντικά nt/pl kahleendeekah 110

toilets τουαλέττες f/pl tooahlehtehss 32, 37, 67

toilet water ω ντε τουαλλέτ f o deh tooahleht 111

toll διόδια f dheeodheeah 79

tomato ντομάτα f dommahtah 42, 43, 49

tomato juice χυμός ντομάτας m kheemoss dommahtahss 60

tomb τάφος m tahfoss 82

tomorrow αύριο ahvreeo 29, 136, 150

tongs τσιμπίδα f tseembeedhah 107

tongue γλώσσα f ghlossah 46, 137

tonic water τόνικ m tonneek 60

tonight απόψε ahpopseh 86, 87, 96

tonsils αμυγδαλές m/pl ahmeeghdhahlehss 137

too πάρα πολύ pahrah pollee 14; (also) επίσης ehpeesseess 15

tooth δόντι nt dhondee 144

toothache πονόδοντος m ponnodhondoss 144

toothbrush οδοντόβουρτσα f odhondovoortsah 111, 119

toothpaste οδοντόπαστα f odhondopahstah 111

torch (flashlight) φακός m fahkoss

tough (meat) σκληρός skleeross 61

tour περιοδεία f pehreeodheeah 16, 80

tourist office γραφείο τουρισμού nt ghrahfeeo tooreezmoo 19, 80

tow truck ρυμουλκό nt reemoolko 78

towards προς pross 15

towel πετσέτα f pehtsehtah 111

tower πύργος m peerghoss 82

town πόλη f pollee 19, 21, 76, 105

town hall δημαρχείο nt dheemarkheeo 82

toy παιχνίδι nt pehkhneedhee 128

toy shop κατάστημα παιχνιδιών nt kahtahsteemah pehkneedheeonn 99

tracksuit φόρμα f formah 117

traffic light φανάρι nt fahnahree 77

trailer τροχόσπιτο nt trokhospeeto 32

train τραίνο nt trehno 18, 66, 67, 68, 69, 70, 73, 152

tranquillizer ηρεμιστικό nt eerehmeesteeko 142

transfer (bank) μεταβίβαση f mehtahveevahssee 131

transformer μετασχηματιστής m mehtahskheemahteesteess 119

translate, to μεταφράζω mehtahfrahzo 12

transport μεταφορά f mehtahforrah 74

travel, to ταξιδεύω tahkseedhehvo 93

travel agency πρακτορείο ταξιδίων nt prahktorreeo tahkseedheeonn 99

traveller's cheque τράβελερς τσεκ nt trahvehlehrs tsehk 18, 62, 102, 129

travelling bag σακβουαγιάζ nt sahkvooahyeeahz 18

travel sickness ναυτία f nahfteeah 108

treatment θεραπεία f thehrahpeeah 142

tree δέντρο nt dhehndro 85

trim, to (beard) κόβω kovvo 31

trip ταξίδι nt tahkseedhee 71, 151

trolley καροτσάκι nt kahrotsahkee 18, 70

trousers παντελόνι nt pahndehlonnee 117

trout πέστροφα f pehstroffah 44

try, to δοκιμάζω dhokkeemahzo 59, 115, 135

T-shirt τι-σερτ nt teessehrt 117

tube σωληνάριο nt solleenahreeo 120

Tuesday Τρίτη f treetee 150

tuna τόννος m tonnoss 41, 44

tunny τόννος m tonnoss 41, 44

Turkey Τουρκία f toorkeeah 145

turkey γαλοπούλα f ghahloppoolah 48

turn, to (change direction) στρίβω streevo 21, 77

turquoise τουρκουάζ nt toorkooahz 122

tweezers τσιμπίδι για φρύδια nt tseembeedhee yeeah freedheeah 111

twelve δώδεκα dhodhehkah 146

twenty είκοσι eekossee 146

twice δύο φορές dheeo forrehss 148

twin beds δύο κρεββάτια nt/pl dheeo krehvahteeah 23

two δύο dheeo 146

typewriter γραφομηχανή f ghrahfommeekhahnee 27

tyre λάστιχο nt lahsteekho 75, 76

U

ugly άσχημος ahskheemoss 14, 84

umbrella ομπρέλα f ombrehlah 117

uncle θείος m theeoss 93

under κάτω από **kahto ahpo** 15
underdone *(meat)* άψητος **ahpseetoss**
61
underground *(railway)* Ηλεκτρικός *m*
eelehtreekoss 73
underpants σώβρακο *nt* sovrahko
117
undershirt φανέλλα εσώρουχο *f*
fahnehlah ehssorookho 117
understand, to καταλαβαίνω
kahtahlahvehno 12, 16
undress, to γδύνομαι **ghdheenommeh**
141
university πανεπιστήμιο *nt* pahneh-
peesteemeeo 82
unleaded χωρίς μόλυβδο *nt* khorreess
molleevdho 75
unresinated *(wine)* αρετσίνωτος
ahrehtseenottoss 58
until μέχρι **mehkhree** 15
up επάνω **ehpahno** 15
upset stomach στομαχική ανωμαλία *f*
stommahkheekee ahnommah-
leeah 108
urgent επείγων/-ουσα/-ον **ehpee-**
ghonn/-oossah/-onn 13, 144
urine ούρο *nt* **ooro** 141
use χρήση *f* **khreessee** 17
use, to χρησιμοποιώ
khreesseemoppeeo 78, 134
useful χρήσιμος **khreesseemoss** 15
usual συνηθισμένος
seeneetheezmehnoss 142

V

vacant ελεύθερος **ehlehfthehross** 14;
άδειος/-α/-ο **ahdheoss** 22
vacation διακοπές *f/pl*
dheeahkoppehss 150, 151
vaccinate, to εμβολιάζω
ehmvolleeahzo 139
vacuum flask θερμός *m* **thehrmoss**
107
valley κοιλάδα *f* keelahdhah 85
value τιμή *f* **teemee** 131
vanilla βανίλια *f* vahneeleeah 54
veal μοσχάρι *nt* moskhahree 46
vegetable λαχανικόν *nt*
lahkhahneekonn 40, 43, 49
vegetable store μανάβικο *nt*
mahnahveeko
vegetarian χορτοφάγος *m/f*
khortofahghoss 37
vein φλέβα *f* flehvah 137
velvet βελούδο *nt* vehloodho 114

venereal disease αφροδισιακό νόσημα
nt ahfrodheesseeahko nossseemah
144
vermouth βερμούτ *nt* vehrmoot 59
very πολύ **pollee** 15
vest φανέλλα εσώρουχο *f* fahnehlah
ehssorookho 117; *(Am.)* γιλέκο *nt*
yeelehko 117
video cassette βίντεο-κασέττα *f*
veedeho-kahssehtah 119, 124
video recorder βίντεο *nt* veedeho
119
view θέα *f* thehah 23, 25
village χωριό *nt* khorreeo 76, 85
vinegar ξύδι *nt* kseedhee 37
vineyard αμπέλι *nt* ahmbehlee 85
visit, to επισκέπτομαι
ehpeeskehptommeh 84, 95
vitamins βιταμίνες *f/pl*
veetahmeenehss 109
vodka βότκα *f* votkah 59
volleyball βόλεϋ *nt* vollehee 89
vomit, to κάνω εμετό **kahno ehmehto**
139

W

waistcoat γιλέκο *nt* yeelehko 117
wait, to περιμένω pehreemehno 21,
95, 108
waiter σερβιτόρος *m* sehrveetorross
36
waiting room αίθουσα αναμονής *f*
ehthoossah ahnahmonneess 67
waitress σερβιτόρα *f* sehrveeterrahss
36
wake up, to ξυπνώ kseepno 70
Wales Ουαλία *f* ooahleeah 145
walk, to περπατώ pehrphahto 74, 85
wall τοίχος *m* teekhoss 85
wallet πορτοφόλι *nt* portoffollee 154
walnut καρύδι *nt* kahreedhee 53
want, to *(wish)* θέλω thehlo 13
warm ζεστός zehstoss 94
wash, to πλένω plehno 29, 114
washbasin νιπτήρας *m* neepteerahss
28
washing powder σκόνη πλησίματος *f*
skonnee pleesseemahtoss 107
watch ρολόι *nt* rolloee 121, 122
watchmaker's ωρολογοποιείο *nt*
orrologhoppeeeeo 99, 121
watchstrap μπρασελέ για ρολόι *nt*
brahssehleh yeeah rolloee 121
water νερό *nt* nehro 23, 28, 32, 38,
75, 90

water flask παγούρι *nt* pahghooree 107

watermelon καρπούζι *nt* kahrpoozee 53

waterproof αδιάβροχος ahdheeahvrokhoss 122

water-ski θαλάσσιο σκι *nt* thahlah-sseeo "ski" 91

wave κύμα *nt* keemah 90

way δρόμος *m* dhrommos 76

we (ε)μείς (eh)meess 158

weather καιρός *m* kehross 94

weather forecast πρόβλεψη καιρού *f* provlehpsee kehroo 94

wedding ring βέρα *f* vehrah 122

Wednesday Τετάρτη *f* tehtahrtee 150

week βδομάδα *f* vdhommahdhah 16, 20, 24, 80, 150

weekend Σαββατοκύριακο *nt* sahvahtokkeereeahko 20, 150

well καλά kahlah 9, 115, 139

well-done *(meat)* καλοψημένος kahlopseemehnoss 47

west δύση dheessee 77

what τι tee 11

wheel τροχός *m* trohkhoss 78

when πότε potteh 11

where που poo 11

which ποιος/ποια/ποιο peeoss/peeah/peeo 11

whisky ουίσκι *nt* "whisky" 59

white άσπρος ahspross 58, 113

who ποιος peeoss 11

why γιατί yeeahtee 11

wick φιτίλι *nt* feeteelee 126

wide φαρδός/-ιά/-ί fahrdheess 118

wide-angle lens ευρυγώνιος φακός *m* ehvreeghonneeoss fahkoss 125

wife γυναίκα *f* yeenehkah 93

wig περούκα *f* pehrookah 111

wind άνεμος *m* ahnehmoss 94

window παράθυρο *nt* pahrahtheero 28, 36, 68; *(shop)* βιτρίνα *f* veetreenah 100, 112

windscreen/shield παρ-μπριζ *nt* pahrbreez 76

wine κρασί *nt* krahssee 40, 57, 58, 61, 64, 127

wine merchant's οινοπωλείο *nt* eenoppolleeo 99

winter χειμώνας *m* kheemonnahss 149

wiper καθαριστήρας *nt* kahthahreesteerahss 76

windsurfer γουίντσέρφερ *nt* "windsurfer" 91

wish ευχή *f* ehfkhee 151

with με meh 15

withdraw, to *(bank)* σηκώνω seekonno 130

without χωρίς khorreess 15

woman γυναίκα *f* yeenehkah 115

wonderful υπέροχος eepehrokhoss 96

wood *(forest)* δάσος *nt* dhahssoss 85

wool μαλλί *nt* mahlee 114

word λέξη *f* lehksee 12, 15, 133

work, to *(function)* λειτουργώ lee-toorgho 28; δουλεύω doolehvo 119

worse χειρότερος kheerottehross 14

wound πληγή *f* pleeyee 138

wrap, to τυλίσσω teeleesso 103

wristwatch ρολόι χεριού *nt* rolloee khehreeoo 122

write, to γράφω ghrahfo 12, 101

writing paper χαρτί αλληλογραφίας *nt* kahrtee ahleeloghrahfeeahss 27

wrong λανθασμένος lahnthahzmehnos 14

X

X-ray *(photo)* ακτινογραφία *f* ahkteenoghrahfeeah 139

Y

year χρόνος *m* khronnoss 148

yellow κίτρινος keetreenoss 113

yes ναι neh 10

yesterday χθες khthehss 150

yet ακόμη ahkommee 15, 16, 24

yield, to *(traffic)* δίνω πρωτοπορεία dheedho prottopporeeah 79

yoghurt γιαούρτι *nt* yeeahoortee 38, 64

you εσύ ehssee, εσείς ehsseess 158

young νέος/-α/-ο nehoss 14

your σου soo, σας sahss 158

youth hostel ξενώνας νεότητος *m* ksehnonnahss nehotteetoss 22

Yugoslavia Γιουγκοσλαβία *f* yeeoonggoslahveeah 145

Z

zero μηδέν meedhehn 146

zip(per) φερμουάρ *nt* fehrmooahr 117

zoo ζωολογικός κήπος *m* zo-oloyeekoss keeposs 82

zoology ζωολογία *f* zo-olloyeeah 83

Ελληνικό ευρετήριον

GREECE

Say BERLITZ®

... and most people think of outstanding language schools. But Berlitz has also become the world's leading publisher of books for travellers – Travel Guides, Phrase Books, Dictionaries – plus Cassettes and Self-teaching courses.

Informative, accurate, up-to-date, Books from Berlitz are written with freshness and style. They also slip easily into pocket or purse – no need for bulky, old-fashioned volumes.

Join the millions who know how to travel. Whether for fun or business, put Berlitz in your pocket.

BERLITZ®

Leader in
Books and Cassettes
for Travellers

A Macmillan Company

BERLITZ Books for travellers

TRAVEL GUIDES

They fit your pocket in both size and price. Modern, up-to-date, Berlitz gets all the information you need into 128 lively pages – 192 or 256 pages for country guides – with colour maps and photos throughout. What to see and do, where to shop, what to eat and drink, how to save.

AFRICA	Algeria (256 pages)* Kenya Morocco South Africa Tunisia	**FRANCE**	Brittany France (256 pages) French Riviera Loire Valley Normandy Paris
ASIA, MIDDLE EAST	China (256 pages) Hong Kong India (256 pages) Japan (256 pages) Nepal* Singapore Sri Lanka Thailand Egypt Jerusalem & Holy Land Saudi Arabia	**GERMANY**	Berlin Munich The Rhine Valley
		AUSTRIA and SWITZER-LAND	Tyrol Vienna Switzerland (192 pages)
		GREECE, CYPRUS & TURKEY	Athens Corfu Crete Rhodes Greek Islands of Aegean Peloponnese Salonica/North. Greece Cyprus Istanbul/Aegean Coast Turkey (192 pages)
AUSTRAL-ASIA	Australia (256 pages) New Zealand		
BRITISH ISLES	Channel Islands London Ireland Oxford and Stratford Scotland	**ITALY and MALTA**	Florence Italian Adriatic Italian Riviera Italy (256 pages) Rome Sicily Venice Malta
BELGIUM	Brussels		
		NETHER-LANDS and SCANDI-NAVIA	Amsterdam Copenhagen Helsinki Oslo and Bergen Stockholm

*in preparation

PORTUGAL	Algarve Lisbon Madeira	NORTH AMERICA	New York Canada (256 pages) Toronto Montreal
SPAIN	Barcelona / Costa Dorada Canary Islands Costa Blanca Costa Brava Costa del Sol & Andalusia Ibiza and Formentera Madrid Majorca and Minorca	CARIBBEAN, LATIN AMERICA	Puerto Rico Virgin Islands Bahamas Bermuda French West Indies Jamaica Southern Caribbean Mexico City Brazil (Highlights of) Rio de Janeiro
EASTERN EUROPE	Budapest Dubrovnik & S. Dalmatia Hungary (192 pages) Istria and Croatian Coast Moscow & Leningrad Prague Split and Dalmatia Yugoslavia (256 pages)	EUROPE	Business Travel Guide – Europe (368 pages) Pocket guide to Europe (480 pages) Cities of Europe (504 p.)
NORTH AMERICA	U.S.A. (256 pages) California Florida Hawaii Miami	CRUISE GUIDES	Caribbean cruise guide (368 pages) Alaska cruise guide (168 p) Handbook to Cruising (240 pages)

DELUXE GUIDES
combine complete
travel guide, phrase
book and dictionary in
one book.
Titles available:
Amsterdam, Barcelona,
Budapest, Florence,
French Riviera, Madrid,
Mexico, Munich, Paris,
Rome, Venice.

SKI GUIDES
Top resorts rated,
where to ski, colour
maps:
Austria
France
Italy
Switzerland
Skiing the Alps*

BLUEPRINT GUIDES
Imaginative new large size guide with mapped itineraries,
special interest checklists, selected restaurant and hotel
recommendations, large-scale road atlas, all in full colour.

France, Germany*, Great Britain*, Greece*, Italy, Spain*.

MORE FOR THE $
Over $ 4'000 worth of discount coupons and gift certificates
from the finest hotels and restaurants for each country
covered.

France, Italy.

*in preparation

PHRASE BOOKS

World's bestselling phrase books feature all the expressions and vocabulary you'll need, and pronunciation throughout. 192 pages, 2 colours.

Arabic	Hebrew	Russian
Chinese	Hungarian	Serbo-Croatian
Danish	Italian	Spanish (Castilian)
Dutch	Japanese	Spanish (Lat. Am.)
Finnish	Korean	Swahili
French	Norwegian	Swedish
German	Polish	Turkish
Greek	Portuguese	European Phrase Book
		European Menu Reader

All of the above phrase books are available with C60 or C90 cassette and miniscript as a "**cassettepak**".

Cassette and miniscript only are also available in the major languages as a "**phrase cassette**".

DICTIONARIES

Bilingual with 12,500 concepts each way. Highly practical for travellers, with pronunciation shown plus menu reader, basic expressions and useful information. Over 330 pages.

Danish	French	Norwegian
Dutch	German	Portuguese
Finnish	Italian	Spanish
		Swedish

TRAVEL VIDEO

Travel Tips from Berlitz are now part of the informative and colourful videocassette series of over 80 popular destinations produced by Travelview International. Ideal for planning a trip, Travelview videos provide 40 to 60 minutes of valuable destination briefing and a Reference Guide to local hotels and tourist attractions. Available from leading travel agencies and video stores everywhere in the U.S.A. and Canada or call 1-800-325-3108 (Texas, call (713) 975-7077; (403) 248-7170 in Canada; 908-66 9422 in UK; (5) 531-8714 in Mexico City).

Printed in Switzerland/1989